VENTRILOQUIZED VOICES

Ventriloquized Voices is a fascinating examination of the appropriations of the feminine voice by male authors.

In a historical and theoretical study of English texts of the early modern period, Elizabeth D. Harvey looks at the tranvestism at work in texts which purport to be by women but which are in fact written by men. The crossing of gender in these ventriloquized works illuminates the discourses of patronage, medicine, madness and eroticism in English Renaissance society, revealing as it does the construction of sexuality, gender identity, and power.

The author brilliantly juxtaposes such canonical works as John Donne's *Anniversaries* and Spenser's *Faerie Queene* with pamphlets on transvestism, midwifery books, and treatises on gynecology and hysteria. By interrogating the fashioning of gender within a broad range of Renaissance culture, *Ventriloquized Voices* investigates not only the relationship between men, women and language, but also crucial twentieth-century feminist debates such as essentialism and the female voice.

This is a powerful and original work. It will be of vital interest to scholars and students of the Renaissance, as well as a wide range of feminist readers.

VENTRILOQUIZED VOICES

Feminist Theory and English Renaissance Texts

Elizabeth D. Harvey

London and New York

First published 1992 by Routledge
First published in paperback in 1995 by Routledge
11 New Fetter Lane, London EC4P 4EE

Simultaneously published in the USA and Canada
by Routledge
29 West 35th Street, New York, NY 10001

Typeset in 10/12pt Garamond by
Ponting–Green Publishing Services, Chesham, Bucks
Printed in Great Britain by
T. J. Press (Padstow) Ltd, Padstow, Cornwall

British Library Cataloguing in Publication Data
Harvey, Elizabeth D.
Ventriloquized Voices: Feminist Theory and English Renaissance Texts
I. Title
809

Library of Congress Cataloging in Publication Data
Harvey, Elizabeth D.
Ventriloquized Voices : feminist theory and English Renaissance
texts / Elizabeth D. Harvey
p. cm.
Includes bibliographical references and index.
1. English literature—Early modern, 1500–1700—History and
criticism—Theory, etc. 2. Women—England—History—
Renaissance, 1450–1600—Historiography. 3. English
literature—Men authors—History and criticism—Theory, etc.
4. Feminism and literature—England—History—16th century.
5. Feminism and literature—England—History—17th century.
6. Women and literature—England—History—16th century.
8. Authorship—Sex differences. 9. Point of view (Literature)
10. Sex role in literature. I. Title.
PR418.W65H37 1992
820.9'352042–dc20 92-4510

ISBN 0 415 12793 9

For Mark

CONTENTS

ACKNOWLEDGEMENTS

At many moments during the writing of this book I was aware of the numerous voices who served as inspiration, who offered correctives, skeptical questions, and encouragement. They have sometimes become so internalized as to be indistinguishable from my own, but I can enumerate many of my teachers, colleagues, and friends who contributed: Sharon Cameron, Jonathan Crewe, Jonathan Goldberg, Stanley Fish, Timothy Hampton, Linda Hutcheon, Katharine Maus, Janel Mueller, William Oram, Patricia Parker, Balachandra Rajan, Nancy Vickers, and the late Richard B. Young. I need to record a special debt of gratitude to Lee Patterson and Stephen Orgel, under whose expert direction I wrote an early version of the Sappho chapter. It was Lee Patterson who first urged me to think about the question of ventriloquism, and Stephen Orgel then and since has provided a continually challenging model for reading Renaissance texts. Kristin Brady's friendship, wise counsel, and vital support, especially at a number of critical junctures, have been invaluable. Carole Farber was a source of bibliographical lore and supplied an important cross-disciplinary perspective. Margaret Ferguson, Mary Nyquist, Richard Regosin, and Miglena Nikolchina all read the manuscript, and their generous and perceptive comments, as well as those from anonymous readers for Routledge, sent me back to rethink both specific details and the larger premises of my argument. My students at the University of Western Ontario (in the English Department, the Center for Women's Studies and Feminist Research, and in the Center for the Study of Theory and Criticism) have left a permanent imprint on the book through their engagement with its arguments. Two research assistants, Elizabeth Sauer and David Kinahan, were extraordinarily diligent, precise, and creative in their work on the book. The audiences to whom I delivered oral versions of Chapters 1, 3, and 4 offered helpful suggestions for revision and reconceptualizing, especially at the Modern Language Association, the Renaissance Society of America, the Association of Canadian University Teachers of English, Trent University, and the University of Alberta.

Various institutional bodies allowed me the time and wherewithal to complete the project. A University of Western Ontario Faculty of Arts Research Professorship gave me a respite from teaching for a year, when my obligations threatened to silence me completely; I am especially grateful to Dean Thomas M. Lennon for his vision in creating this award. A postdoctoral fellowship and a subsequent Research Award from the Social Sciences and Humanities Research Council of Canada enabled me to do a large portion of the research and gave me the necessary time to explore my topic and develop my ideas.

I owe profound thanks to my parents, Sheila Shea Harvey and Lawrence Elliot Harvey (1925–88), who were my first teachers of literature and whose insights have shaped mine, sometimes even from beyond the grave. My son Nicholas was the inspiration for the chapter on birth and a beguiling distraction during the final stages of writing. My greatest and most enduring gratitude is to Mark Cheetham, whose sustaining presence has nourished me throughout the conception and writing of this book, whose editorial perspicacity and intellectual acuity rescued me from numerous impasses, and whose belief during my moments of doubt helped to make this book possible.

An earlier version of "Ventriloquizing Sappho, Or the Lesbian Muse" appeared in *Criticism*, Spring 1989, 31 (2). I am grateful to Wayne State University Press for permission to reprint.

INTRODUCTION
The voice of gender

This book is a historical and theoretical study of male appropriations of the feminine voice in English texts of the early modern period. Its focus on voice derives both from post-structuralist preoccupations with authorial presence or absence and from Anglo-American and French feminist concerns with gender and language. This double theoretical orientation provides a framework for exploring a number of classical and Renaissance texts that share a common feature: although written by male authors, they are voiced by female characters in a way that seems either to erase the gender of the authorial voice or to thematize the transvestism of this process. This phenomenon, which I call transvestite ventriloquism, accentuates the issues of gender, voice, and authorial property in ways that illuminate both Renaissance conceptions of language and their relation to the gendered subject, and also twentieth-century notions of the author and their link (or lack of connection) to the gendered body.

My use of the term voice refers in the most obvious sense to the metaphors of speaking that appear so pervasively in Renaissance texts. The trope of voice is frequently metonymized in the tongue, or conversely in silence, and it is often embodied in mythical figures associated with voice or rhetoric – the Sibyl, Echo, Philomela, Medusa, the Muse. These figures possess a reflexive dimension, pointing as they do to an author and to the way he (or she) represents and thematizes the conception or production of the text. This subject has been treated evocatively by Jonathan Goldberg (1986) in *Voice Terminal Echo: Postmodernism and English Renaissance Texts*, where he explores the complicated intertextual relationship between voices and text, between character and letter, between authorial voice and the imaging of its origin. In his study, Goldberg notes the frequent registering of "the poet's voice in other voices – particularly in the voices of women, descendants of Echo and Philomela and Syrinx" (1986: 12), but he does not elaborate on the implications of this crossing of genders. Patricia Parker does consider the gender of voice in *Literary Fat Ladies: Rhetoric, Gender, Property*, in particular, the contiguities between the body of the text and the female body. Arguing that language and rhetoric seem to issue from, or are at least figured in, a dilated feminine body, she claims that the deferral or errancy that characterizes romance as a form is linked to woman's fabled garrulity (1987). Rhetorical amplification, exemplified in the Erasmian notion of *copia*, is thus not only represented by the expanding or opening of a woman's body, but this trope also points to the social dimensions of language, especially the regulation of discourse and its circulation or commodification.

While both Goldberg's and Parker's books have been formative in Renaissance studies and certainly to my own understanding of voice, neither has addressed explicitly the disturbing problem of ventriloquistic cross-dressing that I will examine here. An author's speaking through the voice of the other gender opens up what I argue is a discrepancy in the etymological sense of "sounding differently." Perhaps the best way of describing this space of difference is through an example from drama because, in a sense, drama furnishes the quintessential paradigm for this study, since it is an orchestration of various characterological voices by an "invisible" author. John Webster's *The Duchess of Malfi* is a particularly apt instance because its thematization of the dramatic and the self-conscious playing of parts calls attention to its meta-dramatic dimensions; both Antonio and the Duchess "play" particular roles in order to preserve the secrecy of their marriage, while Bosola is continually casting himself as different characters and manipulating plots so that he might uncover secrets. The discrepancy between the character and the various roles each enact is registered in the spatialization of voice, in what Ferdinand initially calls "whispering-rooms" (1.2.240), that is, the space behind the visor or mask. The Duchess reinvokes that space, when, as she is being led away to imprisonment, she tells Bosola that if she were a man she "would beat that counterfeit face into thy other" (3.5.116); just before she is strangled, she tells Bosola that any way she dies will take her out of his "whispering" (4.2.212). In other words, voice, especially the hushed voice of gossip, spies, and secrecy, emerges from the disjunction between the face and the masks it wears, and it is in these whispering rooms that the notion of an essential self and its linkage to language is problematized. The thematization of created voice stands not in opposition to an authentic self or voice, but in opposition to the figure of the actor, who is himself already wearing an invented mask and speaking in another's voice. The whispering room is also the locus of a female sexuality that is made illicit by its propagation in rumor, a promiscuity intimately allied to voice. Of course the disjunction between speaking and gender is intensified in *The Duchess of Malfi* because the Duchess would have been played by a male actor, and the gap that is opened up by this transvestism disturbs the illusion of continuity between the gender of the body and the voice that speaks it.

While the disjunction in drama between the representation of women and their actual cultural circumstances, or between their feminine speech and the male author who produces it (or the male actor who utters it), has been influentially analysed by such critics as Lisa Jardine (1983) and Catherine Belsey (1985), among others, the discrepancy between gender and voice in non-dramatic Renaissance poetry has received little attention.[1] The male impersonation of the feminine voice in non-dramatic writing is usually explained with reference to a *persona*, which, while useful as a distinction, is neither historicized nor gendered as a theory. T.S. Eliot in "The Three Voices in Poetry," to cite an early but paradigmatic instance, describes the germ of sympathy that exists between an author and a fictional voice, an affinity that is, he says, not necessarily restricted by temperament, age, or sex (1957: 93–4). In emphasizing the similitude rather than the difference between the sexes, Eliot tends to collapse the cultural construction of gender as a category that distinguishes and divides; this dissolution absorbs women or feminine voices into a gender-neutral (or male) category, just as the female character's voice tends to become a refracted version of the male author's. Although the idea of the *persona* goes back to Plato and Aristotle, Eliot's reference to Ezra Pound's use of the term links it with voice, making *persona* virtually synonymous with the Eliotic definition of the "third voice," the poet's speaking through a dramatic character (Eliot 1957: 89). Despite Eliot's stress in "The Metaphysical Poets" on the inseparability of thought and feeling (or ideas and the body) for poets writing before the second half of the seventeenth century and the dissociation of sensibility, his notion of voice is a curiously disembodied one for a critic who described Donne and Racine as looking into "the cerebral cortex, the nervous system, and the digestive tracts" (Eliot 1975: 66) for the source of their art. Indeed, as I will be arguing in this book, although much post-structuralist theory has striven to divorce the author's body (and voice) from his (or her) writing, the constructed voices within the texts I will be considering vigorously reassert their (feminine) bodily origins.

The feminine voice that is represented in early modern texts by male authors speaks because it purportedly issues from a female body that gives it life and currency. Examined within the cultural discourses of the period, woman's voice or tongue – what Richard Brathwaite in *The English Gentlewoman* called "that glibbery member" (Goreau 1984: 38) – is seen to be imbricated with female sexuality, just as silence is "bound up" with sexual continence. I am exploring what we might designate as hysterical texts (in the root sense of that word), works that are intimately connected to the functioning of the uterus. That organ was considered by writers such as Plato, Hippocrates, and Aretaeus of Cappadocia to possess a life of its own and the capacity to migrate within the female body. Even though Galen's writings, which had the greatest impact on Renaissance notions of sexual difference, stress the homology between men and women (woman's sexual organs are exactly like men's except that they are internal instead of external), the interiority and invisibility of the womb gave it a special status. That a woman's sexual organs remained within the claustral space of her body reflected a whole series of physiological "facts": her relative lack of heat, the colder, moister humors that dominate her make-up, menstruation, her physical shape, her higher voice, her propensity to age more quickly, her weaker powers of mind, her imagination (Maclean 1980: 31–41). The medical representation of female physiology overlapped with cultural ideology in ways that make it impossible to dissever one from the other. Our notions of bodies are, after all, constructed primarily through their descriptions in the discourses of medicine and science, representations that are themselves implicated in and serve to perpetuate ideological structures. The intersections of gendered bodies, their linguistic expression, and a particular cultural matrix have much to tell us about the operations of gender in history. Far from being an essentialist project, then, my investigations into the link between female physiology and the feminine voice emphasize the fabricated nature of this connection, and they do so by focusing on the division – rather than the contiguity – between an actual body and its voice. In other words, my attention to transvestite ventriloquism allows me to explore the way male authors create a feminine voice that seems to be – but is not – linked to a whole set of feminine characteristics (a sexualized body, an emotional make-up, an imagination). Indeed, ventriloquizations of women in the Renaissance achieved the power they did partly because so few women actually wrote and spoke, but the representations of feminine speech that were current in literary and popular accounts, as well as in ventriloquizations, fostered a vision that tended to reinforce women's silence or to marginalize their voices when they did speak or write.

The linkage (or lack of connection) between language and the female body is a frequent and vigorously argued topic in French feminism and in Anglo-American feminist debates. Voice is often used as a powerful metaphor for the rebirth of what has been suppressed by patriarchal culture. As women struggle to repossess a power taken from them, as they challenge patriarchal institutions that have deformed them and limited their potential, the synecdochic expression of that liberation is often localized in the voice. Carol Gilligan's immensely important study of psychology and moral development, *In a Different Voice*, for example, which challenges the androcentrism of traditional psychological models, uses voice as a marker of sexual difference. *Women's Ways of Knowing: The Development of Self, Voice, and Mind* (Belenky *et al.* 1986) is organized methodologically and thematically around the metaphor of voice, Tillie Olsen's *Silences* charts the impediments to the emergence of voice as a synonym for self and creativity, and, in French feminist theory, Hélène Cixous's (1986) "Sorties" describes femininity in writing as "a privilege of voice" (92). On the one hand, this seems like a natural move, since language provides the currency in society and because voice registers in an immediate way that linguistic power. Yet post-structuralist theory has repeatedly challenged the stability of the categories that appear to lend "voice" its coherence as a metaphor by interrogating notions of subjectivity, the author, the reader, the text, and gender. We can no longer assume that the authorial "voice" resides in the text to which a particular signature is affixed, or that a text is the same for different readers, or that there is a clear correlation between the gender of a body and the gender of a text. The problem in theoretical terms, then, is one of reconciling the imperatives of Anglo-American feminism – with its project of integrating women's experience and women's "voices" into traditional systems of knowledge and understanding – with French feminist theory, with its reliance on deconstruction, marxism, and psychoanalytic paradigms. One stumbling block to this reconciliation is that voice has itself become a monolithic construction that seems to be construed in the same way whether it is used in twentieth-century arguments about women's epistemology, as the linch-pin for a theory of gynocritics, or as it appears to emerge from the female body in French feminist writings. This integration is further complicated by the intricacies of history; just as "voice" remains constant across different disciplines and cultures, so, too, does it tend to be envisioned as stable over time, seeming the same whether it is represented in the Middle Ages, the eighteenth century, or the twentieth century.

I argue specifically against this apparent transhistoricality of voice, and I seek to make self-conscious the various metaphorical usages of "voice" in feminist theory. This book, therefore, like the instances of voicing it examines, is characterized by doubleness. I move with a kind of transgressive abandon between the historical context of the early modern period and twentieth-century feminist theoretical writings. If history (and the history that shapes literary criticism) is a narrative, constructed from the perspective of a present that is itself governed by cultural factors specific to its own historical moment, then what one chooses to focus on in the past, what elements one privileges and the arguments that emerge from the literary and cultural evidence one fashions or discovers, are largely determined by present preoccupations. My interest in voice, and the female voice in particular, has been made possible by feminist criticism in the first instance, which has recognized the gender of an utterance as crucially determining how it is received and even what it means. Historical reconstructions are always a kind of ventriloquization, then, a matter of making the past seem to speak in the voice that the present gives it. Rather than suppressing this enabling twinship, I foreground it by pairing texts of the early modern period with late twentieth-century considerations of what I claim are analogous issues.

Chapter 1 gathers a series of writings that link voice and cross-dressing. The chapter is framed, on the one hand, by my analysis of Elaine Showalter's theoretical writings on voice, gynocritics, transvestism, and gender, and, on the other, by my explication of Sarah Kofman's ventriloquization of Freud's theories of bisexuality and hysteria. The central portion of the chapter treats two different problems of transvestism in Renaissance texts: a male author's (Spenser) figuration of cross-dressing as a way of expressing the ambivalences of power and desire incumbent upon a male poet writing under the patronage of a female sovereign, and, in the Jacobean context, the problematic of authorship in anonymous texts about transvestism. The chapter thus begins and ends with feminist writers who explore the question of language, gender, and the possibility of political change that could be effected through language. I start with Showalter because, in her theory of gynocritics, she employs an influential but inadequately theorized notion of voice that is partly inherited from male ventriloquizations of feminine voices; I conclude with Kofman because she redeploys the very strategies of ventriloquism that created this illusory feminine voice as a historical legacy. She makes ventriloquism into a reflexive weapon, using it to argue against Freud's authoritative pronouncements on femininity, and revealing in the process the doubleness of Freudian theory, its simultaneous claim for the purely speculative nature of sexual difference (its reliance on the thesis of bisexuality), and its masculine wish to disavow the "taint" of femininity. All the texts with which I am concerned in this chapter call into question the gender of the voice that speaks and the power (or lack of power) a given (gendered) voice therefore possesses.

In Chapter 2, the most "duplicitous" of the chapters, I address the relationship between hysteria and voice. I begin by looking at Erasmus's ventriloquization of Folly, whose connections with laughter, women, sexuality, and madness link her to a whole series of marginalized discourses. Erasmus's *Praise of Folly* may seem like an odd choice in this consideration of English texts. I have included it first because it provides an example of ventriloquization that had (and continues to have) wide influence. That Erasmus wrote it in England, that its crucial first audience was English, and that it invokes Thomas More both in its title and prefatory epistle makes clear its important connection to the English context. Equally important, the humanism that brought it into being and that it embodies depicts a community that crosses the boundaries of nationality and the vernacular, an intellectual solidarity that is evident in the currency of Latin as the language of humanism. Latin is a privileged language with patriarchal affiliations, and Folly's voice thus sets up a kind of internal tension between the vernacular "mother tongue," what women speak, and the adopted patriarchal linguistic medium of classical learning. *Folly*'s "double" voicing is multiple, then, since it is figured not only in the transvestism of the voice that speaks, but also in the interplay between Latin and Greek and between English and Latin. Multivocality or polyglottism is, of course, one of the characteristics of hysteria as Freud described it, exemplified, for example, in Anna O.'s linguistic disruptions; she forgets German, her "mother tongue," reading French and Italian, and speaking and understanding English perfectly instead (Freud 1974: 79). The second half of Chapter 2 examines the "trope" of hysteria in Clément's and Cixous's *La jeune née*. Although I contrast this French feminist text with Erasmus's mock encomium, I am also interested in the continuities between the early modern imaging of hysteria and its Freudian and post-Freudian manifestations. Is it possible, as Cixous implicitly claims, to reappropriate the discourses that characterize women as hysterical and employ them as a strategy for change? While Cixous does not ventriloquize in the overt way that Irigaray and Kofman do, she does nevertheless subversively occupy the cultural discourses to which women are relegated, making this phallocentric cultural lexicon the basis for a bisexual language that is designed to dismantle the economy of the proper. Both Folly and Cixous employ a many-tongued voice, one that is mirrored in their violations of textual property, and which, in Cixous's case, becomes the enactment of a feminist intertextuality.

After examining the pathology of the uterus in my consideration of hysteria, I turn in Chapter 3 to its positive, creative powers. My focus is the trope of male birth, which I seek to understand by contextualizing it within the historical debate on midwifery. This chapter brings bodies and voices together in their most overt and complicated alliance, because the poetic (and some of the medical) texts that I examine use the metaphor of pregnancy and birth to image their own textual origins at the same historical moment that birth and the interior of the female body were becoming subject to male medical scrutiny and economic control. This historicization of the metaphor of male birth illuminates the way such male poets as Sidney, Milton, or Donne represent their poetic voices as analogously or metaphorically bound up with female reproduction. In the last section of the chapter, I set John Donne's *Anniversaries* against Julia Kristeva's writings on motherhood. There is a special relevance, I suggest, to the double structure of Kristeva's "Stabat Mater," with its two columns that seem to divide motherhood into the experience of the mother, registered in lyrical fragments, and the historical and theoretical analysis of maternity, represented in the right-hand column. Both Kristeva and Donne rely on the image of the Virgin Mary, a figure that represents the bifurcation of maternity and sexuality; where Donne uses a virginal maternity as the source of his (ventriloquized) voice, Kristeva provides a historical and psychoanalytic explication of the Virgin's contribution to a more general theory of maternality. My juxtaposition of these texts interrogates motherhood as a discourse or an act that can be owned or appropriated, either by the male midwives and physicians who colonize and eventually medicalize childbirth, or by feminists who seek to repossess the experience of maternity in language.

The fourth chapter, "Ventriloquizing Sappho," also raises questions of literary property. In this case, they coalesce around the figure of Sappho, whose history is fragmented and occluded by the censorship of her writings and her lesbianism, and by the ventriloquism that this silencing enabled. The male poets who speak in her voice appropriate the power of her poetic reputation, while subjecting her either to male disdain within a heterosexual economy (Ovid's Phaon), or the voyeurism implicit in male constructions of lesbianism (Donne's "Sappho to Philaenis"). Although this analysis examines the specific interaction between Sappho and her male ventriloquizers, its ramifications concern the sexual status of the female muse, the relationship between her chastity and her poetic fecundity. Just as Luce Irigaray (in a feminist reworking of Lévi-Strauss) argues that the circulation of women subtends and supports a heterosexual economy, so too does the production and circulation of poetry depend upon the exchange of female representations, whose sexuality is both guarded and displayed in the contest of male poetic rivalry. This chapter concludes by comparing Donne's ventriloquized Sapphic love letter to Luce Irigaray's lyrical "When Our Lips Speak Together," her meditation on the female body and language. Apostrophizing an unnamed woman, Irigaray's speaker interrogates the imprisoning, homogenizing sameness of patriarchal language, replacing it with a transgressive linguistic medium that in turn seeks to dissolve the division between self and other, to fuse women into a new unity that is at once erotic and linguistic.

A central interpretive focus in all of the chapters is my attention to the problem of intertextuality. Intertextuality, as Julia Kristeva defines it, stands for the transposition of one (or several) sign systems to another, a passage that in turn demands a new theorization of enunciation. Kristeva says that "every signifying practice is a field of transpositions of various signifying systems (an intertextuality)," and that the "'place' of enunciation and its denoted 'object' are never single, complete, and identical to themselves, but always plural, shattered, capable of being tabulated" (Kristeva 1984: 59–60). Rather than describing the bounded property of a stable author, as source studies or influence studies do, then, intertextuality focuses on utterances whose possible sources are illusory points of origin, or whose origins are either infinitely regressive or at least multiple, so that they cannot be identified as belonging either solely to a particular author or even to a particular historical moment. My attention to the intertextual elements of the works I discuss is designed to draw attention to the various authorial and cultural voices that inhabit these texts, voices that undermine the illusory sense of closure and stability sometimes attributed to them. In this respect, ventriloquism and intertexuality overlap, for, in both cases, a putatively single and bounded utterance is destabilized by questions of origin, authorship, and ownership; an intertextual allusion opens a text to other voices and echoes of other texts, just as ventriloquism multiplies authorial voices, interrogating the idea that a single authorial presence speaks or controls an utterance. I return repeatedly to the classical intertexts in Renaissance writing because the presence of these allusions testifies to the often self-conscious construction of Renaissance culture as the inheritor, voice, and disinterrer of the classical past.[2] It is not accidental that the classical author to whom I refer most often is Ovid, for he was manifestly self-reflexive about his use of intertexts, in his parodic rewriting of Virgil in *The Metamorphoses*, in his encyclopedic use of myth, and especially in his densely intertextual and ventriloquized letters from the mythical heroines of the *Heroides*.[3]

My focus on intertexuality is further complicated by gender, a factor central to my readings of the *Heroides* and to the Renaissance rewritings of it. I am particularly interested in what happens to a male-authored text when its intertexts are authored by a woman (such as Ovid's allusions to Sappho), spoken in the feminine voice (Erasmus's references to Virgil's Sibyl), or spoken in a cross-dressed or transvestite voice. In these cases, not only are authorial and textual autonomies transgressed by subtexts, but the stability of gender itself is revealed to be what Judith Butler has recently termed a structure of impersonation (Butler 1991: 21). Just as intertextuality suggests a kind of infinite regress in which there is no original, so too does this transvestism of voice imply that "gender is a kind of imitation for which there is no original" (Butler 1991: 21, italics removed). In other words, what ventriloquistic cross-dressing makes clear is that, while transvestism is seen as a copy of an original (a man dressed as, or speaking as, a woman), when we examine the original, it too turns out not to be original, but a copy of itself. The naturalistic dimensions of heterosexual gender identities are thus imitations, performatively constituted as reproductions of "phantasmatic idealizations" of what "man" and "woman" are supposed to be in a given culture (Butler 1991: 21).

The texts I have selected as examples of transvestite ventriloquism are representative of particular problems or issues (transvestism, hysteria, maternity, lesbianism) rather than constituting a comprehensive survey of male poets speaking in the feminine voice. I have not, for instance, considered the numerous examples of cross-dressed voices in pastoral, a collection that might include not only Sidney's *Arcadia* and Ralegh's "The Nymph's Reply to the Shepherd," but also Marvell's "Nymph Complaining for the Death of her Fawn" and, as Rosemary Kegl argues, the silenced voices of Juliana and her contemporaries in the Mower poems (Kegl 1990: 102–5). Ventriloquized voices that speak in a pastoral context call up a representation and vocalization of nature that is both ancient and pervasive; indeed, the violations of nature that Marvell's Mower laments figure an intrusion or intervention between essence and its covering, "between the bark and tree," that recalls the arguments against transvestism in the *Hic Mulier/Haec-Vir* pamphlet debate. The "green seraglio" populated with eunuchs in "The Mower Against Gardens" represents a contaminated sexuality, an ability to reproduce without sex, or, conversely, an adulterated sexuality that is barren. The monstrousness of this vision is akin to ventriloquism (which is, after all, one of the symptoms of demonic possession or witchcraft), in its violation of the principle of correspondence, the ability to correlate a particular tree with a particular fruit, or a specific voice with a body to which it should belong.

Rather than offering a global account of why male writers might wish to speak in a woman's voice, I have anchored my explications in specific historical and generic contexts. The phenomenon has temporally local causes and manifestations, so that Samuel Richardson's ventriloquism in *Pamela* would need to be understood differently from, say, John Updike's use of it in *S.* (although both overlap with the epistolary tradition), or indeed, from its manifestation in the early modern period. There are, nevertheless, linkages across history, as A.S. Byatt's juxtaposition of a study of male ventriloquism and literary haunting in her recent novel, *Possession*, makes clear. Although the initial allusion to male ventriloquism in *Possession* is satiric, referring as it does to an undergraduate essay on the representation of women in the work of a male Victorian poet, the context makes it apparent that meaning depends upon imputations of gender.

The essay is, ironically, judged as a female ventriloquism of a male student's ideas and discounted accordingly (Byatt 1990: 12). The incident hilariously and pathetically anticipates the more sophisticated versions of ventriloquism with which the novel concerns itself: the complex relationships between biographer and subject, between literary critic and poet, between the past and the present, between professors and students, and the rivalrous feuding among members of the international academic community. As the various senses of the novel's title suggest, ventriloquism as a motif is most often invoked in and around issues of authorial property, especially as property intersects with history in the recreation – and often enshrinement – of the past, in the animation of the dead by the living, or in the way the living are "possessed" by the historical figures they study. Thus, although our construal of transvestite ventriloquism needs to be historically and ideologically inflected, its interpretation in a particular context will nevertheless be contingent upon the intersection of three factors: gender, property, and the author. The interrelationships among these elements, while already complex, are further complicated by history, by the temporal gap between interpreter and ventriloquist, and by the historical (and intertextual) distance between ventriloquizer and ventriloquized.

While my study focuses on ventriloquism in order to explore the construction of gender in the early modern period, especially as it overlaps with property and as it implicitly reveals an idea of the author, I also argue that ventriloquism is an appropriation of the feminine voice, and that it reflects and contributes to a larger cultural silencing of women. This argument could sound narrowly essentialist in its reliance on an unstated identity politics: only women can legitimately speak for themselves, because only they have access to their own experience. As Edward Said and Diana Fuss have both asserted, such an adherence to rigid definitions of identity breeds an exclusivity that is designed to silence outsiders (Fuss 1989: 114–16). But my claim that transvestite ventriloquism expresses a cultural suppression of the female voice is not based upon epistemological premises; in other words, I am not asserting that men cannot know what it is to be a woman and therefore should not speak on their behalf (no matter how beneficent their motives are). Rather, I argue that the issue is not epistemological at all, but ethical and political. It is not whether male poets *can* adequately represent the female voice, but the ethics and politics of doing so. Like Fuss, I believe that essentialism and constructionism are mutually implicated; I thus historicize essentialist definitions of the female voice, adhere to an idea of a constructed and contingent subject, but I also support a tactical essentialism, the belief that even while we recognize the constructed nature of gender, we can still adhere to a conviction that women and men (and their respective voices) are not politically interchangeable.

Although my analysis of transvestite ventriloquism has located its operations in language, the connection between representation and gender transposition is not limited to the linguistic. My cover image expresses in painting many of the issues that have been central to this study. Entitled *Le Silence*, the almost androgynous figure at the center of the womb-like space holds her fingers to her lips in a gesture that mimics the personifications of silence found in Renaissance and Baroque emblem books such as Cesare Ripa's *Iconologia* (Reff 1967: 361).[4] The gesture recalls the classical figure of Harpocrates, the Greek god of silence and secrecy, a fitting reminder of the cultural silence of women that subtends and enables male ventriloquizations of their voices. The context of Redon's painting seems to capture the fundamental ambiguity that also haunts the ventriloquized voices I examine in this book. Redon apparently conceived and painted *Le Silence* in 1911, when his wife was extremely ill and just recovering from a major operation. The otherworldliness of the portrait seems to point to an awareness of death's proximity, just as its title suggests that the barrier between life and death is one that cannot be bridged by language.

This sense of crossing is captured in another picture by Redon also painted in 1911. Entitled either *Le Soleil Noire* or *Le Silence*, it portrays two hooded figures, "like Dante and Virgil about to embark on their momentous journey" (Reff 1967: 363). The first title, as well as the eclipsed sun in the painting, may allude to the image of the black sun in Gérard de Nerval's 1853 poem "El Desdichado," (The Disinherited), for in that poem, the disconsolate speaker is imaged as a widower. The narrator depicts himself as having twice crossed the Acheron alive, and it is the power of the Orphic lyre he carries that allows him to traverse from one world to the other (Kristeva 1989: 140–1). Poised between one world and the next, the figures in Redon's painting also seem to embody liminality and a sense of momentous and inexpressible passage. Yet there is another sense of crossing at work as well. The face depicted in my cover image is "unmistakably that of Mme. Redon" (Reff 1967: 366), but the preparatory drawing depicts a male face that looks like Redon himself. In other words, the painting seems to figure a kind of superimposition or mask, with Redon's own face metaphorically standing beneath the image of his silent wife. It appears from the palimpsestic image that Redon imaginatively occupied his wife's position, as if he – like Orpheus – had crossed the boundary between worlds, or between genders, in order to prepare himself for her passage from the world. The transposition of gender reveals the pathos and emotional investment implicit in this crisis, a sense that actual death might become the spiritual death of melancholia for the widower. The evocativeness of the image, with its array of pictorial and literary intertexts, suggests as well the depth and complexity of discourses buried in the figure of silence.

1

TRAVESTIES OF VOICE

Cross-dressing the tongue

> Nick Greene, I thought, remembering the story I had made about Shakespeare's sister, said that a woman acting put him in mind of a dog dancing. Johnson repeated the phrase two hundred years later of women preaching.
>
> (Virginia Woolf, 1929: 56)

In the introduction to their ground-breaking study of the woman writer in the nineteenth century, *The Madwoman in the Attic*, Sandra Gilbert and Susan Gubar argue that culture, literary history, and literary theory have combined to exclude women, to make them passive and merely represented rather than active participants in literary creativity. They cite Chaucer's Wife of Bath's famous remark that, if women had written stories instead of men, literature would have been very different, for then wickedness would have been seen to be at least as much a masculine as a feminine characteristic. They compare the Wife of Bath to Anne Elliot in Jane Austen's *Persuasion*, suggesting that both demonstrate "our culture's historical confusion of literary authorship with patriarchal authority" (1979: 11). Later on in their analysis, despite references to Chaucer, the Wife of Bath seems to take on a life of her own, for, unlike other represented feminine characters, she has her own "voice," and repeatedly utters memorable and quotable feminist maxims. Chaucer is described as giving her "a tale of her own," which projects "her subversive version of patriarchal institutions into the story of a furious hag" (1979: 79). "Five centuries later," we are told, "the threat of the hag... still lurks behind the compliant paragon of women's stories"; in the next paragraph, Gilbert and Gubar seamlessly emend "women's stories" to "women writers" (1979: 79), making the conflation between feminine voice and female author complete. Even though they claim both explicitly and implicitly that male literary experience is fundamentally different from female literary experience, the Wife of Bath appears to transcend these categories, paired as she repeatedly is with female characters created by female authors who similarly articulate their wish to escape from an oppressive system.

What are we to make of this and similar slippages between characterological and authorial voices (Molly Bloom is another instance of a female character who in the writings of some other theorists – such as Hélène Cixous (1980) – comes to stand for the irrepressible female spirit), especially in a feminist criticism that seems increasingly to privilege and take for granted the female voice? To address these and related questions, I want in this book to extend and complexify the relationship between voice and gender by examining in detail the common but largely unremarked phenomenon of what I call transvestite ventriloquism, which the Wife of Bath exemplifies: the use of the feminine voice by a male author in a way that appears to efface originary marks of gender. Is there necessarily a difference between a feminine voice constructed by a female as opposed to a male author? If so, where – or in what – does that difference reside? Is there an essential distinguishing mark (a recognizably distinct female language), or is the difference signalled in its reception by the reader? What difference does it make who is speaking and who fashions a literary "voice"? What are the theoretical and political implications of male authors ventriloquizing the female voice? To start to answer some of these questions, I focus my study on the intersection between ventriloquized texts of the English Renaissance and twentieth-century theoretical works that treat the linkage between gender and voice. This intersection of concerns is possible because of the historical doubling or convergence of attention to gender, language, and essentialism in both historical frames. Just as the Renaissance was preoccupied with clothing as an indicator of sexuality (as well as class), with the relationship between gender and speech, and with the crossing of genders, so, too, is late twentieth-century western culture concerned with issues of essentialism, transvestism, and the link between gender and authorship. The implications of these intersections are complex, engaging as they do the connection between gender and subjectivity, and the connection between language and alterity. The issues they raise are not only epistemological (can one know or speak of experiences of otherness?) but also methodological, ethical, and political.

In this chapter I will address these questions by pairing a series of texts that examine transvestism: I begin by analysing four essays by Elaine Showalter, two of which study transvestism as a trope in critical and theoretical writing. I juxtapose her two earlier essays on gynocritics, "Toward a Feminist Poetics" and "Feminist Criticism in the Wilderness," with these essays on transvestism, "Critical Cross-Dressing: Male Feminists and the Woman of the Year" and her introduction to *Speaking of Gender*, "The Rise of Gender," because I am interested not only in the question of essentialism, but also in the fundamental implications of that question for understanding historical constructions of gender and feminist methodology. I am particularly concerned to explore the efficacy of a gynocritical model for Renaissance studies, and I thus examine the presuppositions subtending gynocritics and its methodological limitations. The Renaissance texts I set against gynocritics are preoccupied with transvestism: the *Hic Mulier/Haec-Vir* (1620) pamphlets, the Radigund episode in Spenser's *Faerie Queene*, and its Ovidian subtext, Deianira's epistle to Hercules in the *Heroides*. All of these works represent cross-dressing and its relationship to speech, and, in their ventriloquistic dimensions, they thematize issues central to this book: the link between signature and authorial voice and the way this connection is complicated by gender. The male poet's transvestism of voice is, I argue, at once a strategy for confronting the narrowness of the imprisoning bounds of gender definitions, and also (paradoxically) a way of coping with the anxiety generated by the radical instability of gender difference within a particular cultural context. The final section moves from Renaissance figures of the transvestite to Sarah Kofman's (1985) French feminist rereading of Freud's theories of bisexuality, a text in which she repeatedly ventriloquizes Freud's voice as a strategy for illuminating and rebalancing the asymmetry of Freudian bisexuality.

I

Elaine Showalter's 1979 essay "Toward a Feminist Poetics" propounds the binarity that was to shape a decade of Anglo-American feminist criticism and that remains influential in Renaissance studies;[1] on the one hand, she defines a mode of feminist analysis that she calls "feminist critique," which is concerned with woman as reader, and, on the other, a critical mode that centers on woman as writer, which, borrowing from the French, she christens "gynocritics" (1979: 128).

Citing a metaphor originally invoked in a dialogue between Carolyn Heilbrun and Catharine Stimpson, Showalter describes the relationship as typological: feminist critique is aligned with the Old Testament and gynocritics is affiliated with the New Testament. Her gloss on the analogy is that just as feminist critique is focused on "'the sins and errors of the past,'" so, too, is feminist critique intent on revealing the omissions of attention to women or the propagation of stereotypes about them in literature and criticism produced by men. Gynocritics, in contradistinction, is, like the New Testament, "seeking 'the grace of the imagination,'" and it is suffused with the celebratory possibility of arriving in the "promised land of the feminist vision" (1979: 129). Where Heilbrun and Stimpson had insisted on the necessity for both types of feminist criticism, on the interdependence of the righteous, ideologically oriented feminist critique and the liberating "disinterestedness" of gynocritics, Showalter, relying on the evolutionary trajectory that subtends so much of her early criticism, tends to see gynocritics *as* the promised land. This is especially evident in "Feminist Criticism in the Wilderness," where she spends less than a page on feminist critique, while the rest of the essay is devoted to establishing an impressive taxonomy of four "schools" of gynocentric feminist criticism. Her metaphors are equally revealing; while all of theory is a wilderness in which feminist "theoretical pioneers" must make their home, feminist criticism without theory was an "empirical orphan in the theoretical storm" (1981: 244). The "firm theoretical ground" that she claims for feminism is gynocritical: it is "genuinely woman centered" and "independent," it relies on female "experience," it avoids androcentric models in favor of gynocentric ones, and it seeks to discover "its own subject, its own system, its own theory, and its own voice" (1981: 247).

Yet as compelling a theoretical model as this was in 1981, as urgently necessary as it was in that political climate, and as alluring as this vision of stable theoretical domesticity is, there are nevertheless difficulties both with Showalter's vision and with the gynocritical model she has bequeathed to so many feminist critics. One of the most disconcerting and disabling features of her theory is her desire for theoretical and ontological stability (evidenced most clearly in her recurrent references to a "permanent home" (1979: 142)). In her dismissal of feminist critique, for example, she expands what had been a latent metaphor; feminist critique, she tells us, concerns the woman as reader or "consumer of male-produced literature" (1979:

128), whereas gynocritics is a more active enterprise, involved as it is with woman as producer. In "Feminist Criticism in the Wilderness," she spins out the dangers of the consumer side of this capitalist equation, arguing that "in the free play of the interpretive field, the feminist critique can only compete with alternative readings, all of which have the built-in obsolescence of Buicks, cast away as newer readings take their place" (1981: 246).[2] Not only is feminist critique relegated to the "passive" side of the dichotomy (which would seem, then, to align gynocritics with the active – or masculine – half of this binarism), but its major handicap is the ephemeral nature of its work. It cannot effect real change, because in a market economy that thrives on novelty, it will always be displaced by another, newer reading. The vision of competition that Showalter displays is a kind of nightmare of endless change where neither judgment nor political (or moral) imperatives have any force in arresting an endless succession of readings that exist only to be displaced.

The antidote to this pluralistic world is, in Showalter's view, the establishing of a basic model, making definition out of the plethora of competing visions, arriving at a consensus (1981: 246). The problem is for her chaos, change, multiplicity; the solution must then be stabilizing, unitary, and coherent. The basis becomes female experience, which, unified under the embracing rubric of gynocritics, seems to disarm the threat of change and division. At the end of "Feminist Criticism in the Wilderness," she proclaims that the goal some feminists had foreseen in which gender would lose its specificity and texts would become as sexless as angels was a "misperceived" "destination" (1981: 266); instead, we now understand that "the specificity of women's writing" is not "a transient by-product of sexism" but "a fundamental and continually determining reality" (1981: 266). The promised land turns out not to be the "serenely undifferentiated universality of texts," but is instead "the tumultuous and intriguing wilderness of difference itself" (1981: 267). Despite the rhetoric, however, this wilderness and tumult is in fact the theoretical home for which Showalter ardently longs, one that she is prepared to defend against interlopers and unwanted houseguests. Yet its foundations and its walls are even from the beginning infiltrated with complications and intimations of change that will ultimately force Showalter to take refuge in another, more expansive theoretical shelter.

We can see the difficulties in embryonic form in Showalter's early essay, "Toward a Feminist Poetics." There she summarizes her argument from *A Literature of Their Own*, which outlines the historical emergence of a female voice that is the cornerstone of gynocritics. It is a tripartite evolution, with each stage designated by the label that corresponds to a particular phase of development. The trajectory of change begins in 1840 and extends to the present, but Showalter makes no reference to earlier historical periods, which seem either to be non-existent or to be subsumed into the first category. The first two stages are neatly divided into forty year chunks: the "feminine," which extends from 1840 to 1880, and the "feminist," which covers the decades between 1880 and 1920. The phase from 1920 to the present is called "female," and, like the notion of the promised land or the home, seems to signify arrival, where women no longer depend or protest, but turn rather "to female experience as the source of an autonomous art" (1979: 139). As Showalter herself notes, however, this new-found autonomy can become imprisoning, and, citing Woolf's description of life as a "'semi-transparent envelope,'" she strikes an admonitory note about the danger of converting the space of liberation into a claustrophobically enclosed "Room of One's Own," or, indeed, since she sees the Woolfian envelope as a uterine metaphor, a womb of one's own. No such cautionary tone attends her triumphant evolutionary schema, which is a kind of feminist *bildungsroman*, a narrative of progressive independence, in which women detach themselves from their dependence on and imitation of men, becoming artistically united finally with their biological selves and female experience.

Most telling is her discussion of the so-called "feminine" phase, which is distinguished by women striving to equal male achievement (1979: 137). The characteristic mark of this stage, Showalter tells us, is the use of the male pseudonym, a trend that is so prevalent that Showalter wittily claims to have considered calling feminist criticism concerned with the female writer "georgics" instead of gynocritics (1979: 129). She sees the male pseudonym as a way of coping with "a double literary standard," (1979: 138), but the strategy is much more than practical. Its "disguise" "exerts an irregular pressure on the narrative, affecting tone, diction, structure, characterization" (1979: 138). The nature of this disguise – which is, after all, a kind of literary transvestism – produces a literature that is oblique and subversive, and that requires a particular skill in reading, an ability to look for gaps, silences, a capacity to read between the lines (1979: 138). Although Showalter recognizes the use of the male pseudonym as a historically necessary phenomenon, she is eager to see it supplanted by the authenticity of the female voice that emerges in later phases, a judgment that is registered in her designations of "feminine" and "female" as differentially evolved historical stages. "Feminine," for Showalter (and other feminist critics) is taken to signify the cultural construction of femininity in relation to masculinity, whereas "female" has been used to describe innate, biological difference. In the relegation of each term to a particular historical slot within a teleological paradigm, the "female" category gets invested with particular value. Showalter elsewhere disparages the method of reading that the feminine "disguise" necessitates, arguing that the "holes in discourse, the blanks and gaps and silences, are not the spaces where female consciousness reveals itself but the blinds of a 'prison-house of language'" (1981: 256). In other words, she privileges female language or voice over the disguised "feminine" voice, which is in turn valorized in relation to silence. The value these designations carry is assigned within a specific historic range, and the privileging of authorial voice is made possible by the historical phenomenon of a burgeoning of female writers and the publication of their works, an historically specific circumstance that is not shared by writers in the early modern period.

Before turning to the issue of transvestism in more detail, I want to digress briefly to consider Showalter's conception of the author, a factor that, I will argue, compromises the value of the gynocritical model for Renaissance studies. In *Sexual/Textual Politics*, Toril Moi offers a critique of Showalter's reading of Woolf's *A Room of One's Own* that reveals Showalter's dependence on traditional humanism. Showalter's chastisement of Woolf's so-called flight into androgyny – her avoidance of her own female experience – reflects a view of history in which "the text become(s) nothing but the 'expression' of this unique individual: all art becomes autobiography, a mere window on the self and the world, with no reality of its own" (Moi 1985: 8). Showalter's reliance on a "seamlessly unified self" (Moi 1985: 8) is evident in her irritation at Woolf's use of multiple perspectives in *A Room of One's Own*, as Moi astutely points out, because the shifting personae frustrate Showalter's search for the authentic "voice" she claims Woolf wants to find (Showalter 1977: 281). While I would certainly agree that *Room* is preoccupied with voice, it is less concerned with the discovery of Woolf's personal artistic voice than it is with the thematization of the historical silencing or disguising of *women's* writing in general. Showalter's emphasis on the revelation of the female humanist self means that she cannot focus on Woolf's complex and subtle dramatization of this fragmentation of voice. For example, the figures of "Mary Beton," "Mary Seton," and "Mary Carmichael" are never treated by Showalter as anything more than signifiers that stand for particular people, and she is eager to peel away the masks that obscure their identities. "Mary Beton" becomes the persona of the author (which Showalter rapidly conflates with Woolf herself), and Showalter struggles valiantly to assign a determinate identity to the other Marys, making "Mary Seton" Woolf's cousin, Katharine Stephen, while "Mary Carmichael," she says, is probably a "parody or a composite figure" (1977: 283). In fact, "composite" is the very word Woolf uses to describe the representation of woman in fiction, where woman's imaginative importance in literature is inversely correlated to her insignificance in life (Woolf 1929: 45–6). It is thus not surprising that what "identities" we can ascribe to the Marys of *A Room of One's Own* are precisely not reflections of "real" women at all, or at least, their origins are multiplicitous and complicatedly mediated by anonymity and history.

The fragmentation and scattering of the Marys and their voices throughout *Room*, and the way each name gathers specific reference at particular junctures only to emerge later on in different guises, signals the intertextual origin of the Marys and elaborates the parable that lies at the heart of Woolf's essay. Mary Beton, Mary Seton, and Mary Carmichael are three of the four Marys of the eighteenth-century Scottish ballad, "Mary Hamilton" (Child 1965: No. 173), a ballad that seems to have been inspired by an incident in the court of Mary, Queen of Scots (Child 1965: III; 386). The narrative, which, significantly, recapitulates the plot of Shakespeare's sister's story, tells of a young woman, living in the court, who became pregnant, murdered her illegitimate child, and was condemned to die for the offense. The refrain in one variant encapsulates the relationship among the Marys:

> Yestreen Queen Mary had four Maries,
> This night she'll hae but three;
> She had Mary Seaton, and Mary Beaton,
> And Mary Carmichael, and me.
>
> (Child 1965: 386)

The ballad as a form is, of course, closely associated with multiple voicing, since its origins are obscure, since its relationship to myth and history are both rich and unclear, and since it exists in multiple variants, for it was transmitted orally and was not codified in writing until the eighteenth century. It stands as the ideal vehicle for Woolf's argument about women writers, because it encodes an anonymous narrative about female social destiny in a form that is oral and that is as transmittable or as suppressible as rumor itself (and rumor is, after all, one of the main agents of Mary Hamilton's demise). The "voice" that narrates the ballad in many of the variants is that of Mary Hamilton herself, a voice that will be silenced by execution (and in the Russian variants, torture as well), but that continues to propagate itself after death in the fictional "voice" of the ballad. Fittingly, Mary Hamilton is the name that is excised from *Room*, but its absence informs the essay and is its subject. The specificity of her name is subverted by her association with the other Marys, for the repetition of the first name accentuates the interchangeability of the four maids-of-honor (and the queen); Mary Hamilton's fate could as easily have been theirs. Mary Hamilton's narrative functions, then, as *A Room of One's Own*'s mute subtext, whose silence is at once amplified and displaced into the narrative of Shakespeare's sister. The hypothetical narrative that Woolf offers of what might have happened if Shakespeare had had a sister is itself a mute ventriloquism, one in which not a word that Shakespeare's sister might have spoken is uttered. Instead, the circumstances of her fabricated life are given as testimony to her tragic silence, a kind of historical dumb show, in which her muteness is ventriloquized and reenacted.

A similar problematization of voice is apparent in my epigraph to this chapter, where Woolf cites Nick Greene – the actor-manager who befriends and impregnates Shakespeare's sister – who remembers Woolf's own narrative (in which he plays a part) and says that a woman acting reminds him of a dog dancing. Woolf's claim that Samuel Johnson repeated the analogy two hundred years later to describe women preachers, playfully subverts pieties about origin, citation, chronology, literary property, and gender, for the source of the remark is now a character Woolf herself invented, which, among other things, makes Johnson a plagiarist. Woolf's recontextualization of the analogy, situated as it is within the literary product of this travesty of nature (a woman writing is like a woman preaching or a dog dancing), makes a difference, for it is ventriloquized (and variously mediated – Woolf, Mary Beton, Nick Greene, Johnson) by a female voice created by a female author. Woolf thus enters this misogynistic epithet from the very perspective that it seeks to erase through its satiric humor, enacting the travesty of nature the analogy describes. As I will argue at the end of this chapter, this is a strategy that Luce Irigaray (1985b) has called mimicry, and it is the mechanism that both she and Sarah Kofman (1985) use to reread Freud from the point of view of the silenced and disempowered woman of his theories. In the case of Woolf, this practice of subversive miming allows her to read Johnson against himself, exposing Johnson as a ridiculous figure by measuring him against his own narrowness of judgment.

Despite (or perhaps because of) Woolf's thematization of silence in *Room*, it could be argued that the parable of Shakespeare's sister is a kind of founding text for gynocritics. Gilbert and Gubar's volume, *Shakespeare's Sisters: Feminist Essays on Women Poets*, examines the achievements of Shakespeare's "many sisters" (1979: xv), women who wrote poetry even though patriarchal strictures attempted to impose silence on them. I want to emphasize that the gynocritical endeavor is unmistakably a laudable one, both for feminist critics working in the nineteenth century as well as for those whose task is the recovery of the works of female authors writing in the early modern period. The gynocritical imperative is responsible for the recuperation of the reputations of such poets as Lady Mary Wroth and Aemilia Lanier, as well as the discovery and publication of all kinds of previously undervalued writing by women (autobiography, diaries, sermons, letters, pamphlets), and the pressure gynocritics has exerted both on the traditional canon and on the theoretical principles that underlie it is prodigious. But because gynocritics, as it has been propounded and practiced by Showalter (and Gilbert and Gubar), takes nineteenth-century literature as its model, there have been a number of unfortunate repercussions, especially for feminists working in earlier historical periods. First, gynocritics valorizes the female author, construed as a stable, historically verifiable woman. Yet as Woolf herself reminds us, "Anon, who wrote so many poems without signing them, was herself a woman" (1929: 51). The desire to correlate signature with historical personage means that authorial indeterminacy – transvestism of signature, absence of signature, or disguised signature – and the differing status of an author with respect to textual "property" are disregarded, often with the result of flattening or erasing crucial distinctions. The gynocritical privileging of the unitary author also ignores literary collaborations and the richly intertextual character of literary production. Second, although this is not a necessary fruit of gynocritics, because it is a recuperative program, it is inscribed with a competitive urgency, a desire to provide a canon of female authors as worthy as the existing canon of male authors. Since it is difficult to undertake an authorial and generic challenge simultaneously, gynocritics has often limited itself to traditional genres. Third, perhaps because Anglo-American feminist criticism is so strongly grounded in the nineteenth century, that century tends to furnish the historical paradigm for feminist criticism and theory. As I suggested earlier, Showalter is particularly prone to evolutionary metaphors, as if a disturbing Darwinian subtext were shaping her theories. In Gilbert and Gubar's *Norton Anthology of Literature by Women* we can see the practical effects of the evolutionary pattern: the Middle Ages and the Renaissance are sparsely represented by thirty-eight pages, the seventeenth and eighteenth centuries are more amply depicted in one hundred and twenty-two pages, and female literary production positively burgeons in the nineteenth and twentieth centuries, so that the remaining two thousand plus pages can barely contain the efflorescence. This evolutionary pattern is an instance of what Marguerite Waller – in an analysis of the way the ideological operations of critical discourse sometimes replicate those of the texts under examination, a "rhetorical moebius loop" – has dubbed the "TOOTSIE trope" (1987: 2), and it is to this trope of transvestism and ideological replication that I want now to turn.

Showalter's influential 1983 essay "Critical Cross-Dressing; Male Feminists and the Woman of the Year" was originally presented as a review of a number of books, three of which were male authored and treated feminist theory. The 1982 film, *Tootsie*, starring Dustin Hoffman, serves – in the way the narrative of Shakespeare's sister informs Woolf's essay – as the cautionary exemplum of male feminism and the dangers of transvestism. Showalter's trenchant analysis of the film reveals Hoffman not as the ideal feminist some reviewers claimed he was, but rather as a phallic woman; his cross-dressing becomes "a way of promoting the notion of masculine power while masking it" (1983: 123). Hoffman's masquerade as a woman paradoxically reveals his masculine privilege, and the gap between the feminine disguise and the man who inhabits it is the space in which the film's comedy flourishes (Michael Dorsey's lowering of his "voice" to a male register in order to hail a cab effectively), and the space in which anti-feminism is displayed. That is, Dorothy Michaels is a more interesting and effective character than any of the "real" women in the film, and the dilemma of her transvestism exposes the vulnerabilities of women even as it provides an antidote to the anxieties such (real) feminine weakness provokes. Hoffman mimes feminine disempowerment, but he always overcomes it, not as a woman, but as the man beneath the disguise. Marguerite Waller has perceptively argued that the spectator's position is masculinized by the film, associating viewers with the unseen, shadowed male figures, and thus effectively erasing the female perspective (1987: 3). Showalter similarly suggests that in the film's unwitting message – that feminism is more palatable and interesting when it comes from a man (1983: 123) – there is a lesson to be learned about the dangers both of transvestite disguise and male feminism.

Showalter goes on to apply this monitory parable to a number of male literary critics who use feminist theory. She sets up a comparison between Jonathan Culler's use of feminism in *On Deconstruction* (1982) and Terry Eagleton's (1982) competitive usurpation of feminism in *The Rape of Clarissa*; her approval of Culler's explication rests primarily on his lack of disguise, for he writes not as a woman, but as a man and a feminist (1983: 126). In contradistinction, Eagleton practices a kind of "rape" of feminist criticism, an appropriation that declines to acknowledge self-reflexively his own (male) subject position. Just as Eagleton sees the rape of Clarissa as an act in which Lovelace recovers the lost phallus, so Showalter reads Eagleton as "possessing" feminist criticism as a way of containing his own anxiety about the so-called effeminacy of writing (as opposed to revolutionary action) (1983: 128). Despite Showalter's endorsement of Culler and of Eagleton's use of feminist theory in his *Literary Theory: An Introduction*, she nevertheless implicitly claims that men and women read differently; she juxtaposes Eagleton's interpretation of the rape of Clarissa with Terry Castle's reading of the rape, arguing that the novel polarizes readers along gender lines, and (with Castle) that rape is a kind of cultural silencing, an interpretation to which "female/feminist readers" are especially responsive. While I would certainly agree with Showalter that many male critics have sought to use feminism to support rather than confound patriarchal domination in literary studies, the theoretical implications of her insights are more problematic. At the end of her essay, she sets French feminist theory against Anglo-American feminism, claiming that the decentering of the human subject, the purported death of the author, and the insignificance of the gender of the signature in *écriture feminine* have made feminism more available for male appropriation (1983: 131). Anglo-American feminism must, on the other hand, continue to stress the importance of women's writing and the crucial significance of the author's signature as a way of protecting feminism's special province, female writing. The issue she raises is one of canonicity and political change; she fears the cooptation of feminism by male critics and the erasure of the female voice in history.

Showalter's insistence on the propriety of distinct sexual categories ("the question of whether a man or a woman wrote a text is of primary importance" (1983: 131)) carries forward an uneasiness about cross-dressing that is observable in earlier essays. For example, she criticizes even Virginia Woolf's exploration of androgyny in the "tedious high camp of *Orlando*" (1977: 291), and she pronounces in "Toward a Feminist Poetics" that feminist theory "cannot go around forever in men's ill-fitting hand-me-downs, the Annie Hall of English studies, but must, as John Stuart Mill wrote about women's literature in 1869, 'emancipate itself from the accepted models, and guide itself by its own impulses'" (1979: 139). (The irony of invoking a male voice as an authority at precisely this moment of liberation goes unremarked.) While Showalter's anxieties about male feminism have been shared by a number of important and influential feminist theorists (Alice Jardine, Tania Modleski, Nancy Miller, and others), her political concerns about feminism, as I have already argued, take the particular form of an anxiety about instability and chaos, about the crossing of categories, be they sexual or national (the uneasy alliance of French and Anglo-American feminisms). Her conclusion to "Critical Cross-Dressing" is a futuristic vision inspired by the surrealistic cover illustrations to a *Diacritics* special issue on gender, one of which portrays a figure that is ambiguously dressed (a tuxedo and high heels) and headless, while the other depicts various items of female clothing that cover (or discover) the absence of a (sexed) body. For Showalter, these illustrations hint "at the ephemera of gender identities, of gender signatures" (1983: 132), as if her worst fear had come true, and the gender of the author would cease to be important, or worse, verifiable. Her nightmare of the "feminist literary conference of the future" features a woman who mutates, the diacritical woman without a head, and a man wearing a dress, all figures that transgress the categories to which they seem to belong.

I have focused at some length on Showalter's theorization of gynocritics, especially as it is expressed in the metaphorics of domesticity and the home, the authenticity of voice, and the trope of fashion. These metaphors seem to point to Showalter's longing for stability, her dislike of disguise, and her conviction that change is teleological, that it ultimately arrives at a destination that is more satisfying than its point of origin or departure. Her impatience with disguise – whether of literary identity, or of men masquerading as feminists – suggests a profound belief in the stability of the human subject and of the permanence of gender assignation. Even her response to Terry Eagleton's infuriatingly oblique but interesting allegory about class rather than gender (which is offered as a response to her critique of him in "Critical Cross-Dressing") is couched in terms of sexual difference: men and women have different conversational styles in our culture, and Eagleton's putative failure to engage with her is a symptom of male conversational tyranny (Showalter 1987: 136). It is as if Showalter's view of clothing as disguise or as covering of essential biological difference were also a comment on fashion (and literary critical fashions); if it changes – as Buicks are produced, and become obsolete so that they can be replaced by new ones – it must be lacking permanence and hence value. The desire for ontological stability that informs Showalter's writing on gynocritics has, ironically, made it too inflexible a model to survive change. In many ways, gynocritics recapitulates the monolithic qualities of patriarchy by setting itself up as a private society in which admission is granted only to those who possess the proper anatomical equipment. Its untheorized valorization of voice pays little attention to the definition of what voice is in relation to an author, a signature, a reader, a text, not to mention the complexities of voice within the text. Nor does it consider the way gender and sex change across cultures and time. Male feminism is not, after all, only a phenomenon of the late twentieth century, as is apparent in Gilbert and Gubar's (1979) reference to the Wife of Bath or Showalter's own citation of John Stuart Mill. Does male feminism become more palatable when the author is dead? Or, is it a question of reappropriating a voice, where citation and recontextualization lend it an intertextual "double-voicing," so that the female voice that quotes a male text provides an antidote to its maleness?

To try to answer these questions, I want to turn now to Showalter's discussions of gender and double-voicing. Given her attack on transvestism in "Critical Cross-Dressing," it is somewhat surprising – but not unanticipated – to see Showalter's *volte face* in the introduction to *Speaking of Gender*. There she speaks retrospectively and magisterially about the "rise of gender" as a category of analysis in the 1980s, and her writing is characterized by a new kind of expansiveness and inclusiveness. Instead of collapsing sex and gender into barely discernible separate categories, she pulls them apart, making sex, gender, and sexuality different from each other. She further problematizes the relationship among these terms by invoking transsexual operations, which, she argues, deconstruct the "natural" linkage among sex, gender, and sexuality, although the intertwining of these categories is even more subtle than Showalter has time to explore. Gynocritics turns out to be a stage rather than an end in itself; she says that in 1981 "it was far too early and dangerous to give up the demanding task of reconstructing women's literary heritage" (1989: 5), but the retrospectiveness and distance of her discussion (produced partly by quoting other critics rather than herself) make it clear that the historical efficacy of gynocritics is a thing of the past. She cites the dangers of ghettoization implicit in gynocritics, arguing that only by examining gender in relation both to men and women can we begin to understand its operations. Myra Jehlen's call to examine women and men's writing in the same historical period in order to reveal the contingency of patriarchal domination was prophetic but premature, she argues, since there was no body of theory upon which to base such a methodology. The major enabling factor for the rise of gender is, according to Showalter, critical attention directed to the marks of gender in male writing, a perspective that makes evident for the first time the historical and cultural contingency of patriarchal privilege. This critical attention is made possible partly by feminist criticism and partly by the new attention to race, class, history, and sexual preference (codified theoretically in "Afro-American" criticism, New Historicism, and gay studies (1989: 7)). This, Showalter tells us, enables men to examine their own position as men, rather than as participants in male feminism, which "looked a lot like the old misogyny dressed up in Woolf's clothing" (1989: 7). Despite this unflattering reference to transvestism, Showalter cites approvingly studies of metaphorical cross-dressing as one of the places in feminist criticism where "gender" first began to appear as a critical category (1989: 5). Her introduction of gender studies into feminist theory marks a new stage, however, where it seems that the binarities of outside and inside, of clothing and what it covers, and of men and women, are deconstructed in favor of a sophisticated sense of the interplay of these elements. Although Showalter's introduction rightly ends on a cautionary note about the dangers of the new (potentially post-feminist) critical community she sees forming around issues of gender (and class, race, and sexual orientation),[3] dangers she had anticipated in "Critical Cross-Dressing," she also seems eager to affirm a community that is inclusive of difference. Showalter doesn't overtly embrace French theory and the instability of the subject, and she still argues for the moral and political imperative that authors take responsibility for their own subject positions, but it is a theory that, perhaps because of its potential for exploring the shifting boundaries between the specificities of sexual difference – especially as they are inflected by such factors as sexual orientation – offers more flexible possibilities for Renaissance studies.

In "The Rise of Gender," Showalter cites "double-voicing" as a feature of gynocritics. I want to back up for a moment to consider that description, because the idea of double-voiced texts provides a way out of the sometimes constricting bind of gynocritics. She claims that gynocriticism was "'bi-textual'" and "double-voiced" in the sense that female-authored texts are always in dialogue with a matrilineal and a patrilineal heritage (1989: 4–5). She had elaborated this idea in "Feminist Criticism in the Wilderness," where, drawing on the writings of Edwin Ardener, a cultural anthropologist,[4] she discussed the overlapping of muted (female) and dominant (male) discourses. Articulated as intersecting circles, "X" describes the sphere of dominant order, whereas "Y" designates the circle of the muted group. There is a crescent of each circle that does not overlap with the other, a separate space that is inaccessible to the other group, and these crescents are valued asymmetrically, depending on their gender. Where the "X" crescent refers to a "zone of male experience alien to women" (1981: 262), which can be known by women even if it cannot be seen, the "Y" crescent stands for a "wild zone" of female experience that is unknowable by men. The basis of the gynocritical project is this wild zone, which is "the address of a genuinely woman-centered criticism, theory, and art, whose shared project is to bring into being the symbolic weight of female consciousness, to make the invisible visible, to make the silent speak" (1981: 263). While Showalter later admits that this zone is a "playful abstraction" and that feminist critics must understand women's writing as a "'double-voiced discourse' that always embodies the social, literary, and cultural heritage of both the muted and the dominant" (1981: 263), it is nevertheless fair to say that her emphasis is more on the "female" crescent that exceeds the overlapping circles than on the intersection of discourses. Even when she invokes a model of literary parentage, she notes the imbalance at work: "a woman writing unavoidably thinks back through her fathers ... only male writers can forget or mute half their parentage" (1981: 265). As she acknowledges in her later theorization of the problem in "The Rise of Gender," however, the difficult but crucial task for feminist critics is to understand the sexual difference that divides male from female experience as not so much a static division into separate spheres of experience as the relationship between gender and its social construction. The emphasis is thus shifted from a territorialization of difference (what makes men and women distinct) to an analysis of social power and the hierarchization of gender (1989: 4).

Teresa de Lauretis has likewise reminded us that a theoretical focus on sexual difference operates at the expense of other differences that divide women, such as class, race, and sexual preference (1987: 2). The danger of a theory of sexual difference is that it moves rapidly toward effacing historical and cultural specificity, tending toward the metaphorization of Woman that is such a prevalent feature of postmodern (and postfeminist) French philosophy. This displacement of gender on to a textual figure of femininity (de Lauretis 1987: 24) is what Alice Jardine has brilliantly analysed as gynesis, a space coded as feminine or maternal that becomes a locus in which (male) theorists (such as Derrida, Lyotard, and Deleuze) confront the breakdown of the paternal "Master Discourses" of religion, philosophy, science, and history (Jardine 1985: 25–7, 34). She argues that the problem with gynocritics is the impossibility of separating "the two sexes and their imaginations" (1985: 40), and her solution is to elaborate a "new theory and practice of the speaking subject," one that can accommodate the ethical concerns of American feminists and the emphasis on language and process in French feminism. Or, to put it another way, American feminism tends to emphasize the empirical, "external" study of female language, where French feminist theorists concentrate on the internal process of signification, the way the gender of the speaking subject is constructed by language (Jardine 1985: 44–5). Jardine, like de Lauretis, cautions against the reinscription in feminist theory of male narratives of gender (de Lauretis 1987: 25). Unlike Showalter, whose theory of gynocritics emerges from a similar anxiety about being absorbed into the male theory she relies upon, de Lauretis sees the interaction of male gender narratives and feminist theory as inevitable. Her solution is a continual strategy of resistance, a rewriting of cultural narratives, the creation of new spaces of discourse, what she terms – using a cinematic metaphor – the "space-off," the area not visible in the frame but inferable from it (1987: 25). Where gynocritics inevitably (and sometimes unwittingly) reproduces what it seeks to eradicate, the strategies advanced by feminist theorists like Jardine and de Lauretis (and Showalter in her most recent writing) provide ways of undoing the hegemonic discourses of sexuality and gender.

My focus on voice is thus multiple. I am interested in "double-voicing," not in Showalter's definition of the term as genealogical influence, but in the interaction between an "author" and the constructed voice through which he or she speaks, especially as that intersection crosses genders and is imaged as transvestism. In a sense, I am investigating the historical use of the *Tootsie* trope in the Renaissance, not because I want to unmask men who speak as women, but because the phenomenon of transvestite ventriloquism itself – the gap between the male voice and the female voice it takes on – has much to say about cultural constructions of gender.[5] The crossing of voices encodes what de Lauretis calls the "interstices of institutions," "the chinks and cracks of the power–knowledge" system (1987: 25), a kind of historical "space-off" In male appropriations of feminine voices we can see what is most desired and most feared about women and why male authors might have wished to occupy that cultural space, however contingently and provisionally. That men did so provides a legacy of gynesis, a metaphorization of woman, that has at least partially shaped what gynocritics now identify as the "female voice." To recognize this legacy is not, however, to deny the importance of the gender of the author. On the contrary, I argue that transvestite ventriloquism is asymmetrically disposed in relation to the sexes: it is different for a man to ventriloquize a woman's voice than for a woman to speak in a masculine voice, since gender itself is asymmetrically constructed in relation to power. Far from wishing to sever the links between body and voice, author and text, voice and text, and text and reader, I want to affirm and interrogate them. At the same time, however, I recognize the constructed nature of each of these categories, as well as the historical and cultural contingencies of the ligatures between them.

II

I begin by considering a scene of double transvestism, the moment in Book V of Spenser's *Faerie Queene* when Britomart (a woman dressed as a man) rescues Artegall (a man dressed as a woman) from his shameful enslavement to the Amazon Radigund (a woman who transgresses the boundaries of her sex). It is important to remember that Renaissance conceptions of the sexes were based on the Galenic principle of homology. That is, the genitals of men and women were considered to be basically the same, except that women's reproductive organs were internal, whereas men's were external to the body. Not only were their sexual organs homologous, but their sexual experience was analogous, since both experienced orgasm, and orgasm was necessary not only for ejaculation but also for conception (Laqueur 1986: 1; Orgel 1989: 13). The distinction between men and women in the Renaissance lies not in an ontological difference, but rather in the way gender is hierarchized within a common physiology. As Thomas Laqueur puts it, "There was still in the sixteenth century, as there had been in classical antiquity, only one canonical body and that body was male" (1990: 63). The difference between men and women was, then, not a matter of kind, but of degree: women are imperfect (men) because they lack the generative heat that would cause their reproductive organs to be extruded (Maclean 1980: 32; Laqueur 1986: 5). Because heat is associated with perfection in Galen's account, the hotter temperature of males produced a more perfect being: "The male grows faster *in utero*, is of darker and harder flesh, more hirsute, more able to sustain extremes of temperature, has larger arteries and veins, a deeper voice, is less prone to disease, more robust, broader, comes to full maturity more slowly and ages less quickly than the colder female" (Maclean 1980: 32). The female's relative coldness, on the other hand, is responsible for menstruation, her high voice, her paler and fattier flesh, her physical shape (broader hips, narrower shoulders), her propensity to reach puberty earlier and to age more quickly (Maclean 1980: 35).

Despite the physiological divergences generated by heat and its lack – differences that are codified medically and ideologically so that they become "natural" – what is striking about Renaissance conceptions of gender is that, because of the anatomical similarities, there exists the dangerous possibility of one sex turning into the other (Orgel 1989: 14). While women were capable of being transformed into men through prodigious activity or excitement, a teleological progression that worked to enhance representations of masculinity, the reversal of this trajectory – where men degenerated into women – was an ignominious and dangerous state that threatened the patriarchal system. What I wish to consider is the way this gender transformation is effected by and represented in clothing. As John

Guillory has argued, "The institution of clothing, while it conceals anatomical difference, may be said to institute sexual difference, as a properly semiological distinction, as socially constructed" (1990: 76). The ideology of clothes meant that writers of the period saw sexual distinctions of dress as naturally rather than culturally prescribed, so not only is biblical authority frequently invoked to underwrite the truth of these sartorial categories, but adulteration of dress is seen as a contamination of essence and nature.[6] In English Renaissance culture, clothing became an external marker of class and occupation (codified in sumptuary laws), as well as gender, and it is therefore not surprising that dress in *The Faerie Queene* becomes a crucial system of identificatory signs, which may or may not register consistency, or accurately project what it also covers. It is this discrepancy between inner and outer with which I am most concerned in the Radigund episode.

Radigund, herself, of course, embodies sexual transgression, not only because she behaves like a man, but also because, as an Amazon, she is associated with a society always situated at the margin of the known world (Montrose 1983: 66). She stands as a borderline figure – part history, part myth – an embodiment in the Renaissance of the unknown. Some of her enigma is linguistic: according to Herodotus, Amazons were known for their ability to master other men's languages, but men were, in contradistinction, unable to learn the Amazonian tongue (Showalter 1981: 254). Spenser's mention of the Amazon river in the Proem to Book 2 situates it in lands only recently colonized. The reference is ostensibly a justification for his creation of the land of Faery (for, although it is not yet known to exist, it too may one day be discovered as a "real" place); yet the allusion to the Amazon (as well as to "fruitfullest *Virginia*" (2:2)) links it to the act of colonization, an overcoming of a foreign people, in Radigund represented as a different and barbaric sexual custom. As an Amazon, Radigund exemplifies simultaneously masculine and feminine traits: she fights like a man and is clearly accustomed to the exercise of power, but her battle-dress is alluringly and femininely ornamented, and she experiences a characteristically female erotic passion. Her behavior is thus ambiguously gendered, and the blend of male and female elements is imaged as irregular, discordant, and anomalous. Rather than enhancing her female status through its inclusion of masculine attributes, she is figured as incompletely assimilated ("halfe like a man" (5.5: 36)), a sexual misfit. The result of this sexual incongruity is perhaps most easily seen as its effects are mirrored in other characters, especially Artegall.

When Artegall first encounters the troop of Amazons leading Sir Turpine (a name cognate with the Latin *turpis* or shame) to the gallow tree for his refusal to submit to the "proude oppression/ Of womens powre" (5.4: 26), Artegall displays no inclinations toward effeminacy. On the contrary, he initially berates Turpine in a series of questions that seem already incriminating; addressing him as a "haplesse man," he asks whether Turpine has "lost" his "selfe" (an absence of identity that is dramatized in Turpine's first appearance, where his bared head and covered face renders him unknowable). The choice of "haplesse" is apt, as Turpine indicates in his application of the epithet to himself, for in addition to the obvious sense of "unfortunate," "hap" also carries the Middle English sense of clothing or covering. That Turpine has refused to put on women's clothing is, of course, what brings him almost to death. Despite Artegall's initial scorn and his implicit indictment of Turpine's presence among the Amazons, it is as if he changes places with Turpine, since, by going to Radegone to avenge this shame on mankind, Artegall suffers a fate even worse than Turpine's by agreeing to dress as a woman. Not only does he clothe himself in their garments, but he also occupies a woman's place, subjects himself to a female ruler, uses feminine wiles to survive, and, finally, allows himself to be rescued by a woman dressed in male armor. The process of this transformation is not, however, immediate. When Artegall originally arrives at the city of Amazons, he engages in fierce battle with its inhabitants, striking Radigund a blow of such force that, had she not warded it off, it would have killed her. The similes used to describe the encounter inscribe a gender hierarchy: Artegall is likened to a "kingly" eagle driving Radigund, a "Goshauke," from her prey (Turpine) (5.4: 42). When night comes, Radigund gathers her followers within the city walls, and Artegall sets up his rich pavilion outside the gates, in a scene that invokes the Petrarchan conceit of the amorous siege. The Petrarchan echo is, in fact, proleptic of the eroticism that will suffuse the single combat between Radigund and Artegall the next day, and it also links Radigund to Spenser's Queen through the activation of the Petrarchan ideology that Elizabeth cultivated in her relations with her courtiers.

The erotic nature of the duel is signalled in the account of Radigund's battle attire, which, while it alludes to the epic hero's preparation for war, also displays a "feminine" preoccupation with ornament. The prelude to the account of Radigund's dressing alerts us to the discrepancy between the combatants' sartorial preparations:

they dressed, "The Knight, as best was seeming for a Knight,/ And th'Amazon, as best it likt her selfe to dight" (5.5: 1). Mimicking their respective concerns for attire, Radigund's dressing is described at length, where Artegall's is given half a line. Radigund's camis of purple silk woven with silver – which is quilted on white satin and trailing with ribbons – and her gold buskins recall the depiction of Belphoebe in Book 2, except that where a harmonious blend of masculine and feminine attributes distinguished Belphoebe's costume,[7] Radigund is motivated by perversion, and she expresses the monstrous, discrepant union of the sexes within her person, divided as she is between presenting herself as a woman in appearance and a man in action. The duel between her and Artegall is initially savage in its fury, but Artegall's strategy is to defend himself, waiting for her to wear herself out: "The more she rag'd, the more he did abide" (5.5: 6). Like a smith, who, seeking to "subdew" metal, waits until the metal is "mollifide with heat" before he beats it with his iron "fledge," (5.5: 7) so Artegall sets upon Radigund once the fire of her rage has softened her. Here we can see an apparent inversion of the Galenic principle in which heat converts women into men, since the hotter Radigund grows, the more capable she is of being defeated by Artegall's male strength. The ostensible parallelism of the simile is misleading, however, because the second half does not accord with the first: "So did Sir *Artegall* upon her lay,/ As if she had an yron anduile beene" (5.5: 8). The double meaning of "lay" – either "to beat down" or "to place in a position of recumbency" – provides an ambiguous pivot point. If Radigund is an anvil – the iron block upon which the metal is hammered – then Artegall, not Radigund, becomes the metal to be beaten and softened, and it is he, not she, who will be mollified. The process of mollification is what this battle (and the entire Radigund episode) is about; the possible etymological connection between the Latin "mulier" (woman) and the verb "mollire," to become soft and flexible, is analogous to the process by which Radigund renders Artegall soft and pliable, and ultimately turns him into a woman. We need, though, to consider the question of agency, which is what the discrepancy at the juncture of the parallelism reveals. Although Radigund does wound Artegall in the thigh, that symbolic castration is made possible by a process of effeminization that is already at work. That is, as Artegall's later behavior in the duel makes clear, he submits freely to Radigund, laying himself across the very anvil that he had destined for her ultimate shaping. The moment of acquiescence is ostensibly when Artegall removes her helmet and "dis-covers" her face, since it is in that glance that her feminine beauty overpowers (the word Spenser uses is, again, "mollifie" (5.5: 13)) his masculine bellicosity. But we can see that the process of mollification begins much earlier. It is Radigund's martial fury that inspires Artegall's strategy of waiting, and it is, presumably, the action of waiting, a position induced by her activity, that begins the effeminizing transformation. In other words, Radigund's (heated) masculine behavior forces Artegall to occupy the position of the other (woman), and, even when he seems most to be opposing her, he is powerless to choose a masculine site of resistance.

Once the dispositions of power in the battle change, so, too, do the similes. Where the eagle–goshawk pair pointed to a hierarchy of gender, Radigund now becomes a "puttock," a buzzard or kite, attacking a "gentle" bird, a disabled falcon, a divergence of attitude that suggests not only gender (Artegall has mutated from eagle to gentle (female?) falcon) but also class. Ironically, Artegall's aristocratic nature is accentuated through linguistic ornamentation (simile) at the same time that he is stripped of the sartorial markers of rank. Radigund's fierce wrath does not abate until he delivers his shield, and thus "was he ouercome, not ouercome,/ But to her yeelded of his owne accord" (5.5: 17). The sign of his submission is the "warelesse word" of acquiescence that he utters, and where he uses language to signal his yielding, she accepts his humiliation with a warlike gesture of her sword. In a kind of parodic echo of the creation of a knight, Radigund strikes him with the flat of her sword, signalling his "true subjection to her powre." Radigund's creation of a vassal in her "thraldome" ironically reverses Artegall's status; far from making him a knight, it unmakes him. He is then stripped of "all the ornaments of knightly name" and clothed in "womans weedes, that is to manhood shame" (5.5: 20). Thus clad, Radigund leads him to a chamber filled with brave knights similarly attired, all of whom are engaged in spinning and carding.

The narrator invokes the pathos of this metamorphosis through an allusion to Hercules's cross-dressing: "Who had him seene, imagine mote thereby,/ That whylome hath of *Hercules* bene told,/ How for *Iolas* sake he did apply/ His mightie hands, the distaffe vile to hold/ For his huge club" (5.5: 24). Spenser's subtext is ostensibly Hercules's enslavement to Omphale, the Lydian queen who forces him to dress in women's clothing and serve her. As Ovid (1976) recounts it in the *Fasti*, Omphale and Hercules are preparing to celebrate a festival of Bacchus; when they reach the grove and the attendants are preparing their repast, Omphale and Hercules retire to a nearby cave, where they exchange clothing. Ovid describes in witty detail how Hercules's great waist is too large for Omphale's dainty belt, how his strong wrists break her bracelets, and how his large feet split her delicate shoes. She, in turn, dons the lion's skin and Hercules's quiver of weapons, and, thus arrayed, they sit down to eat. After their meal, they retire to separate but adjacent beds, still dressed in each other's clothes. When they are asleep, Faunus, who is lusting after Omphale, creeps into the dark cave, gropes in one bed, and, feeling the rough lion's skin, recoils. He then comes to the second bed, where the soft drapery beguiles him. As he explores further, Hercules awakens, knocks him on the floor, and everyone laughs at the hilarity of Faunus's mistake. The function of the story, according to Ovid, is to explain why Faunus has ever after insisted that worshippers come naked to his rites, for he has since shunned garments that betray, that conceal what lies beneath them. Although the incident has a comic outcome, its "disguised" homoeroticism is a frequent motif in figurations of transvestism, since, just as cross-dressing transgresses the boundaries of gender, so also can it cross the boundaries of heterosexuality by providing titillating – if brief – sexual encounters between members of the same sex.

While transvestism and the moral have some relation to Artegall's enslavement, it does not explain Spenser's confusion of Omphale with "Iola." The conflation is probably derived from Ovid's other recounting of Hercules's cross-dressing, Deianira's epistle in the *Heroides*.[8] The opening lines of the letter describe a rumor spread to all the Pelasgian cities: that although Hercules has vanquished Oechalia, Iole has placed him under her yoke. Deianira goes on to complain of Hercules's other amorous exploits, but the one for which she reserves her ultimate bitterness is Hercules's subjection to Omphale, who, interestingly, is named only periphrastically (therefore enhancing the possibility of confusion). The epistle is thus framed by its indictment of Iole, who subjugates Hercules erotically, even though he has conquered her people. Within this frame, Deianira recalls the shame Omphale's humiliation of Hercules brought, an ignominy made especially vivid by Deianira's imagining Hercules recounting his heroic deeds even as he is arrayed in the girdle and turban of a woman. At the same time that she lists the heroic labors about which he supposedly tells Omphale, Deianira chastises his speech, urging him to maintain a silence in accord with his feminine attire.

> Haec tu Sidonio potes insignitus amictu
> dicere? non cultu lingua retenta silet?
>
> (These deeds can you recount, gaily arrayed
> in a Sidonian gown? Does not your dress rob
> from your tongue all utterance?)
>
> (Ovid 1977b: 114–15)

The irony of Deianira's rebuke is that her own speech is ventriloquized, since Ovid stands behind the vengeful, querulous voice that is supposedly hers. At the same moment that she enjoins Hercules to be silent because of his shameful "womanish" dress, Ovid cross-dresses himself as Deianira, providing the very language that counsels silence. This supposed inscription of the feminine psyche in the *Heroides* – Ovid's liberation of these abandoned and complaining heroines from the representational bondage of a traditional mythology that constrained their expression – reveals itself at junctures like these for the masquerade it is. Ovid's thematization of silence and cross-dressing exposes his own presence as male author, "dressed" in a woman's voice.[9]

Linda Kauffman has persuasively claimed that the *Heroides* are characterized by doubleness. She sees this duplicity at work in the tension between the uniqueness of each heroine's plight and the repetition of their common situation in the collection as a whole, in the simultaneous employment of logic and emotional rhetoric (filiated respectively with the rhetorical exercises *suasoria* and *ethopoiiae*), and, most pertinent for my purposes, in Ovid's subversion of Augustan values through his invention of an epistolary genre that challenges the hegemony of epic (Kauffman 1986: 42, 44, 61). This last insight is a feminist variation on the revisionary thesis advanced by Richard Lanham in *The Motives of Eloquence*, which argued that Ovid's choice of change for the subject matter of the *Metamorphoses*, his intercalation of erotic matter into the Virgilian material in the poem, and his profound skepticism about the stability of individual or Roman identity, interrogate not only epic as a genre but also the values upon which Augustan Rome was built (Lanham 1976: 48–64). Kauffman transposes this insight to the *Heroides* and the issue of gender, asserting that "to write like a woman is to challenge conventional notions of tradition, of origins, of fathers, of paternity, of authority, of identity" (1986: 61). While this statement captures Ovid's strategy perfectly, the fundamental duplicity that makes it work remains unarticulated in Kauffman's account. Ovid can write from the perspective of the woman precisely *because* he is not himself a woman; he metaphorizes the figure of woman, associating her with a constellation of attributes that are already traditional and will remain so: erotic passion, abandonment, desire that cannot be satisfied, rhetorical skill, especially as expressed in the complaint. The very characteristics that Ovid uses to define these women are also the qualities that render them marginal in Roman society (and in subsequent cultures), and it is the recognition (and perpetuation) of their marginality that makes Ovid's impersonation of them subversive. Ovid, like Hoffman in *Tootsie* or Derrida in *Spurs*, uses the metaphor of woman as a lever for dismantling certain patriarchal values, but, unlike the heroines he ventriloquizes, he simultaneously partakes of the very privilege he seeks to expose.

Yet just as Artegall effeminizes himself at a cost, so too, does Ovid. Kauffman joins Howard Jacobson in speculating that it may have been Ovid's portrait of an "*impius Aeneas*" in Dido's Heroidean letter that provoked Augustus to banish him to the inhospitable shores of the Black Sea (Kauffman 1986: 49). His exile literally puts him in the position of the Heroidean women he depicts, for as Kauffman astutely points out, the *Tristia* are full of the sentiments voiced by the abandoned heroines: longing, despair, and grief at the injustice of their plight (1986: 33). Roland Barthes wrote in *A Lover's Discourse* that the "man who waits and who suffers from his waiting is miraculously feminized" (1978: 14), but it is crucial to recognize that occupying the metaphorical position accorded to Woman (the one who waits) is not the same as becoming a woman. We can see this distinction acted out in violent detail at the end of Deianira's letter, where, even as she writes, she hears a report of Hercules's death throes. She berates herself for her deed, since it is her wedding gift to Hercules of a robe impregnated with the poisoned blood of the satyr Nessus that brings about his agonizing end. As Ovid tells it in the *Metamorphoses*, once the burning poison begins to permeate his skin, Hercules "tries to tear off the deadly tunic; but where it is torn away, it tears the skin with it and, ghastly to relate, it either sticks to his limbs, from which he vainly tries to tear it, or else lays bare his torn muscles and huge bones" (Ovid 1977a: 15). While we might be tempted to read this episode as an allegory of the inseparability of the clothing one wears and one's skin or "essence," therefore suggesting that cross-dressing can permanently transform the sex of the wearer, Hercules's fate portrays an opposite sense. That is, the robe that Deianira sends is masculine clothing, but it is permeated with a feminine vengefulness; what is revealed as Hercules tries to strip off the poisoned cloth is the masculinity of the body beneath and the male fury of his pain. When at last Hercules lies on his funeral pyre and is consumed by the flames, what is purged are the traces of his (mortal) mother: "no shape of Hercules that could be recognized remained, nor was there anything left which his mother gave" (Ovid 1977a: 21). He retains qualities from his father only, and, like a serpent that sloughs off its old age with its skin, Hercules shines in resplendent glory, acquires heroic stature, and is set among the stars by Jove.

That Hercules can subjugate himself to Omphale, dress in her clothes, and still redeem himself as a quintessentially male hero does not, however, completely undo the threat his effeminacy poses. Like Renaissance writers, Barthes makes passion, especially erotic passion, the property of Woman. Barthes says that Woman "gives shape to absence, elaborates its fictions, for she has time to do so; she weaves and sings; the Spinning Songs express both immobility (by the hum of the Wheel) and absence (far away, rhythms of travel, sea surges, cavalcades)" (1978: 14). Artegall, in his effeminized captivity, perfectly exemplifies this role, since he must wait for Britomart (as warrior) to rescue him. As Barthes notes, spinning, weaving, and waiting are also figures of writing (Penelope embodies this conjunction in *The Odyssey*), and Artegall is by extension linked with Spenser himself. To represent Artegall as imprisoned by a cruel and capricious queen, forced to earn a meagre existence by repetitive and effeminate work, and constrained to negotiate the possessive and unwanted attentions of the Queen (whose communications are distorted by her go-between) provides dangerous parallels with Spenser's own situation, one that he could hardly have portrayed unless veiled in the darkest of allegories. It is customary for critics to note the figuration of Elizabeth in Gloriana, Belphoebe, and, to a more limited extent, in Britomart, and to see Radigund as a perversion of womanhood, but this interpretation does not take into account the complex linkages between them and the Amazon. Radigund recalls Belphoebe in her attire, and, when Britomart engages in battle with Radigund, not only are they described in similes that suggest equality, but, at certain moments, they become virtually indistinguishable. At one point, their names drop out, and each is referred to by the pronoun "she," effecting a syntactic confusion that mirrors the conflation of their identities. That Britomart is herself wounded in the encounter suggests that Radigund is not just a caricature of the masculine woman, but a genuine threat to Britomart. Louis Montrose argues that, because Britomart is Radigund's double, she incorporates and personifies everything in Britomart that is threatening to Artegall (1983: 76). When Walter Ralegh compared Elizabeth to an Amazon in his *Discoverie of Guiana*, he insinuated that the Queen could free herself from negative associations with the Amazons only if she sanctioned their subjugation (which, of course, would underwrite Ralegh's colonial enterprise) (Montrose 1983: 76), and it is this battle between Amazon figures that Spenser represents in the combat between Radigund and Britomart. In other words, only by setting women against each other can female supremacy be defeated and the "proper," patriarchal order be restored.

After Britomart has successfully vanquished Radigund and freed Artegall from his shameful enslavement, thus enacting "true Iustice" by repealing women's liberty (5.7: 42), we are given a warning of the way female beauty and the love it inspires can "mollify" men. The catalogue of examples includes Samson, Hercules, and Antony; in contrast to them, Artegall will not be restrained by imprisoning love, for nothing can hold him "from suite of his auowed quest,/ Which he had vndertane to *Gloriane*" (5.8: 3). Although he frees himself from Britomart and "her strong request" (5.8: 3), Artegall still labors in the service of Gloriana. Significantly, it is Artegall's voice that Spenser borrows in the proem to Book 5 to address his queen: "Pardon the boldnesse of thy basest thrall,/ That dare discourse of so diuine a read,/ As thy great iustice praysed ouer all:/ The instrument whereof loe here thy *Artegall*" (11). While Spenser was well rewarded by Elizabeth for his poetic offering – receiving a pension of fifty pounds a year after he presented the first three books of *The Faerie Queene* to her – he chose to see his Irish career as a bitter exile and his monetary reward as paltry (Goldberg 1981: 171). Spenser's use of Artegall's voice erases the figure of the poet only to displace it on to the knight of justice in this "most uncompromisingly public" of the books of *The Faerie Queene* (Helgerson 1978: 904). Richard Helgerson, among others, has pointed to the increasing bifurcation of the public and private ideas of the poet in the last two books of the poem, a split between private inspiration and public duty, and an increasing divorce between heroic action and virtue or love (Helgerson 1978: 902–5). Although Spenser's representation of his Queen was multiple and for the most part celebratory, we can read the Radigund episode as depicting the darker aspect of a poet in the service of a female sovereign. Where he subjects her to his veiled, unflattering figurations (her spurned love that is converted to Amazonian misanthropy, her inability to manage her spies, her personal vanity), he depicts himself (through Artegall) as her effeminized subject. The voice through which Artegall speaks is the instrument that condemns him to servitude (the "warelesse word"), a subjugation that he himself invites, just as Spenser's own career as a poet in search of patronage placed him in the service of a sovereign renowned for her dilatoriness. Above all, Artegall's enslavement to Radigund is characterized by waiting – waiting for her to tire in battle, for her to decide his fate when he is in prison, for Britomart to rescue him – a position that humiliates and effeminizes him. Spenser's cross-dressed voice stands, then, among his other often effusive celebrations of Elizabeth's power and wisdom as a disguised and "silent" complaint, an allegorized portrait of one of the consequences of female rule.[10] Where Ovid in the *Heroides* uses a feminine position as a way of exposing and subverting the values of (male) Augustan Rome, Spenser implicitly condemns transvestism in the Radigund episode as the inevitable consequence of his own role in Elizabethan society, a position that violates nature and demeans men. Ovid borrows the metaphor of Woman and the strategies of eroticism in order to contest patriarchal rule, while Spenser's depiction of Radigund as a ruler distorted by thwarted desire and capricious judgment registers an unease with gynocracy and presents the patriarchal alternative to Amazonian power as liberating.[11]

For my second example of voice and transvestism in the Renaissance, I turn to a different problem. Where with Spenser and Ovid, I read the cross-dressed figures against the authorial "voice," which, while historically and culturally constructed, is nevertheless discernible, the two Jacobean pamphlets on transvestism that I will now consider are anonymous. The circumstances surrounding the publication of *Hic Mulier* and *Haec-Vir* are well known. In January of 1620, John Chamberlain reported in a letter that the Bishop of London had called his clergy together and told them that he had received express orders from King James that they should all condemn in their sermons the recent trend in which women dress like men (Woodbridge 1984: 143). Chamberlain enumerates the details that especially attracted the king's displeasure: in addition to their female insolence, he cites "theyre wearing of brode brimd hats, pointed dublets, theyre haire cut short or shorne, and some of them stillettaes or poinards" (Woodbridge 1984: 143). In February, 1620, a pamphlet entitled *Hic Mulier: Or, The Man–Woman: Being a Medicine to cure the Coltish Disease of the Staggers in the Masculine–Feminines of our Times* appeared, and its purpose seemed designed, like the diatribes from the pulpit, to remedy the monstrousness of nature that expressed itself in women's "mannish" dress. The declamation – as it calls itself – is an apostrophe to *Hic Mulier*, which opens by defending the false Latin of its title. The oration converts the Man–Woman into a grammatical subject, arguing that women have become masculine in declension and conjugation: in gender, number, case, mood, and tense (1620: Sig. A3). The conflation of women and language accentuates the representational status of the feminine category, since, just as its deformation is expressed in linguistic corruption, so is its remedy ostensibly achievable through a social purification by means of language. Before the speaker begins his rhetorical flagellation, he pauses for a moment to consider the women he does not include in his condemnation, those good women who are the "crownes of natures worke, the complements of mens excellencies, and the Seminaries of propagation." These women "are Castles impregnable, Rivers unsaileble, Seas immoueable, infinit treasures, and inuincible armies" (1620: Sig. A3v), and for them will be reserved praise written with a golden pen on leaves of golden paper. The author exhorts virtuous women to protect themselves by the clothing they wear, which offers an impenetrable shield and closes off all points of access: "shield [your charms] with modest and comely garments... hauing euery window closed with a strong Casement, and euery Loope-hole furnisht with such strong Ordnance, that no unchaste eye may come neere to assayle them" (1620: Sig. B4). The mannish women who are the subject of his declamation, on the other hand, are imaged in their full deformity in order that they might be called "back to the modest comelinesse in which they were" (1620: Sig. A4v). Where the chaste woman uses the shield of her innocence to protect her, the masculine woman wears a weapon, which figures her aggressive (and sexually assertive) nature.[12]

The shape of their transgression is expressed repeatedly as a distortion of the relationship between inside and outside. While the "good" woman is depicted as unknowable, impregnable, and invincible – images that suggest simultaneously containment, inviolability, and stability, and that do not differentiate between bodies, their coverings, or the spaces inside the body (mind, soul, feminine essence) – the speaker's derision specifically targets ornamentation, cosmetics, particular items of dress, and hair styles, and the carrying of weapons. In other words, the terms of abuse contrast the immutable essence of Woman with the historical and cultural vicissitudes of fashion, thus linking fashion with the dangers of change. Further, these "hermaphrodites" of fashion are criticized both for covering and uncovering their bodies: the modest straight gown has been exchanged for a French doublet, which is unbuttoned "to entice," yet "all of one shape to hide deformitie," and is in addition "extreme short wasted to give a most easy way to every luxurious action" (1620: Sig. A4v). Women use clothes to advertise what is beneath, but what lies under what they wear turns out to be not just sexuality but "deformity," as if female sexuality *were* deformity. The contamination of their feminine nature is represented as disguise, mimicking, and imitation (disguising "the beauty of their creations" "with the glosse of mumming Art"), an "infamie of disguise" whose marks "sticke so deepe on their naked faces, and more naked bodies, that not all the painting in *Rome* ... can conceale them, but every eye discovers them almost as low as their middle" (1620: Sig. Bv). It is as if disguise penetrated the very flesh it covered and then manifested itself as a sign of shame that could be discerned by all eyes. What began as a concealment turns into a transparency of deformity that makes inside and outside once more contiguous. At other points in the pamphlet, however, women's bodies are also as protean as the fashion they wear (they mould "their bodies to euery deformed fashion," [1620: Sig. Bv]), and it is this changeability that is most condemned.

The speaker quotes from Spenser's *Faerie Queene* to support his censure of the masculine woman, citing the lines about the cruelty of women who have shaken off the "shamefast band" with which nature bound them (5.5: 25). The cited lines are the narratorial aside just after Radigund has dressed Artegall in female clothing, and they refer in the first instance to the effeminizing consequences of female power, rather than to the monstrosity of masculine women. In other words, it is the effect on men as much as the act of cross-dressing that is condemned, since transvestism effectively inverts the roles of both sexes. As Linda Woodbridge has observed, however, the clothing the author of *Hic Mulier* describes and the costumes depicted on the frontispiece are precisely not masculine disguises; the difficulty with these images (both pictorial and discursive) is that they are hermaphroditic, for they depict a female body beneath male attire, and they figure women partaking of male privilege and engaging in male pursuits (e.g. the carrying of weapons) (Woodbridge 1984: 145). The fear that is voiced is that costume will become essence, that women will really turn into men, but the threat registered in the disturbing representations of gender hybridism is a more fundamental threat of ambiguity, of sexual indeterminacy. One aspect of this ambiguity is, of course, the irregularity of erotic exchange, so that a woman may be attracted to a man, only to discover that s/he is a woman (as, for instance, Malecasta's wooing of Britomart), or a man may pursue a woman, only to discover a boy beneath her clothing, thus expressing a cultural fear at the heart of transvestism, "that the basic, essential form of erotic excitement in men is homosexual" (Orgel 1989: 17). Clothing that appropriately expresses the anatomy beneath prevents the breaching of these sexual boundaries, and the speaker thus urges women to do away with their foule disguises and "vizards" (1620: Sig. B3v) and reconceal their female charms modestly from the eye, just as nature hides her treasures in "hidden cauerns of the earth." In keeping with the linguistic analogy with which he begins, the author invokes a textual metaphor: "Let not a wandring and lasciuious thought read in an inticing Index the contents of an unchaste volume" (1620: Sig. B3v). Women, like books, ought to disclose their subject matter only to the engaged reader, not lewdly advertise what is within to every passer-by. What the society most fears – especially a culture rent asunder by epistemological, religious, and economic shifts that undermine its foundational certainties – is displaced onto the female body, where it is contained as the (stable) locus of unknowability. Like Lacanian lack, which is ascribed to Woman in order to secure the fiction of a coherent male subjectivity, the Jacobean female body is burdened with the anxieties of change and ambiguity that disturb its myth of itself as stable and knowable. What transvestism threatens, then, is the possibility of making woman the repository of this fear; while the author speaks of transvestism spreading like the plague (1620: Sig. Bv-B2), the imagery of infection figures a no longer containable anxiety about order and stability that becomes as contagious as the transvestism he actually describes.

Where *Hic Mulier* presents itself as conventional misogynist fare, *Haec-Vir*, the pamphlet that answered *Hic Mulier* one week later, is more difficult to evaluate. Rather than the single-voiced apostrophe to transgressive women of *Hic Mulier*, *Haec-Vir* is a dialogue between the effeminate man and the masculine woman. The dialogue opens with a confusion of identities – as if the fear articulated in *Hic Mulier* had been realized – in which the effeminate man mistakes the mannish woman for a man, and she initially believes him to be a woman. When they discover their mistakes, they introduce themselves, although this clarification has the effect of intensifying the confusion when Haec-Vir addresses Hic Mulier as a "most courageous counterfet of *Hercules* and his Distaffe" (1620: Sig. A3v). The two cross-dressed figures begin to debate, Haec-Vir reiterating the charges levelled in the first pamphlet, and Hic Mulier demanding the right to reply. The first and most pertinent defense s/he offers is to the accusation of being a "Slave to Nouelty" (1620: Sig. A3v). This defense of fashion and change reads like a manifesto for the liberation of women from the bonds of patriarchy. "For what is the world," s/he asks, "but a very shop and ware-house of change?" (1620: Sig. B). Since the world is nothing but change, why should "poore woman" stand as "a fixed Starre, that shee shall not so much as moue or twinkle in her owne Spheare"? (1620: Sig. B). Such fixity is indeed what is contrary to nature, s/he argues, for everything in nature alters continually. In defense of "her" "naturalnesse," s/he invokes custom, as the contingent process by which a society affirms its particular habits as natural. Her description of custom has a parallel in Louis Althusser's definition of ideology as representing "the imaginary relationship of individuals to their real conditions of existence" (Althusser 1971: 162). That is, both ideology and custom have the function of constituting individuals as subjects with particular identities, and in the cases s/he cites, the identities are national: just as the English wash their hands before a meal, Romans are accustomed to annointing their arms and legs; as the English sign of mourning is black, Romans signal bereavement by the color white (Sig. B2, B2v). If custom defines national habits, it also codifies gender distinctions within a particular nationality.[13] The common etymological root of custom and costume points to the importance of clothing in registering sexual difference, a linkage that argues for a similar contingency in codes of dress. Where the author of *Hic Mulier* refers to the biblical injunction (*Deuteronomy* 22) that the sexes wear clothing appropriate to their different genders, Hic Mulier argues that practicality (thrift and warmth) ought to govern the selection of attire for men and women alike. Rather than embracing the radical implications of her speech, however, s/he ultimately condemns the contingency of custom ("To conclude, *Custome* is an idiot" (Sig. B2v)), figuring custom or fashion as a capricious, unfaithful, and changeable servant, thus laying the groundwork for the pamphlet's final arguments for the restoration of a traditional gender balance.

Haec-Vir accepts the arguments about custom, but he turns them back upon Hic Mulier by arguing that women do not, in fact, choose their clothes with an eye to practicality, but are governed by the whims of fashion. He insists that cross-dressing confers not liberty but shame, and women will only be treated well if they behave (and dress) like women: "if you will walke without difference, you shall live without reverence" (Sig. B4v). Hic Mulier proceeds to attack his effeminization of dress, also an effect of fashion (and this is presumably a topical reference to the notoriously effeminate dress and behavior of some of James's courtiers), claiming that women are wearing masculine clothes only because they have been cast off by men (Sig. C2v). Hic Mulier and Haec-Vir then exchange clothes and adjust their Latin names to suit the restored harmony of their respective genders. What are we to make of this capitulation to tradition, especially after Hic Mulier's impassioned speech celebrating change and recognizing the relativity of custom? Linda Woodbridge reads this moment as a harbinger of feminism:

> When Hic Mulier cried "Custom is an idiot," she flung open the door to reveal vistas of freedom and equality. And then her creator, growing alarmed, bustled in and shut it again... Someday it would be opened again, and through it would march Mary Wollstonecraft and Emmeline Pankhurst, Susan B. Anthony and John Stuart Mill, Simone de Beauvoir and Betty Friedan, and all of us who can thank the dubious feminism of the English Renaissance for at least one indisputable battle-cry: *Haec-Vir*'s "We are as free-borne as men".
>
> (1984: 149)

Yet, as Woodbridge recognizes, Hic Mulier's feminist manifesto is dampened by her later capitulation to custom; given that reversal, how are we to read this conversion to propriety in relation to the gender (and the feminist convictions) of the pamphlet's author?[14]

Jonathan Dollimore has recently addressed this movement to contain the transgression of the pamphlet's most challenging statements. He argues that to privilege Hic Mulier's final judgment (if men become masculine, women will become feminine again) over her defense of transvestism "is probably to interpret the pamphlet according to modern and anachronistic notions of authorial intention, character utterance, and textual unity (all three notions privileging what is said finally as being more truthful than what went before)" (Dollimore 1991: 298). He suggests that in fact the final, conservative gesture of the pamphlet "still partakes of the same fundamental challenge to gender division" as the preceding statements because it acknowledges that sexual difference can be maintained by means of cross-dressing. To do so is, of course, to undermine the idea that sexual difference is a function of divine or natural law rather than social custom. Thus, according to Dollimore, Hic Mulier's seeming capitulation ironically incorporates the original challenge (1991: 298).

Haec-Vir's argument for equality rests on a claim that both sexes should have access to and delight in the mutability that is Nature's essence. Such encomia on variety were not uncommon in the Renaissance, of course, especially when change was associated with women. We can think here of John Donne's "Confined Love," his elegies "Change," "The Anagram," and "Variety," or Ben Jonson's ventriloquized "Another. In Defence of Their Inconstancy. A Song." Jonson's poem, spoken in the voice of "womankind" maintains that women's "proper virtue is to range" (Jonson 1975: 138). The changeability the speaker ascribes to her sex turns out to be sexual variety of a confined sort, the "frequent varying of the deed." Jonson's cross-dressed voice thus imputes to women all that is most feared and most desired, domesticating the threat of mutability by converting it to a kind of natural (and infinite) sexual inventiveness. That change is identified as a particularly feminine attribute is rendered especially plausible when it is articulated in a feminine voice, since the mutation of voice (masculine to feminine) becomes an "invisible" feature of the poem, masking the patriarchal origin of the utterance by cross-dressing it so that it appears to emanate from the female body. Yet we cannot read *Haec-Vir*'s defense of change, as we can Jonson's, against a male authorial voice that stands behind it, because the pamphlet is anonymous. The sex of the author is not only indeterminate, but that indeterminacy is thematized, I would argue, in the transvestism of the voices in it. Although the speakers do revert to their "true" genders at the end, the pamphlet opens by dramatizing the undecidability of sexual identity. Speech, clothing, behavior, and social status are determined in relation to an attribution of gender, and, while it is impossible to suspend one's judgment about the gender of a voice (or an author), the transvestism of the interlocutors in *Haec-Vir* insists that we consider the mutually constitutive nature of gender construction, the sexual orientations on which they depend, and the contingent nature of these gender identifications. It is crucial, then, that we read *Haec-Vir* as anonymous, for, in its refusal to present itself as the property of a (proper) name, it forces us to recognize the role custom plays in fashioning gender, and dressing the voice that speaks it.

III

So far, I have considered transvestite ventriloquism from the perspective of male appropriations of feminine voices, or of anonymous authors using transvestite voices. I want to conclude this chapter by looking briefly at one instance of a woman ventriloquizing a male voice, the French feminist philosopher Sarah Kofman, who borrows Freud's voice in *The Enigma of Woman: Woman in Freud's Writings*. The epigraph to Part One of the book provides a useful introduction to its argument and a gloss on the title: Kofman quotes a line from Derrida's *Glas* that defines the enigma as "'the structure of the veil suspended between contraries'" (1985: 9). While Woman is ostensibly the enigma that Kofman sets out to anatomize, it quickly becomes apparent that Woman is inseparable from the enigmatic nature attributed to her both by tradition and by Freud. Far from being able to answer the riddle of what woman *is*, Kofman is concerned to investigate the "veil" of misunderstanding and obfuscation that is suspended between the sexes, a veil that both is and is not Woman. A central focus of Kofman's investigation is Freud's theory of bisexuality. Bisexuality, like psychoanalytic discourse itself, becomes a double-edged "weapon" in the "internecine" war within psychoanalysis, a struggle between Freud and women analysts (and feminists) over the "woman question" (Kofman 1985: 11–13). Where feminists have repeatedly challenged the androcentric bias of Freudian psychoanalysis, charging that Freud's claim to scientific objectivity is compromised when he considers femininity because he is a man, the thesis of bisexuality functions as an implicit defense that is rooted at the heart of psychoanalytic theory. That is, Freud's claim that both sexes contain elements of the other in them – which is developed with respect to women in his 1933 lecture, "Femininity" – allows Freud to imply that he is not simply a man, for he contains feminine elements within himself. The theory of bisexuality seems to dismantle the fixed, metaphysical binarities of the sexes, displacing that stability in favor of a more speculative and constructed opposition (Kofman 1985: 15). But, as Kofman brilliantly demonstrates, while Freud celebrates the universality of bisexuality, he also uses it against his female colleagues, imputing an unflattering masculinity (if not homosexuality) to their intelligence, with all the attendant implications of pathology and arrested development. Yet he never applies the thesis directly to himself, never exposes his own femininity, and this curious reluctance functions, Kofman argues, "to disguise his silent disavowal of his own femininity, his paranoia" (1985: 15).

The "double-edged" weapon of bisexuality would thus seem to make psychoanalysis invulnerable to feminist incursions into its territories. Kofman's feminist strategy for undoing the protective, self-confirming androcentrism of psychoanalytic discourse is to employ exactly the same duplicities of argumentation that Freud uses, except that she turns them back on Freud in order to deconstruct theories that have remained implacably hostile to feminism, creating in the process a "space" for feminist speech.

The central tool in her endeavor is ventriloquism, an infiltration of the Freudian voice, a metaphoric occupation of the Freudian mind. Her text is made up of a variation of voices: her own analysis (which predominates), her quotation of Freud's works – which is suitably indicated with diacritical marks and off-set text – and her occasional assumption of Freud's voice, usually announced by "I, Freud," followed by a passage spoken by Freud/Kofman. These moments are clearly much more than paraphrase; they constitute a double-voiced text, in which Kofman speaks through Freud, reshaping his words through her own interpretation of them, and manipulating his speech so that he seems to be engaged in passionate debate with her. For example, in one such passage, she ventriloquizes his resolution to guard psychoanalysis against women by turning the discourse back upon them:

> I, Freud, Truth, I speak, and Truth will soon be able to resist all pressures, all more or less hysterical "feminist" demands; for, O, women, if you seek to use psychoanalysis against me, I shall be much better prepared to turn it back against you, even while I pretend to be granting you some concessions, agreeing to some compromises in order to put an end to the battle of the sexes between us, and to reestablish among male and female psychoanalysts a "polite agreement": in my lordly fashion I freely grant you that "pure femininity" and "pure masculinity" are purely theoretical constructions and that the content of such speculative constructions is uncertain. I am prepared to grant, too, that most men fall far short of the masculine ideal, for "all human individuals, as a result of their bisexual disposition and of cross-inheritance, combine in themselves both masculine and feminine characteristics" ("Consequences," p. 258).
>
> (Kofman 1985: 13)

The passage is doubled against itself, for we can hear Kofman's value judgments shaping Freud's tone ("in my lordly fashion"), and her direct quotation from "Some Psychical Consequences of the Anatomical Distinction Between the Sexes" at the end imbues it with irony, coming as the words do from a woman's perspective. It is one thing for Freud to recognize that most men fall far short of the masculine ideal, and another for Kofman to say the same thing. Further, Freud's enactment of bisexuality is decidedly asymmetrical because the masculine is obviously the privileged term. Kofman enters the discourse at the exact point where Freud erects a theory that will supposedly render psychoanalysis invulnerable to "hysterical" feminist demands, turning Freud's "weapon" on himself by forcing him to accept the consequences of the theoretical constructions of "pure" masculinity and femininity.

Since Kofman holds Freud to his thesis of bisexuality, she can read his writings on women not as an attempt to describe an eternal essence, but as a process of understanding how the differentiation between the sexes came about. Freud postulates three paths by which the little girl becomes a woman (the normal path, the neurotic or hysterical path, and the path of masculine overcompensation, in which the woman refuses her feminine "destiny") (Kofman 1985: 123). That these divergences exist at all suggests the gap between anatomical endowment and psychical organization, and the complicated process by which a girl becomes a woman signals her greater predisposition to hysteria. Hysteria, like (and of course closely related to) bisexuality, is a condition of doubleness, somatically expressed in the hysteric's simultaneous holding of her dress to her body (the female response) and her attempt to pull it away (the male response) (Kofman: 1985: 123). Just as the hysteric seeks to cover and uncover her body at the same time, so, too, does hysteria conceal and reveal simultaneously (Kofman 1985: 123). Kofman argues that the way Freud uses his thesis of bisexuality "mimics" the behavior of the hysteric, because he reveals the presence of both sexes in each one, even as he conceals his own femininity, a strategy that allows him to break down the metaphysical opposition between masculinity and femininity, while maintaining the privilege of masculinity (1985: 123). Hysteria predisposes women to silence, forcing them to express somatically what they cannot utter in language. This silence is the enigma or riddle that the psychotherapist seeks to discover, and the true hysteric is she who becomes complicitous with her analyst, confessing her secret. He, in turn, becomes the hysteric's accomplice by guaranteeing to change her name if he publishes her case history, thus preserving her anonymity (even as he displays it) (Kofman 1985: 44–5). But if Freud is complicit with the hysteric, or even, at certain points, mimics her behavior, so, too, is Kofman. The ventriloquized Freudian voice in *The Enigma of Woman* is a hysterical voice, a bisexual voice, and its function is to represent Freud's insight about the speculative, provisional nature of the masculine/feminine opposition. The strategy partakes of what Luce Irigaray has called mimicry, the deliberate assumption of the feminine role, which has the capacity "to convert a form of subordination into an affirmation, and thus to begin to thwart it" (Irigaray 1985b: 76).[15] It is by self-reflexively occupying the very attributes that cause psychoanalysis to relegate the feminine to the inferior, the neurotic, and the hysterical that Kofman can challenge Freudian dogma. At the end of her reading of Freud, she observes that, in becoming obsessed with a fixed idea of woman, he immobilizes her, "imprisons her in her 'nature' as in a real yoke of iron," opposing that fixity to the "flexibility and plasticity" of man (Kofman 1985: 222).

While the sexual hierarchy that produces this paralysis is a function of anatomical difference that stems from an origin of similarity (bisexuality), the differences quickly efface what the sexes share. Just as the Freudian standard of comparison is the penis (to which the female "penis," the clitoris, is invidiously compared), so is the Renaissance standard the male body, with its sexual organs externally displayed. The inferiority of the female body, with its internalized reproductive system, is as apparent to the eye as the lack of a penis is in Freudian theory. Despite the emphasis on bodies in Freud, however, the discourses of transvestism and psychoanalysis both make it clear that bodies are as historically constructed as the clothing that covers them. Transvestism and hysterical or bisexual discourses alike allow us to see in the crossing of genders where and how the boundaries between the sexes have been set, and it is at these junctures that the gender system is most vulnerable. While there is nothing inherently subversive about transvestite ventriloquism – indeed, as we have seen, it can be used to affirm phallocratic rule – it has the radical potential to expose the contingency of gender, opening cultural discourse to the "voices" it otherwise marginalizes and silences.

2

FOLLY AND HYSTERIA

Duplicities of speech

Near the beginning of Erasmus's *Praise of Folly*, Folly makes a bilingual pun that encapsulates much of the mock encomium's irony. Joining the Greek words for fool and lover of wisdom ("morosoph"), she creates a hybrid word, which Thomas Chaloner in his 1549 English translation rendered as "foolosopher" (Erasmus 1979: 13). Folly embeds this Greek term in her Latin text, and she says that, in doing so, she is imitating the rhetoricians who sprinkle Greek tags throughout their Latin works, "like bright bits in a mosaic" (1979: 14), and therefore come to think of themselves as virtually divine in their learning. These rhetoricians, whose claim to erudition rests upon their ability to use esoteric phrases or obsolete words to baffle their readers, are likened by Folly to horseleeches, since both use two tongues. Erasmus's reference to the horseleech may well be derived from *The Book of Proverbs*; the first of the numerical proverbs says "The leech has two daughters: 'Give, give!' their cry" (30.15). As glossed by Renaissance commentators, the two daughters become two tongues, and the horseleech becomes a symbol of the insatiability of female demands, registered both in its putative thirst for blood and in its doubling of that quintessentially female attribute, the tongue.[1] The double-tongued horseleech points not only to the rhetoricians Folly satirizes, however, but also refers self-reflexively to *The Praise of Folly* itself, which is, after all, a double-voiced text, spoken through Erasmus's ventriloquization of Folly. In this chapter, I will be investigating the trope of double-voicing as it is expressed in ventriloquism and in irony, the mode that governs *The Praise of Folly*. I am particularly concerned to explore the relationship between Folly and the feminine voice that Erasmus invents for her, since it is my contention that Folly's gender expresses a cultural construction of woman that makes the feminine voice particularly suitable to

Erasmus's purposes, especially as that voice seems to emerge from a female body that clearly manifests an uncensored female sexuality and as it is associated with marginalized or repressed aspects of culture (madness and folly).

In the second part of this chapter, I examine the linkage between voice and the "trope" of hysteria in a French feminist text, Hélène Cixous's and Catherine Clément's (1986) *La jeune née* (*The Newly Born Woman*). Although Freud's celebrated writings on hysteria (his own as well as those written in collaboration with Breuer) have tended to make it seem like a nineteenth-century phenomenon exclusively, hysteria does, of course, have a long history; references to the condition go back as far as 1900 B.C. (Veith 1965: 2). Throughout much of that history, speech and its pathological manifestations are associated with the female body, a ligature that is registered in the etymological connection between hysteria and the uterus (Gk *hystera*). Clément's contribution to *The Newly Born Woman* examines this history in anthropological, mythic, and psychoanalytic terms; she argues for the similarities between the figures of the witch and the madwoman or hysteric, and she also notes a kind of transposition of gender between hysterical women and the men who depict them or speak on their behalf. Clément asserts – following Michelet and Freud – that there exists a particularly powerful bond between these women and history or memory. Just as Freud thought the hysteric's body was a theater of forgotten scenes, so also for Clément is the sorceress the site of what is repressed in culture (1986: 5). In her chapter on the sorceress and the hysteric, Clément notes (again picking up on Freud's own sense of history) the historical continuities between nineteenth-century descriptions of the hysteric and medieval or Renaissance accounts of related cultural pathologies, particularly witchcraft and particularly as that phenomenon is codified in the *Malleus Maleficarum*. The doubleness of women, which, according to Marcel Mauss, results from their simultaneous alliance with order and disorder, lends them a special power, and it is this power that some French feminists seek to make the special property of the feminine (Clément/Cixous 1986: 8). Instead of being the cause of their marginalization (as it was historically), female duplicity is recuperated as the source of liberation, a liberation that is at once effected in and through language and also involves a restoration of the female body. Yet such a strategy always risks reinscribing traditional representations, and it is only through a vigilant self-reflexivity that formerly imprisoning definitions of women can be employed to create space for new discourses. A celebration – or even fetishization – of the hysteric can ultimately become a conservative gesture, since, because the hysteric threatens the social fabric, but is then contained by it, she cannot effectively dismantle the very structures that produce her in the first place.

Even though both Clément and Cixous celebrate the hysteric, they also recognize the dangers of that acclamation, and this double stance is mirrored in the double structure of the book. *The Newly Born Woman* is made up of two main texts, Clément's treatment of hysteria and Cixous's more rhapsodic meditation on woman, voice, and bisexuality. It concludes with a dialogue between them, which, far from representing consensus, accentuates their differences on such issues as language, hysteria, and political action. This exchange is divided into two parts ("A Woman Mistress" and "The Untenable"), and it is further doubled by dividing the page into two, so that the top part records the conversation between Cixous and Clément and the bottom part consists of a series of citations of other "voices" (including those of Cixous herself). Both the structure of the book and the individual texts within it interrogate the idea of authorial property, the relationship between women and language, and the connection between the gender of the body and the gender of the voice. Cixous's section, which is entitled "Sorties," defines the thread – or "double braid" (1986: 63) – that organizes discourse into the same hierarchized oppositions that structure western metaphysics. "Thought has always worked through opposition" (1986: 63), Cixous asserts, an observation that can apply as easily to this penchant for thinking in binarities as to her own endeavor to undo it, either by opposing the system (hence the submerged military reference in her title) or by dismantling it (hence the sense of exiting that *sorties* implies). One of the pairs of oppositions that Cixous cites is speaking/writing, the binarity that, as Jacques Derrida has so memorably argued, subtends the phonocentrism of western culture, the privileging of voice or speech over writing. Derrida's critique forcefully exposed the reliance on presence as a guarantor of meaning's stability, and to privilege voice has subsequently seemed to endorse a belief in presence and the immutability of signification.[2] This deconstructive critique of voice informs Toril Moi's criticism and ultimate dismissal of Cixous in *The Newly Born Woman*. Reading Cixous's description of voice within a strict Derridean framework, Moi argues that Cixous deconstructs phallogocentric discourse through her distinction between the "gift" and the "proper," but that Cixous's theorization of writing and femininity vacillates between a deconstructive approach and "a full-blown metaphysical account of writing as voice, presence, and origin" (Moi 1985: 119).

I will offer an alternative interpretation of Cixous's writings on voice in *The Newly Born Woman*, one that investigates the historical and metaphorical constructions of the relationship between voice and the female body. Cixous and other French feminists (such as Irigaray) have been criticized for being essentialist, for locating their revolutionary impulses within a female physiology that always has the potential to become imprisoning. Ann Rosalind Jones, for instance, accepts Cixous's attribution of women's nurturant instincts, but is made understandably nervous by Cixous's mention of the female drive toward gestation, with all its historical echoes of a "coercive glorification of motherhood" (Jones 1986a: 368–9). My analysis of Erasmus's *Praise of Folly* and other Renaissance writings on voice is designed to demonstrate that the feminine voice has historically been imaged as emanating from a sexualized female body, and that French feminists like Cixous participate in that (usually misogynistic) tradition. There is an uncanny resemblance, for instance, between Folly's voice and the hysterical language that Clément praises. Clearly, however, there is a difference between being consigned to a marginalized position by the patriarchal order and voluntarily (and self-consciously) occupying that position as a strategy for subverting the dominant discourse. At the same time that I recognize the construction of the female body and the female voice as metaphors of Woman freighted with the baggage of misogyny, I also argue that there is nothing essentially or ineluctably patriarchal about those metaphors, nothing that necessarily precludes their conscription for feminist purposes. Their political force depends upon a context of enunciation that is recognized or even produced by readers, and part of that enunciatory context is the delicate and complicated interaction between the speaking voice and the author figure. The issue this chapter addresses is one that is also topical in recent theorizations of irony: how in the ironic mode does one identify agency and audience, and to what extent is irony's political efficacy contingent on communities of knowledge and interpretation?

I

Despite Erasmus's self-reflexive attention to the creation of Folly's voice and his attempt to preempt misunderstanding through his prefatory letter to Thomas More, *The Praise of Folly* was greeted in some quarters with outrage and accusations of heresy or blasphemy. The commentary that was added in 1515 (written partly by Gerard Listrius and partly by Erasmus), as well as the letter to Dorp, three of Erasmus's other letters, and Erasmus's later additions to the commentary, seek to defend *Folly* on the grounds of literary decorum, genre, and the nature of irony (Erasmus 1979: xii). His opponents tended to ignore the literary merits of the work, and their strategy of attack was to extract sentences from *Folly* as exhibits that supported their charges of blasphemy; far from being ineffective, the accusations eventually resulted in the Sorbonne's condemnation of *Folly* in 1543 and in the paradoxical encomium's appearance in at least fourteen indices of censored books for the next fifty years (Erasmus 1979: xii–xiii). The attacks were made possible by a conflation of Folly's voice and the author's, a reading that collapsed the distinctions that are so carefully manufactured in *The Praise of Folly* through its thematization both of the nature and propriety of speaking and also the decorum of interpreting or listening.

The ability to listen and interpret correctly is alluded to in Folly's multiple references to the myth of Midas, a narrative whose central character cannot discriminate "properly" between the music of Pan and Apollo. That Midas prefers Pan's playing makes him Folly's ideal inscribed reader, since Folly aligns her own discourse with Pan's rustic pipes (as opposed to the more sublime notes of Apollo's lyre), urging her auditors to "lend" their "ears," "just as [her] protégé Midas did long ago to Pan" (Erasmus 1979: 10). Yet the allusion is implicated not only in the issue of judgment but also of disguise, since Midas sought to hide the shameful sign of his musical preference – his ass's ears – by concealing them beneath a turban. As Ovid tells it, only the slave who cut Midas's hair knew of the metamorphosis; unable to contain the terrible secret, he dug a hole in the ground, whispered the clandestine news of his master's ears into it, and then covered it over, burying "the evidence of his voice" (Ovid 1977a: 133). Folly sets herself against Midas, claiming that she is never in disguise, but is always identical with herself in physical appearance and speech; in contradistinction, those who "arrogate to themselves the character and title of wisemen" (1979: 13) always eventually reveal the tips of their Midas-ears. In other words, Folly's encomium is directed especially to those who profess wisdom but whose "real" taste is obscured by their pretense of learning.

Yet the paradoxical, inverted logic of *The Praise of Folly* offers a more complicated model of voice than this explication would suggest. Despite Folly's protestations about the recognizability of her image and language, she is, of course, already a disguised figure, concealing behind her ingenuous rhetoric her creator, Erasmus. Mikhail Bakhtin defined this "double-voiced discourse" as serving two speakers at the same time, expressing the constructed and inscribed needs of the speaker, as well as the "refracted" wishes of the author (1981: 324). Folly's voice is thus "internally dialogized," just as the ironic mode of *Folly* is double, working simultaneously to reveal (among other things) the wisdom of folly and the folly of wisdom. The disguise of wisdom is linked by Folly to Midas's foolish choice, and the concealment of that judgment (the ass's ears) is associated with the production of voice. In Ovid's *Metamorphoses*, we are told that, although Midas's barber buried his secret deep in the earth, reeds sprang up on the site, and, when the wind blew, the story of his master's ears was broadcast for all to hear (Ovid 1977a: 133). In some subsequent recountings of the story, the figure who cannot keep the humiliating secret is not the trusted barber, but Midas's wife. In Chaucer's Wife of Bath's tale, for instance, the wife so desires to tell the uncontainable secret, that, full of an urgency like the need to give birth, she whispers it into a swamp. Lee Patterson argues in his analysis of this Chaucerian retelling of Ovid that the wife is made into an image of feminine speaking, and her garrulity is imbricated with her sexuality in ways that reveal the indecency and untrustworthiness of both (Patterson 1983: 656–8). Like Midas's wife, Folly is closely linked with speech and sexuality, and the ventriloquization of her voice affords Erasmus opportunities otherwise unavailable to him.

Folly differentiates herself from ordinary speechmakers in the extemporaneous nature of her oration. Rather than labor with her text for thirty years, plagiarize some parts, divide it painstakingly into sections, and then pretend that it was "dashed off in a couple of days," as some orators do, she decides to "blurt out whatever pops into [her] head" (Erasmus 1979: 12).[3] Not only is Folly thus imaged as a source of unpremeditated speech, but her absence, or an orator's failure to enlist her support, appears to render even eloquent men mute. Socrates, for instance, was purportedly driven away by the crowd's raucous laughter, Plato was so disconcerted by the noise of the people that he could utter only half a sentence on behalf of his teacher in his hour of mortal danger, Isocrates never dared to speak at all because of his timidity, and Cicero – "the father of Roman eloquence" – began each speech paralyzed by trepidation (1979: 37). Just as Folly removes the obstacle of fear that stands in the way of knowledge, so, too, is she capable of dissolving the anxieties that reduce the rhetorician to silence (1979: 42). As Erasmus suggests in his account of the writing of *Folly*, he apparently borrowed her impromptu compositional method, or, at least, he purportedly wrote with a speed that is less characteristic of the orator's drawn-out labors than of Folly's particularly feminine "disorganized" outpouring (Erasmus 1979: ix-x).

His voice is in fact allied with Folly's in a relationship that is imaged by an allusion in one of Folly's asides to herself. After cataloguing a series of examples of madness, she asks herself rhetorically why she has embarked on this endless task: "'Not if I had a hundred tongues, a hundred mouths,/ A voice of iron, could I survey all kinds/ Of fools, or run through all the forms of folly'" (1979: 66). Folly is, of course, adapting the words of Virgil's Sibyl as she guides Aeneas through the underworld, and the Sibyl's use of the inexpressibility *topos* registers the innumerability of crimes and the punishments those who perpetrate them suffer in this underworld. The image of multivocality (a hundred tongues, a hundred mouths) is itself a multiple intertext, since Folly is quoting Virgil (6: 625–7), who is in turn citing Homer (*Illiad* 2: 489–90). That Virgil has the Sibyl utter (and reshape) the Homeric phrases, and that Erasmus makes Folly echo the Sibyl's words, designates the figure of the prophetess as a conduit of voices, both intertextual and divine. She is a medium for Apollo's words, and Virgil describes her seeming madness before she succumbs to the god's will and allows him to speak through her. In an analogous way, Folly is a mouthpiece for Erasmus; she, too, enacts the folly she personifies through the disruptions of her rhetoric, especially in the first part of *Folly*, and she, too, eventually submits to being a conduit of voice. (It is worth noting that some commentators[4] have seen a merging of the Erasmian voice and that of Folly in the latter two sections of the work, where Folly anatomizes first the folly of academic and social classes and then Christianity itself.) Erasmus uses the sibylline allusion to foreground the nature and origin of the speaking voice, dissociating himself from the property of his utterance through the interventions of the Homeric,

Virgilian, and prophetic voices, a point he makes more bluntly in his prefatory letter to Thomas More (1979: 5). He thus heightens the distinction between his own voice and Folly's, a differentiation that is further accentuated by the difference of sex.

It is crucial for Erasmus's purposes that Folly be a woman. She celebrates those aspects of humanity traditionally relegated to the feminine: emotion, pleasure, laughter, childlikeness, and significantly, sexuality, which is synecdochized in the genitalia, those parts which are "so foolish and funny" that "they cannot even be mentioned without a snicker" (1979: 18).[5] This bodily site of generation, not the Pythagorean tetrad or some other abstract principle, is the "sacred fount" of life, for without the folly of eroticism, men would be unlikely to submit to the "halter" of matrimony, and, without eroticism (and the influence of Lethe), women would be reluctant to endure the pains of childbirth (1979: 18–19). Not only is Folly the "nursery of life" (1979: 19), but she has special affinities with religious madness or ecstasy as well. Because women, children, old men, and "retarded persons" are more open to religious matters (1979: 132), it is more likely that they will experience the ecstatic transport that Folly describes, a state very close to madness: "they talk incoherently, not in a human fashion, making sounds without sense. Then the entire expression of their face vacillates repeatedly: now happy, now sad; now crying, now laughing, now sighing – in short, they are completely beside themselves" (1979: 139). This description of ecstatic language, like the Sibyl's voice, is an echo from the *Aeneid*, where Juno shapes an eidolon of Aeneas, a phantom designed to deceive Turnus (Virgil 1978: 10. 640). It speaks with just such an otherwordly voice, one similar to sibylline utterances, mad (or hysterical) speech, or indeed, Folly's voice. Folly, like the eidolon, is a phantom figure, whose words, at times seemingly wild or incoherent, are made up of a patchwork or motley of intertextual citations and proverbs. Her language thus appears to stand apart from her in a kind of "ecstatic" relation, metaphorically enacting her relationship to Erasmus. This difference from her author, or indeed from herself, turns out to be an inherent part of her femaleness.

As Folly recounts it, she counseled Jupiter to join woman to man, since women, being "foolish and silly creatures," could provide an amusing and pleasurable antidote to the extra rationality with which men are endowed (Erasmus 1979: 28). Women are "naturally" foolish, and no matter how hard they try to disguise it, it is impossible to work against the "inborn bias of the mind": quoting a

Greek proverb, Folly intones "'An ape is still an ape, even if it is dressed up in royal purple'; just so, a woman is still a woman – that is, a fool – no matter what role she may try to play" (Erasmus 1979: 29). Yet Folly's logic here, as elsewhere, is as faulty as her identity is unstable. She goes on to argue that women's folly is actually a positive quality; it is to folly, for example, that women can attribute their beauty, the aspect that they "correctly" value above all things. Beauty is what distinguishes them from rough, coarse, and hairy men, and beauty – registered in their soft cheeks, delicate complexions, and high voices – is what lends them the aspect of eternal adolescence (1979: 29). While these signs of unchanging youth seem in this passage to be "natural" to women, Folly turns a moment later to the extraordinary effort necessary to preserve the illusion of youthfulness: the female desire for attractiveness is the reason "for so many toiletries, cosmetics, baths, coiffures, lotions, perfumes, so many clever ways of highlighting, painting, disguising their faces, eyes, and skin" (1979: 29). Disguise appears to be as much a property of women, then, as the putatively adolescent quality of their appearance, and this illusory, deceptive nature provides insight into Erasmus's strategies of presentation. Women appear to be undisguisable ("a woman is still a woman... no matter what role she may try to play") even though their nature is to present the disguise of a certain unchanging image. In an analogous way, Folly claims that she never conceals her identity, but always looks exactly like what she is (1979: 13), even though she is never what she seems to be (because her voice refracts the Erasmian voice).

The discrepancy between outside and inside (men who boast of possessing the very attributes they lack, like wisdom) is not only the subject of Folly's diatribe, however, it is also the means by which she reveals this incongruity and then, paradoxically, celebrates it. That is, in the Silenus box image, Erasmus argues that appearance does not necessarily correspond with content; one can open an ugly container to find beauty inside, or conversely, a virtuous exterior can cover internal iniquity. Far from wishing to eliminate this discrepancy, it is seen as essential. Using the trope of theater, Folly explains the indispensability of illusion:

> If someone should try to strip away the costumes and makeup from the actors performing a play on the stage and to display them to the spectators in their own natural appearance, wouldn't he ruin the whole play?... Everything would suddenly

> look different: the actor just now playing a woman would be seen to be a man; the one who had just now been playing a young man would look old; the man who played the king only a moment ago would become a pauper; the actor who played god would be revealed as a wretched human being. But to destroy the illusions in this fashion would spoil the whole play. This deception, this disguise, is the very thing that holds the attention of the spectators.
>
> (1979: 43)

While drama is a metaphor for the life of mortal men, illusion is also what gives life to *Folly*; disguise, in short, enables Erasmus to say what he does.[6] It is according to the transposition of voice, too, that the *Encomium* should be judged, for, as Erasmus reminds us in his *Adages*, what is important in a dialogue is the decorum of the speaker; Moria speaks in *The Praise of Folly*, not Erasmus (Kahn 1985: 223). The borrowing of a female voice allows Erasmus to say with impunity what he might otherwise not be able to articulate openly. Folly functions as an enabling source and also as a shield; she lends Erasmus a freedom of subject and style, while always providing the very excuse that produced the voice in the first place: "But if you think my speech has been too pert or wordy," he says at the end of *Folly* and then reminds us again in the letter to Dorp, "keep in mind that you've been listening to Folly and to a woman" (Erasmus 1979: 138, 160).

Appreciating the *Encomium*, as we can see in the scandalized responses it elicited from some of Erasmus's contemporaries, depends partly upon a recognition of its double-voicing and of its irony, features that are closely related to one another but not identical. Irony has been called the trope of doubleness or double-voicing (Hutcheon 1991), most obviously because it operates through the simultaneous cultivation of literal and ironic meanings. Folly's praise of herself and her accomplishments ironically lauds what is considered of least worth in the culture she describes (irrationality, the feminine, youth, old age, the body, pleasure, and so on); this inversion works to expose the foolishness of the dominant values at the same time that this supposed speaking from the margins paradoxically also reasserts the power of privilege. It is possible for Erasmus to take on temporarily the voice or perspective of the disempowered precisely because he is not dispossessed of various enabling factors: he is male, educated, and knowledgeable not only about those subjects he anatomizes (such as the folly of erudition), but also about the modes of expression correlated with each. That he writes in Latin signals his affiliation with a paternal language of learning, a language to which few of Erasmus's female contemporaries would have had access (Ong 1977: 22–30). His foregrounding of classical erudition in the horseleech image with which I began this chapter functions both to describe the doubleness of Greek tags in a Latin text – where Greek becomes a metonym for communities of rarified scholarly understanding (a smaller group within the community of those who write Latin), or conversely, a metonym for the exclusion of those who do not understand – and also to distinguish classical languages from the vernacular. This distinction is obviously gender coded, so Erasmus's coupling of a feminine voice and its Latin speech itself registers a cultural doubleness or incongruity. The devastating force of his subversion depends, then, upon his occupation of the same ideological and cultural position as the subjects of his critique. Irony, as Linda Hutcheon has reminded us, always creates insiders and outsiders: the appreciation of irony depends upon a system of shared cultural values (1991: 11). Although Erasmus can occupy the position of Folly or woman (they are often contiguous) in order to attack the hypocrisies of the church and of learning, he can only do so because he is not a woman, is not relegated to expressing himself in laughter, or the vernacular, and is not imprisoned by the very folly he celebrates.

One of the enabling ideological matrices for Erasmus's representation of Folly is a construction of woman whose capacity for language is inseparable from her female physiology. The linkage between feminine speech and the female body is a staple of anti-feminist writing, articulated unforgettably in such representative texts as the *Malleus Maleficarum*, or a hundred years later, when the idea still had strong currency, in Joseph Swetnam's (1615) *Arraignment of Lewd, Idle, Froward, and Unconstant Women*. The *Malleus* reserves special condemnation for three things: a woman, an ecclesiastic, and the tongue (Kramer 1971: 42). Women and tongues, however, have a particular affinity, for the slipperiness of the female tongue makes her incapable of keeping secrets or indeed of containing language within her (Kramer 1971: 44). Her speech is characterized by duplicity: "For as she is a liar by nature, so in her speech she stings while she delights us. Wherefore her voice is like the song of the Sirens, who with their sweet melody entice the passers-by and kill them" (Kramer 1971: 46). Woman embodies a fundamental doubleness because she possesses two mouths, one containing the garrulous tongue and the other represented by the insatiability of her womb ("There are three things that are never satisfied, yea, a fourth thing which says not, It is enough; that is, the mouth of the womb" (Kramer 1971: 47)). The *Malleus* and other Renaissance writings on witchcraft emphasize woman's natural frailty and the facility with which she might therefore become an instrument of the devil. It is not uncommon in accounts of witch trials, such as *The Wonderful Discovery of the Witchcrafts of Margaret and Philippa Flower*, to see "ventriloqui" listed as one of the manifestations of magic, for ventriloquism – like prophecy – makes the female body into a vehicle for another's speech (Henderson/McManus 1985: 369). Given the alliance between women's two "mouths," it is also not surprising to find that disorders of the uterus appear to produce irregularities of speech. In Edward Jorden's 1603 *Briefe Discourse* on hysteria, for example, we learn that women are particularly susceptible to diseases of the womb and to the "other parts, with which it hath correspondence" (Jorden 1603: Sig. B). Thus, hysteria may manifest itself in symptoms that are often ascribed to witchcraft: "*suffocation* in the throate, croaking of Frogges, hissing of Snakes, crowing of Cockes, barking of Dogges, garring of Crowes, frenzies, convulsions, hickcockes, laughing, singing, weeping, crying, &c" (Jorden 1603: Sig. B2). These disturbances of voice are produced, according to Jorden, by a pathological condition he names "the Mother, or the Suffocation of the Mother," because the condition manifests itself most commonly in a choking in the throat, which is caused by "*the Mother or wombe*" migrating within the body, impinging on other organs, and causing difficulty in breathing or speaking (Jorden 1603: Sig. C–Cv).[7]

Jorden's position on the relationship between witchcraft and hysteria in *A Briefe Discourse* resulted from his involvement in a London trial in 1602. The accused, Elizabeth Jackson, was indicted for having bewitched a fourteen-year old girl named Mary Glover, whose symptoms included speechlessness, fits, swellings of the neck and throat, and an inability to move or feel the left side of her body. Four doctors, including Jorden, were asked to give medical opinions on Mary Glover's condition, and, although Jorden diagnosed her as hysterical, Elizabeth Jackson was nevertheless condemned as a witch (Veith 1965: 120–1). Jorden's treatise is designed to circulate a description of hysteria and its manifestations in order that the disease might be diagnosed correctly rather than being attributed to witchcraft. As he himself says in the dedicatory epistle, his cataloguing of hysterical symptoms shifts the cause of the disorder from an external cause (the devil working through a witch) to an internal one (the migratory uterus). Yet as compassionate as Jorden's motives were, they had the effect of transposing maleficent agency from supernatural causes to the body of woman, converting religious and social disorder into a more localized somatic disruption. Where in prophetic discourses or in witchcraft the female body is vehicular, a receptive conduit for the voices of others – be they gods, demons, or animals – hysteria depicts the body of woman as choked or silenced by her wandering womb. Her "voice" and special propensity for language is transformed into a kind of somatic dumb show, making her particularly dependent upon the men who must translate her bodily signs into language.

II

It is not accidental that the examples I have chosen to characterize Folly's voice (the horseleech, the buried voice in the Midas tale, Virgil's Sibyl, and the incoherent speech of the ecstatic) are all intertextual echoes. While the images filiate female speech with the natural or bestial (hollow reeds, horseleeches) or with the otherworldly (prophets, madness, ecstatic transport), the intertextual nature of the allusions breaks down the notion of language as the exclusive property of the author. Instead, feminine speaking becomes a repetition of proverbial or poetic utterance, a scattering of language, akin to the dispersal of voice in Ovid's whispering reeds. Cixous's idea of *écriture feminine* is intimately allied with this concept of language, a position on linguistic property that she both theorizes and exemplifies in *The Newly Born Woman*. The collaborative nature of the book is registered most obviously by the lack of authorial attribution in the table of contents; without Sandra Gilbert's introduction, the authorship of the sections needs to be inferred from the final dialogue. The exchange between Clément and Cixous at the end of the book only formalizes the implicit dialogue and multiple overlaps between "The Guilty One" and "Sorties" that are already at work. Unlike Clément, who tends to document her sources fairly meticulously, Cixous strives to break down such boundaries of ownership. Not only does she transgress the "laws" of syntax, providing a text that is both lyrical and fragmentary, but she freely appropriates the writings of others – Derrida, Freud, Joyce, Kleist, Shakespeare, for example – weaving their words into her own through (often) unacknowledged direct quotation, paraphrase, and reformulation. She includes herself in this process, so that sections of her essay "The Laugh of the Medusa" are interpolated into the text, or, elsewhere, she treats herself as a separate author, acknowledging a quotation with her initials (1986: 125).[8] As she argues, breaking the "law of individuation" allows her to make "another way of knowing circulate." Cixous's description of what woman must do reads like a gloss on her own text: "she breaks with explanation, interpretation, and all the authorities pinpointing localization. She forgets. She proceeds by lapse and bounds. She flies/steals" (1986: 96).

The well-known pun on *voler* encapsulates the double senses of theft (women's relation to patriarchal language) and flying (an act of joyful transgression). The duplicity of meaning that Cixous activates destabilizes the unitary sense of the word, but where the Derridean pun on *différance* suggests an infinite deferral of meaning, Cixous fuses "bird," "burglar," and "woman" into an amalgamation capable of subverting both linguistic ("hesheits") and cultural (turning "the proper upside down") orders (1986: 96). The other theoretical paradigm that underwrites Cixous's feminist intertextuality is her distinction between the economies of the gift and the proper. Based in the first instance on a law of savings, her analysis of property invokes a phallocentric set of distinctions that subtend the social structure. What conserves the patriarchal order is the system of oppositions organized around property and its linguistic cognates: mine/not mine, clean (*propre*)/dirty, appropriate/inappropriate, proper/improper (1986: 80). Cixous's definition of the realm of the proper quickly expands to include the political and libidinal orders, however, and it is only through her apparent digression into psychoanalytic theories of sexuality that she reintegrates the realms of the proper and the gift with writing. In other words, her theory of writing is grounded in a theory of the body and a corollary theory of subjectivity. Cixous is careful to argue that masculine and feminine political economies belong to a system of cultural inscription that does not necessarily assign men to the masculine or women to the feminine. And she is equally clear about the dangers of a psychoanalytic theory that provides essentialist interpretations of sexual difference (such as Freud's or Jones's), since the thesis of a natural difference based on anatomical distinction functions to support male privilege (1986: 81). She asserts that Freudian theories of difference are already anchored in a scopic economy, because the ascription of anatomical distinctness depends upon vision (seeing a penis or its lack), and that this reliance on what can be seen with the eyes – both for Freud and also for Lacan, whose transcendental signifier also has its point of origin in anatomy – privileges exteriority (1986: 82).

By contrast, Cixous wants to relocate the site of difference to the invisible, to what cannot be referred to the masculine order, that is, to "woman's instinctual economy" (1986: 82). The questions she seeks to address are about the nature of feminine *jouissance*: what it is, and where it inscribes itself in relation to the body, the unconscious, and writing (1986: 82). Far from collapsing the distinctions between the somatic and psychic registers, thereby providing an essentialist "fit" between the (female) body and (feminine) desire, Cixous's *écriture feminine* pulls them apart. It is only through destabilizing the "naturalness" of this conjunction that she can rejoin them and celebrate a female body that can "write itself." The new feminine libidinal register that Cixous sets up in contrast to the realm of the proper is closely linked to her definition of the economy of the gift, but this definition is arrived at only through a reformulation of bisexuality. Cixous's crucial arguments on bisexuality are thus situated as a hinge or pivot point between the economies of the proper and the gift, as if it was possible to pass from one to the other only after achieving an integration of the masculine and feminine in the "other bisexuality." Cixous's "other bisexuality" is formulated in opposition to a Freudian notion of bisexuality as wholeness (which in turn alludes to Plato's myth of hermaphrodism in the *Symposium*); this fantasy, as she notes, "replaces the fear of castration and veils sexual difference," (1986: 84), producing an image of neutrality, where one sex effectively cancels the other. To this vision, Cixous opposes the "other bisexuality," a conception that reaffirms the presence of both sexes within the individual subject and multiplies the "effects of desire's inscription on every part of the body and the other body" (1986: 85).

As this definition suggests, Cixous's reference to the body stands not for an actual physiological entity, since a subject obviously cannot occupy two physical bodies simultaneously, but to an internalized somatic register or to a metaphor of the body. Nevertheless, she goes on to argue that the new theory of bisexuality that she is advancing privileges women, not because of any innate or essential qualities they possess, but because Freudian theory apportions bisexuality unequally to men and women.

Freud claimed that the way the little girl progresses from an original bisexuality to becoming a woman is a more complicated and involuted process than it is for a boy. Where boys retain a single erogenous zone, a girl must transfer sexual pleasure from the clitoral to the vaginal zone. Even when this transfer is accomplished successfully (and Freud's enumeration of the three paths by which the girl becomes a woman indicates that the shift from one zone to the other is by no means automatic), sexuality in a woman simply hierarchizes the zones, subordinating clitoral to vaginal sexuality. This means that adult female sexuality is characterized by its bisexuality, with the clitoris signifying masculine pleasure and the vagina standing for feminine sexuality. This bisexuality predisposes women to hysteria, he argues, a pathology to which men retain a certain resistance because their passage to adult sexuality necessitates a repression of the feminine aspect of their original bisexuality. (Male repression of their bisexual nature, as Cixous notes, is linked to their fear of being a woman, a fear that is imbricated with homosexuality (1986: 85)). Rather than discarding Freudian theory, Cixous – like Sarah Kofman – appropriates his conception of woman's "natural" bisexuality. Instead of seeing this doubleness as the basis for neurosis, then, she turns it against Freud, making the doubleness of woman, rather than the unitary nature of men, the norm.

Cixous's frequent invocation of Freud should alert us to her reflexiveness about the contingency of her formulations. She is careful to assert that her theories represent an interim solution, a way of redefining the subject's relationship to the body (1986: 83). She also reiterates that men as well as women can participate in the "other bisexuality." That her thesis is inscribed on the feminine body is, I believe, a gynetic gesture, in Alice Jardine's sense of the word. Because woman is the locus of lack, castration, and doubleness in psychoanalytic theory, she (as the site of difference, as metaphor) can also be used as a vantage point from which to dismantle the sexual hierarchy that informs Freudian theory. Cixous argues that to assert woman's bisexuality is a way of "displacing" the question of difference (1986: 85). Writing "is woman's" (1986: 85) because of her greater predisposition to bisexuality; writing (and by analogy, woman) is the passageway (or the exit – *sortie*) that allows for the co-existence of the other in the one. As Cixous suggests, this openness has in the past been called "possession" (and here we might think of sibylline prophecy or ecstatic transport), but that inhabitation was also historically a dispossession or erasure of woman, since she became an empty vehicle, alienated from herself (1986: 86).

The idea of co-existence in the feminine of the "same" and the "other" brings us to Cixous's definition of the gift economy. Where in the masculine realm of the proper, a gift always presupposes a return, a gain of masculinity (virility, power, money, pleasure), woman gives without trying to "'recover her expenses'" (1986: 87). Toril Moi's reading of this idea returns it to a kind of basic belief in female generosity (Moi 1985: 112–13), yet this difficult passage seems rather to rely on the sexes' asymmetrical relationship to giving. In a patriarchal system, woman is herself the gift; she is what circulates in order to sustain relations among men (Irigaray 1985b: 170–91). Her relation to the realm of the gift is thus not an essential or biological one, but emerges, instead, from her inscription in the order of the proper. A gift economy, like bisexuality, then, is Cixous's way of entering the system through the place to which woman is assigned, except that she does so deliberately, thus setting up a version of Irigarayan mimicry (Irigaray 1985b: 76). In the realm of the gift, woman has a special receptivity to language: "She lets the other tongue of a thousand tongues speak – the tongue, sound without barrier or death. She refuses life nothing. Her tongue doesn't hold back but holds forth, doesn't keep in but keeps on enabling" (Cixous 1986: 88). Moi sees in this passage a slippage from "'feminine'" to "'female'," evidence for her of the "clear biologism" (Moi 1985: 113) that subtends Cixous's theorization of the gift economy. But I would argue that there seems to be little reason to tether this (admittedly) rhapsodic and utopian language to a female anatomy; at the end of the passage, Cixous writes "I am spacious, singing Flesh: onto which is grafted no one knows which I – which masculine or feminine, more or less human but above all living, because changing I" (1986: 88). What Cixous depicts as woman or the feminine is characterized most of all by its multiplicity and changeability, the elasticity with which it accommodates otherness of various sorts. What interests me about this version of woman and language is its imbrication with the historical male tradition that also represents woman as possessed of a thousand tongues that never cease talking (garrulity) and which sees woman as the essence of change, mutability, and duplicity, a tradition I have just examined in my discussion of *Folly*. Appropriating this conception of the feminine from the economy of the proper, Cixous fashions a version of woman that depends upon a misogynist metaphorization of the feminine, except that, rather than allowing it to construct her, she seizes it, using the epithets traditionally used to keep women confined and silent, and makes them the basis for her utopian manifesto.

> If woman has always functioned 'within' man's discourse, a signifier referring always to the opposing signifier that annihilates its particular energy, puts down or stifles its very different sounds, now it is time for her to displace this 'within,' explode it, overturn it, grab it, make it hers, take it in, take it into her woman's mouth, bite its tongue with her woman's teeth, make up her own tongue to get inside it.
>
> (1986: 95–6)

The economy of the gift guides Cixous's relationship to other texts. Instead of subscribing to a system of authorial property, designated by traditional markers of ownership, she enters into poetic or theoretical discourses with a freedom that seems to abolish boundaries of possession. This is a discursive strategy designed to undo the authority of a male tradition, and it also marks the intersection of the text and the subject. Cixous describes her own upbringing in Algeria, where, as a Jewish woman in a country colonized by France, books become the means for her exit from this "real, colonial space" (1986: 72) of political oppression. Her identifications with poetic figures provide the basis for her construction of herself as subject: she resists the roles of Dido and Joan of Arc, for example, because Dido is ultimately a victim and because Joan of Arc is Christian, but she forges an alliance with Achilles, whose "sexual ambiguity" permits her own (1986: 78). If these early literary "impersonations" allow her to confront a colonized Algeria, this discursive space of liberation later reveals itself as the site of a more pernicious cultural colonization. Alienated from her female body through the "'dark continent' trick," sex becomes frightening for woman, for her body has been "colonized" (1986: 68), both by psychoanalysis and by literature. The remedy is a rebellion that redeploys the weapons of empire against itself, a method of infiltration "where her power of identification puts the same to rout" (1986: 96). Cixous's representation of the "dark continent" simultaneously metaphorizes and literalizes it, for this place is both female sexuality and Africa itself (which in turn contains the Algeria of her childhood), a continent that is also mythologized as "dark" and "unknown" and governed by a rule of "apartheid" (1986: 68). The last sections of *The Newly Born Woman* enact Cixous's traversing or occupation of a variety of mythic or literary figures, from Freud, Freud's Dora, Kleist's Penthesileia, Kleist's Achilles, to Shakespeare's and Plutarch's Cleopatra. She disrupts the proprieties that distinguish characters from their creators, men from women, hysterics from psychoanalysts, analysis from poetry. Each of her lyrical entries into the narratives she evokes calls up the issue of language (frequently metonymized in the tongue) and its relation to the body and to culture.[9]

The ligature between body and language is one that Cixous addresses more directly in her discussion of writing and voice. Near the beginning of her definition of *écriture feminine*, she claims to sense femininity in writing by "a privilege of *voice*: *writing and voice* are entwined and interwoven and writing's continuity/voice's rhythm take each other's breath away through interchanging, make the text gasp or form it out of suspenses and silences, make it lose its voice or rend it with cries" (1986: 92). Toril Moi, working from a predominately Derridean perspective, understands Cixous's references to voice as a privileging of origin and presence (1985: 119). Derrida's deconstruction of the opposition between speaking and writing revealed western metaphysics' valorization of speech. The speaker's presence seems to offer an implicit guarantee of the stability of meaning in an utterance. Writing, on the other hand, produces a kind of textual orphan that is cut off from the source of its production, and is thus susceptible to distortion and misunderstanding. Further, voice signals the subject's self-presence, since to speak is also to hear oneself speak. The proximity of signifier to signified in spoken language thus appears to proffer a sense of mastery or "limitless power over the signified" (Derrida 1973: 80). Yet this self-presence and sense of mastery over meaning in the Derridean definition of phonocentrism is very different from the Cixousian use of voice. For Cixous, voice is a privileged term because it emerges from the body, but it is the voice's connection to the body rather than the match between signifier and signified that is important.[10] Thus, her "voice" at times has little to do with language: "*Voice*! That, too, is launching forth and effusion without return. Exclamation, cry, breathlessness, yell, cough, vomit, music. Voice leaves. Voice loses" (1986: 94). *Ecriture feminine* is a strategy for recovering the discarded female body and its relation to language within a linguistic realm that is immense and elastic, having as it does closer affinities with the Lacanian Imaginary than with Derrida's theories.

Moi's other criticism of Cixous's celebration of voice is that, in positing a female or maternal body as its source, voice becomes an essentialist principle (1985: 118). The search for voice leads woman to a time before the Symbolic, before the law took "breath" away and made it a prisoner of language. Yet the recovery that Cixous urges is not a nostalgic search for origin, nor is it a fusion with the mother:

> listen to me, it is not a captivating, clinging 'mother'; it is the equivoice that, touching you, affects you, pushes you away from your breast to come to language... it is the rhyth-me that laughs you... who is no more describable than god, soul, or the Other; the part of you that puts space between yourself and pushes you to inscribe your woman's style in language.
>
> (1986: 93)[11]

What Cixous seems to be advocating is less a retreat into the Imaginary, then, than an irruption of the Imaginary into the Symbolic. Voice is thus correlated with the body and the instinctual drives, while traditional writing is associated with sublimation and the law. *Ecriture feminine* is a writing that is infiltrated with the silenced voice of the body; it is as if Cixous's psychoanalytic formula has reversed the Derridean terms: voice in Derrida's critique of phonocentrism stands for self-presence, whereas writing is what encodes difference (*différance*), multiple senses, play. Traditional writing, from Cixous's perspective, takes place in a phallocentric order and depends upon the repression of Woman and all the metaphysical baggage heaped upon her: sexuality, bodies, waste, non-discursive sound. In other words, woman makes (phallocentric) language possible by becoming all that the linguistic order exiles or abjects. Throughout this "dumb history," women have been "embodied but still deadly silent, in silences, in voiceless rebellions" (1986: 95). The feminine writing attempts to create a new relationship between the imaginary and symbolic orders by challenging the discourses of mastery that depend upon a muting of the female "voice" and the body it speaks.[12]

Because the female body is the site of what the phallocentric order represses, it is this body that must be brought into writing in all its disruptive, multiplicitous possibility. When Cixous speaks of the woman's "privileged relationship with voice" (1986: 93), then, she is not, as Moi claims, evoking "the essential bond between feminine writing and the mother as source and origin to be heard in all female texts" (1985: 114). Rather, she is recuperating a female body and a definition of woman that already exists in a patriarchal cultural legacy, except that, instead of being spoken or interpreted, the body "speaks" itself in language. Cixous celebrates the hysteric, Dora in particular, because the hysteric is the paradigmatic instance of feminine speaking through the body. She addresses Dora directly in an apostrophe (the trope of voicing):

> It is you, Dora, you, who cannot be tamed, the poetic body, the true "mistress" of the Signifier. Before tomorrow your effectiveness will be seen to work – when your works will no longer be retracted, pointed against your own breast, but will write themselves against the other and against men's grammar.
>
> (1986: 95)

Cixous uses the hysteric as a paradigmatic instance of *écriture feminine* because of the hysteric's suppressed linguistic ability and because of her capacities for disruption. She argues, though, that the hysteric is a metaphor for a certain state and that the linguistic and sexual energy she possesses is distributed along a continuum. At one end of the spectrum, it becomes possible for the hysteric to succumb to her neurosis in such a way that she loses her capability effectively to disrupt. But the qualities of the hysteric, the "very strong capacities of identification with the other, that are scouring, that make mirrors fly, that put disturbing images back into circulation" (155), are elements that all women possess in some measure. It is especially the hysteric's strength that Cixous values, the capacity to make demands in a way that disturbs the functioning of the economies of mastery and the proper (1986: 154–5).

Cixous's method is crystallized in her use of the Medusa head, a figure that is explicitly associated with rhetoric in the Renaissance (Vickers 1985: 110–11). Medusa, according to Freud, is an image of the purportedly hideous female genitalia, so Cixous's appropriation of the image and her conversion of Medusa into a figure of laughter, embodies her desire to repossess the link between female sexuality and language and make it the basis of feminine writing. Clément uses a similar representation in her account of hysteria and witchcraft. She invokes Baubo, the woman with whom Demeter stayed at Eleusis. Because Demeter was searching for her abducted daughter, and was grief-stricken, she refused food and drink. Baubo made her laugh by suddenly lifting her dress over head and exposing her body. Clément, like Freud, sees Baubo as a figure of inversion, for the genitals appear where the head should be. Freud's description stresses the synecdochic aspects of the representation, a derogatory or caricatured image in which the genitals come to stand for the whole person (Freud 1957: 338). Yet for Clément, who inverts Freud, Baubo (like Folly) is linked with the female genitalia and laughter, and is thus a figure of the voice that emerges from censored sexuality, the ineffable sound of feminine *jouissance*. Where Luce Irigaray's desire to transform the symbolic order is effected through mimicry, Cixous's strategy is inversion, turning what has been traditionally subordinated upside down. This process is not simply a reinscription of hierarchy, an inversion that reasserts feminine values rather than masculine ones. Baubo, Medusa, and Folly bring the "double mouths" of the female body together, but the locus of the doubleness is treated differently for Cixous and Erasmus. Cixous self-reflexively pillages tradition, salvaging detritus, infiltrating patriarchal narratives and inverting them. Rather than making herself into an empty receptacle, capable of being "possessed" by others and therefore "dispossessed" of herself, she argues for the co-existence of otherness, a cultivation of nonexclusion and "permeability" that itself constitutes a threat to the order of the same. Although she evokes a representation of voice that emerges from a recognizably patriarchal tradition, one that has been used to insure women's silence, her articulation of the very voice that should render her mute produces an undermining doubling that is at once inversion and recuperation. Erasmus's ventriloquization of Folly (or her temporary inhabitation of him) represents no such threat. His repeated insistence on doubleness, the references to his authorial presence, and the linguistic medium of his oration serve to accentuate his position of authorial privilege. Though the *Encomium* undoubtedly represents a subversive challenge to social institutions, it does so at the expense of the female voice he uses. Functioning merely as the vantage point from which he anatomizes social and ecclesiastical excesses, the representation of feminine speaking serves to perpetuate a metaphor that guarantees the marginalization of female speech.

3

MATRIX AS METAPHOR

Midwifery and the conception of voice

> But the fact that the maternal function is wielded by men – indeed, that literature is one of the ways in which men have elaborated the maternal position – means that the silence of actual women is all the more effectively enforced. With men playing all the parts, the drama appears less incomplete than it really is.
>
> (Barbara Johnson 1987: 142)

> What does it matter who is speaking, someone said,
> what does it matter who is speaking.

Michel Foucault's citation (1984: 101) of an anonymous voice from Samuel Beckett's *Texts for Nothing* points to half of the problem that I will be investigating in this chapter: who speaks a literary text and what is the status of that utterance with respect to origin, representation, and property? In other words, how do authors image their own voice in poetry in order to guarantee its recognizability and hence its survival as their product? Emile Benveniste and Roland Barthes have argued that the "person" of the author dissolves into the linguistic subject of the text (the one who says "I"), and is, according to Barthes, given life only by the reader, and Foucault has pointed to the ideological and historical construction of the author-function; drawing on both of these theoretical positions, I will be examining how the "I" of a text fashions itself and is shaped both by the immediate cultural circumstances of its production and by the history of its readership. The construction of John Donne's poetic voice provides us with a particularly clear example of this problem. Until very recently, critics have tended to read Donne's voice through the authoritative legacy bequeathed to us by T.S. Eliot and the New Critics; in his celebrated essay on the Metaphysical poets,

Eliot situates Donne before the "dissociation of sensibility," so that thought and feeling, expression and experience were unified for the seventeenth-century mind in a way that became impossible for the twentieth-century poet. Where Eliot saw the Donnean text as the pure medium of expression, "a direct sensuous apprehension of thought, or a recreation of thought into feeling" (1975: 63), subsequent critics tended to locate the purity or accessibility of Donne less in the process of poetry than in the presence of the poet. As Thomas Docherty has recently characterized this tradition of reading, "in stressing the purity or instantaneity of Donne's medium, Eliot inaugurated the critical process of restitution of Donne's body, starting not from the cerebral cortex, but from the voice" (1986: 3).

Not only has this critical tradition of assuming that the authorial voice is present and clearly identifiable dominated Donne studies, but the voice that marked the outrageous rhythms and compelling diction of his poetry as his was also, according to his critics, definitively gendered as male. This brings me to the second half of the problem I will be exploring, then, the gender of the voice that speaks. Following the speaker's characterization of his own rhetoric's "masculine persuasive force" in Elegy 16, contemporaries of Donne have applied that epithet to Donne's poetry as a whole. Ben Jonson's censure of Donne's verse "for not keeping of accent" (Jonson 1975: 462) correlates with Jonson's gendering of style in his *Discoveries*, in which the so-called "women's poets" write "a verse, as smooth, as soft, as cream," but in sounding the wits of this verse, one discovers them to be but "cream-bowl" or "puddle deep" (1975: 396). The masculine style distinguishes itself by its eschewing of these effeminizing impulses and its substitution of a muscular power that avoids mere mellifluousness and metrical ornamentation. Thomas Carew's (1989) 1633 "Elegie upon the Death of John Donne" furnishes a similarly gendered depiction of Donne's poetic bequest. Apostrophizing the dead poet, he claims that "Thou hast redeem'd, and open'd Us a Mine/ Of rich and pregnant phansie, drawne a line/ Of masculine expression." Samuel Johnson's famous definition of metaphysical wit incorporates the ingredients of mastery and violence (nature and art are "ransacked for illustrations, comparisons, and allusions") (1967: I:20), and C.S. Lewis's more recent dichotomization of style into two distinct strains reiterates Ben Jonson's categories, associating Donne not with the luxurious style of Spenser's *Amoretti*, but with the "abrupt, familiar, and consciously 'manly' style" of Wyatt's lyrics (Lewis 1966: 144).

Yet this confined description of voice in Donne criticism – even when it has expanded to consider his use of personae – has been largely unable to account for Donne's perplexing and shifting treatment of woman. By focusing on a unitary voice emanating from a contained authorial figure, traditional criticism has paid little attention to the issue of poetic inspiration as it is imaged both culturally and in Donne's poetry. Although my interest in voice derives partly from current feminist debates, there is in recent feminist theory a strong emphasis on the recovery of an authentic female voice, a refrain that has in some cases had the effect of reifying and essentializing voice, as if it emerged from a gendered body and remained thereafter perennially tethered to it.[1] I will question this assumption by arguing that voice is, first, a construction that takes place within a cultural and historical matrix, and, second, that it is often ambiguously and complicatedly gendered, crossing the boundaries between sexes with a freedom largely unacknowledged by current theoretical treatments of voice.[2] For instance, even in the lines I have just cited from Thomas Carew's "Elegy," the "masculine expression" that he claims stamps Donne's verse is modified by what he calls the "Mine/ Of rich and pregnant phansie" that provides the source of subsequent poetic inspiration. Why should this aggressively masculine poetic tradition be seen as springing from an image typically associated in Donne's poetry with the female body and the body of the earth that is pregnant with treasure, waiting to be ransacked? To attempt to answer that question, I will concentrate on the way voice as a construct coheres in a particular constellation of metaphors that is frequently found in Renaissance poetry: the image of the pregnant male poet giving birth to voice, being impregnated or impregnating his muse, or serving as a midwife to poetic birth. I begin by looking at a number of midwifery books from the period in order to contextualize the trope in historical and medical terms. I then examine the particular topicality of the metaphor in a number of Renaissance texts, and I return to Donne's poetry at the end of the chapter, where I look at his imaging of birth and the figure of the midwife in a number of poems, but most specifically in the *Anniversaries*. While none of these texts is ventriloquized in the technical sense, all of them represent their poetic voices as emerging from a feminine source, a source that is imaged – or closely linked to – female reproduction. Where Sandra Gilbert and Susan Gubar in *The Madwoman in the Attic* traced the metaphor of the penis as the organ that generated (male-authored) texts, I am concerned to chart the transvestism (or at least cross-gendering) of literary production, in which woman stands as the silent but enabling condition of writing.

My claim is that poetic use of birth metaphors registers a cultural preoccupation with birth as a new territory, which, like the human body generally, was being explored by science and medicine in ways that were to have profound political, religious, and economic repercussions. What makes (physiological) childbirth particularly interesting for my purposes is that it is gender coded; birth, as a function specific to women, was traditionally set within a feminine space and supervised by female midwives, but this architectural and epistemological space was increasingly encroached upon by men in the late sixteenth and early seventeenth century in England. One element of this encroachment – which was both a vehicle for it and a symptom of it – was the publication of midwifery books translated into the vernacular for the first time during this period. The books disseminated information about pregnancy and birth and provided illustrations both of the inside of birthing chambers and also of the womb's interior. These images provide evidence of the medical curiosity about gestation and birth, they point the way toward the economic and scientific dimension of the struggle to control childbirth, and they also reflect the interpenetration of medical and literary discourses. The midwifery texts, too, employ the familiar metaphor – which is as old as Plato's *Theaetetus* – of book as child, they ground language and creativity in the female body and its reproductive processes, and they reenact in their rhetorical strategies the appropriation both of the female body and the poetic voice that putatively springs from it. We can read a poetic text like Donne's *Anniversaries* in relation to the medical discourses that subtend so much of his metaphorical language, just as we can read the medical texts both for what they tell us about the historical context and for their figuration of language. Put together, these texts allow us to begin to understand the historicist dimension of the strange transvestism of the male poet giving birth to his own voice, as well as to recognize the complexity of the construction of gender in the early modern period.

I

Theoretical attention has been directed in the past few decades to destabilizing the belief that language can be transparent, the belief that what is enunciated is far more important than how it is enunciated. The ensuing focus on the "how" has produced a new attention to the study of rhetoric and specifically to the operations of tropological language. While this renewed interest has had repercussions for many disciplines, it has engendered a special sensitivity to language and text in the study of history.[3] This chapter seeks to question the relationship of metaphor to history by focusing on tropes of male birth and investigating the various economic, scientific, and medical circumstances that helped to give them prominence and circulation. My contention is that these metaphors become a kind of nodal point, a linguistic symptom of a cultural phenomenon broader than its merely "literary" manifestation. Derrida has demonstrated the impossibility of trying to distinguish the figurative from the literal aspects of language, and, while I don't wish to imply that there is a material basis in a given historical moment that can be recovered, I do see metaphor as grounded in other discursive sites, and these discourses can allow us to see the broader operations of culture. Terry Castle, in a study of birth topoi from 1660 to 1820, has argued that the way metaphors of the human body are used by poets changes over time, a change that is symptomatic of alterations in aesthetic theory (1979: 194). Although she convincingly suggests that, for eighteenth-century satirists (and even for critical prose of this period), birth imagery provided a figuration of corrupt cognitive functioning, whereas, for the Romantics, childbirth offered a celebratory image of poetic fashioning, she claims that, with the exception of Plato, "there seems to be no overt attachment of any philosophic significance to the figure until the eighteenth century" (Castle 1979: 194). Despite the "extreme popularity of the poetic birth *topos* in English poetry of the sixteenth and seventeenth centuries," Castle, in an assertion that seems to reiterate T.S. Eliot's dissociation of sensibility argument, claims that "English Renaissance poets are at ease with the metaphor... it remains for them an obviously natural and psychologically convenient mode for designating the act of versifying" (1979: 194, 196). Clearly, to suggest that Renaissance poets were unified with their bodies in such a way that the metaphor was "natural" and unproblematic is to ignore, first, the historical complications of the period and, second, the transvestism of the process, for it is, after all, primarily *male* poets who are impregnated and giving birth.

While it could be said that the fascination with representations of motherhood and figurations of birth in late twentieth-century theory and criticism is produced by a number of historical factors –

including the explosion of technology surrounding conception and birth[4] – the prevalence of birth imagery in Renaissance England is less obviously easy to account for. Elizabeth Sacks has pointed to the political and very public concern with begetting heirs that haunted the Tudor monarchy throughout the sixteenth century, and, although she mentions only Henry VIII and Elizabeth I, Mary Tudor's embarrassing and well-publicized false pregnancies reenacted Henry VIII's obsession with begetting a male heir in ways that must have been painfully reminiscent for her subjects.[5] Elizabeth I's very childlessness caused a similar preoccupation among her subjects, who feared that the political and religious chaos following Henry VIII's failure to produce a healthy male heir would return to England upon her death. The anxiety evidenced by the monarchy about their heirs (or lack of them) was intensified by their political position, but it was hardly a novel situation, since the patriarchal nature of the English aristocracy also depended upon male heirs to perpetuate itself. The sheer number of births among upper-class women, some of whom produced a child a year (the elite woman's use of a wet-nurse would have heightened her fertility) (Harris 1990: 613), the high mortality rate for infants, and the extreme hazard associated with childbirth in the period may well have contributed to the symbolic importance of birth in poetry.[6] Far from indicating a "naturalness" or ease with the body, however, the prevalence of the metaphor signals the beginnings of a cultural change, both in the management of childbirth itself and in the epistemological and medical discourses surrounding the understanding of gestation and birth.

Much of the changing attitude toward female reproduction is crystallized in the debates surrounding midwifery. Female midwives, in addition to their crucial practical functions, occupied a significant symbolic role, since it was they who ascertained virginity, diagnosed pregnancy, certified a child's legitimacy, and, as witnesses, ensured that one child was not substituted for another, that still-born children were properly baptized and disposed of, and could testify that if a child died it had perished of natural causes (Eccles 1982: 14–18). Midwives had been licensed by the church in England since approximately 1512, both because they might need to baptize an infant before it died and because of the moral role they were supposed to perform. The midwifery books of the period stress the excellence and reliability of the ideal midwife's character; one of the requisites is that she be as "sharp-sighted as Argus" (Culpeper 1651: 3), an allusion not only to her skill but also to her role as guardian of chastity within a patriarchal culture. The importance of the midwife as custodian to reproduction and the cultural codes governing it made her a potentially dangerous figure, a danger that is registered in the violent attack on her in the *Malleus Maleficarum*, where the authors assert that "No one does more harm to the Catholic Faith than the midwives" (Kramer 1971: 66). Represented as a witch, she is depicted as having control over sexual intercourse, conception, abortion,[7] and birth, and of either killing or offering newborn children to the devil (Kramer 1971: 141). While the explicit target in the *Malleus* is the midwives' use and perversion of Christian ritual, where baptismal rites are transformed into satanic ceremonies in which the child's body or soul are offered to the devil, Barbara Ehrenreich and Deirdre English have persuasively argued that the accusations against midwives are intimately linked to the rise of the medical profession.

Twentieth-century descriptions of the state of midwifery in England in the early seventeenth century are inevitably informed by ideological positions that reflect not only attitudes towards science and medicine but which are also encoded with assumptions about gender. Histories of obstetrics written by members of the medical profession tend to judge the practice of midwifery before the seventeenth century as dominated by ignorance, superstition, and death. Herbert R. Spencer in his *History of British Midwifery*, for example, describes midwifery in England in 1650 as being "in an unsatisfactory condition and... conducted mainly by women, many of whom had no education, knowledge or character requisite for its proper practice" (1927: 1). Lawrence Stone echoes this condemnation, attributing the danger of childbirth partly to midwives who, he says, "were ignorant and ill-trained, and often horribly botched the job" (1977: 64). This deplorable situation could be remedied, according to Spencer, only by the inclusion of obstetrics and gynecology within the medical establishment, so that the proper education and training of midwives could be ensured. The crisis over the control of childbirth seen from the perspective of feminist scholars, on the other hand, emphasizes the progressive superceding of women by men who excluded them from the very education that could have guaranteed their continued prominent place in midwifery. Alice Clark, in *Working Life of Women in the Seventeenth Century*, argues that midwifery stood out "as the most important public function exercised by women" and it was regarded

> as their inviolable mystery till near the beginning of the seventeenth century. The steady process through which in this profession women were then supplanted by men, furnishes an example of the way in which women have lost their hold upon all branches of skilled responsible work, through being deprived of opportunities for specialised training.
>
> (1968: 242)

Indeed the only training available to aspiring female midwives was apprenticeship, and this "could not supply the more speculative side of training, which can only be given in connection with schools of anatomy where research work is possible, and from these all women were excluded" (Clark 1968: 269). Although in England women were not actually replaced by men as the primary birth attendants until the eighteenth century, the term "man-midwife" enters the language for the first time in the early 1600s (Donnison 1988: 23), and the ideological conditions for this transposition of childbirth management were definitively laid in the seventeenth century. The elements that fed into the ideological shift were many and complexly intertwined. They had to do with education, with the changing status of the human body – especially the female body – as an object of scientific study, with the structure of patriarchal society that made the production of legitimate heirs crucial to its survival, and with the emerging medical and obstetrical profession and the scientific and commercial interests it sought to regulate and protect.

The twentieth-century debate about the historical status of midwives strikingly reiterates the terms that were employed in the seventeenth century, where men aligned with the medical profession represent midwives as dangerously ignorant, intrusive, and inimical to the laboring woman's health and survival, whereas what written records survive from female midwives depict the invasion of the birthing chamber by men with instruments that as often as not stand for pain and death. The confrontation between the midwives and the physicians and man-midwives who increasingly sought control over childbirth is epitomized by the Chamberlen family, who not only invented the midwifery forceps and kept that invention a family secret until the eighteenth century, but who also sought to form a corporation of midwives. Peter the elder and Peter the younger, sons of the Huguenot refugee, William Chamberlen, were trained as barber surgeons. Both of their names appear in the Annals of the Royal College of Physicians for infringements on medicine, for, as surgeons, they were not allowed to administer internal remedies (Aveling 1977: 6–7). It appears that Peter the Elder was imprisoned for his offense, but Queen Anne interceded on his behalf; it seems that he may have attended the Queen during her confinements, since there is a record of a payment of 40 pounds to him, and the gift of a diamond ring from her is recorded in his will. He also acted as surgeon to Henrietta Maria, and there is one mention of his serving as midwife to her when she miscarried of her first child in 1628 (Aveling 1977: 8–9). Like his brother, Peter the younger was in conflict with the College of Physicians on the grounds of practising physic, and he, too, was closely involved with the first attempts to incorporate midwives. In 1616, the College of Physicians of London met to consider a petition by London midwives to incorporate and form a self-governing society, and Peter the younger was present at that meeting, apparently acting as an advocate for the midwives (Aveling 1977: 21). In fact, the idea for the petition may well have originated with him (Donnison 1988: 26), and his interests were hardly completely altruistic; not only would a society of midwives (in which he would probably have served as governor) have consolidated his familial reputation in midwifery, thus creating a specialization that would heal the division between medicine and surgery (rectifying his own exclusion from physic), but the monopoly on licensing would have been extremely lucrative. The petition (which was addressed to Francis Bacon, then attorney general) was ultimately refused, on the grounds that there was no precedent in the commonwealth for such a corporation. Some concessions were made by the College of Physicians to the midwives in education, training, and regulation, however: they were to be allowed to attend anatomies "once or twice in the yeare," the College offered to depute "grave and learned men" to resolve their doubts and instruct them, and it promised to make them subject to censure by the College for any abuses of physic (Aveling 1977: 24).

The efforts of the Chamberlen brothers to form a society of midwives were revived by the son of Peter Chamberlen the younger, who was also named Peter. Unlike his father and uncle, he received a thorough medical education, at Cambridge, Heidelberg, and Padua, and received his degree of Doctor of Medicine, by his own account in *A Voice in Rhama* " 'ere nineteen sunnes had measured out my Nativitie." He claims that God blessed him with extraordinary gifts of healing, which, far from granting him happiness and success, bestowed a fame which in turn engendered envy and "secret enemies" (1647). His fame was increased by his father having bequeathed to him the family secret (the invention of obstetrical forceps). The secret was preserved by observing unusual precautions during deliveries: keeping the forceps in a locked box and then working beneath a sheet, which in this case not only shielded the woman's body from his gaze but also guarded his secret from the inquiring eyes of those within the birth chamber (Arms 1975: 19–20). Peter Chamberlen's medical successes were at least partially precipitated by the envy of his colleagues, for, as he says, "they cunningly allow me a transcendency in the particular of Deliveries, that they may the more securely denie me my due in Physick." Far from losing prestige by specializing in childbirth, Chamberlen made such a success of his particular calling that he became physician ordinary to three kings and queens of England and to various foreign princes as well (the Czar of Russia is said to have requested his services) (Aveling 1977: 123; 32).

Seeking to capitalize upon his expertise and to remedy his financial situation (his profligacy is mentioned by at least one detractor) (Aveling 1977: 33), he seems to have attempted in 1634 to incorporate London midwives and to appoint himself educator and regulator of that society (Donnison 1988: 26; Spencer 1927: v–vi). The midwives themselves retaliated, and two of them, Mrs Hester Shaw and Mrs Whipp, filed a petition of grievances against Chamberlen's despotic treatment of them, a tyranny that they claimed ranged from his insisting on their attending mandatory monthly meetings to his threat that he would not attend distressed women in labor whose midwives had refused his authority (Spencer 1927: vi). They denounced him on a number of counts and sought to make clear that, despite his rhetoric of salvation, his interests were less medical than financial. They argued that:

> Neither can Dr. Chamberlane teach the art of Midwifery in most births because he hath no experience in itt but by reading and it must be by continuall practise in this kind that will bringe experience, and those women that desire to learne must be present at the delivery of many women and see the worke and behavior of such as be skilfull midwifes who will shew and direct them and resolve their doubts.
>
> And further Dr. Chamberlane's work and the work belonging to midwifes are contrary one to the other for he delivers none without the use of instruments by extraordinary violence

> in desparate occasions, which women never practised nor desyred for they have neither parts nor hands for that art.
>
> (Aveling 1977: 40)

The midwives asserted that the promise of being taught anatomy by demonstration was an empty one, since the only bodies that could be dissected were those of criminals, and, because pregnancy temporarily exempted women from execution, the anatomies they were likely to witness would have little bearing on their specialization. They are especially vehement in condemning Chamberlen's extortionary practices, which, according to them, involved making unreasonable demands for large payments from those who could little afford them, usually before he would consent to treat the patient and usually in moments of extremity and vulnerability, where delay might mean death for the laboring woman. He is accused of cultivating especially those midwives who were most ignorant and least skilled, since, if only the expert midwives were allowed to flourish, the need for his particular abilities would be greatly diminished (Aveling 1977: 40–2). The midwives' petition, which was heard by the Bishop of London, was successful in all its arguments. Chamberlen was reprimanded for his unscrupulous and hectoring treatment of midwives (and it was found that the certificates endorsed by midwives who purported to be in favor of his cause were often obtained surreptitiously or by threat), for his unethical demands for payment in advance of services, and for his alleged "immodesty and undecent behaviours" (Aveling 1977: 46). He was further required to obtain a license in midwifery from the Bishop of London and to submit himself to the oaths and duties pertaining to the office of midwifery as it was ecclesiastically dictated.[8] Chamberlen's bitterness is recorded in a hyperbolic defense of his own case, *A Voice in Rhama*, which announces itself as *The Crie of Women and Children, Echoed forth in the Compassions of Peter Chamberlen*. In this supposedly ventriloquized – or at least advocatorial – tract, he laments the blood that is allowed to run freely from women and children because the "uncontroled femal-Arbiters of Life and Death" have made it impossible for a charitable Samaritan (like himself) to bind their wounds. The battle for the control of childbirth was thus fought both rhetorically and literally over (or on) women's bodies, in the sense that, as Chamberlen's threat to the midwives makes clear, the laboring woman was held hostage by the warring ideological positions of those attending her. Although the midwives were initially able to frustrate Chamberlen's monopoly of licensing, the very lack of a system for educating and regulating midwives (apart from the existing system of ecclesiastical licensing, which provided no method for training and only a loose regulatory function) must certainly have contributed to the medical establishment's ultimate appropriation of obstetrics.

As Mrs Shaw's and Mrs Whipp's accusation demonstrates, midwifery forceps and obstetrical instruments in general function as metonymical expressions of male intrusion into the birthing chamber and indeed into the secret recesses of the female body. Men were usually called to assist only at births with complications, and their presence was associated with the instruments they used, such as the crochet, which was designed to extract the fetus from the mother's body piecemeal. While it is certainly true that such procedures sometimes saved the mother's life (just as the caesarean preserved the child's life), the presence of the surgeon or the male midwife often already signalled that there was danger to mother or child and that extreme measures were necessary.[9] A man-midwife's assistance at a birth was regarded as a violation of both modesty and nature, as an anecdote recounted by Louise Bourgeois, the renowned French midwife, attests. She tells of a birth she attended, where the woman at last consented to let a surgeon come on the condition that she did not see him. Louise Bourgeois, afraid that the woman would "die with apprehension and shame," darkened the room, and arranged the bed so that the woman was unaware of the man's presence (Culpeper 1680: 29). Yet, if instruments metonymically express the control man-midwives and surgeons came to wield, vision is equally implicated. Vision is increasingly associated with knowledge in general and especially with a knowledge that can be verified by sight; Bacon's tropology of vision in *The New Organon* ("For I admit nothing but on the faith of eyes" (Bacon 1960: 26)) registers this privileging of ocularity in ways that connect strikingly with the tropes of childbirth I discuss. Indeed, Bacon's lament about the state of learning derived solely from the authority of the ancients is articulated in terms of barrenness: he describes knowledge as like Scylla, whose face and head are of a virgin, but whose womb is "hung round with barking monsters, from which she could not be delivered" (1960: 8). The "issue" and "fruit" of learning can be successfully delivered only by a rigorous attention to the information gathered by the senses. Just as learning in general was "barren" or "miscarried," so knowledge of the female reproductive organs in the sixteenth and early seventeenth centuries in England was largely stagnant, relying as it did on Galen's writings, which saw female genitals as an internalized version of male genitals: "Turn outward the woman's, turn inward, so to speak, and fold double the man's, and you will find the same in both in every respect" (Laqueur 1986: 5). In his elaboration of this homology, Galen provides an illustrative simile, for he likens women's reproductive organs to the eyes of a mole because in both cases the requisite equipment exists and is imperfect for its assigned purpose. The mole possesses eyes that are undeveloped and incapable of vision, and the female organs are similarly insufficient, since, lacking adequate heat, they cannot extrude themselves, and must remain enclosed within the claustral space of the female body. It is perhaps partly because the interior of the female body could not be seen in the ordinary course of events that it was set up as a space to be known, colonized, imagined, and depicted in images.

The generation and circulation of this new knowledge was facilitated by the books on conception and birth that began to be translated and published in the seventeenth century. The earliest English textbook for midwives, *The Birth of Mankind*, was a translation of the 1513 German text of Eucharius Rosslin; it was published in 1540, and went into thirteen editions (the last in 1654) (Eccles 1982: 11–12), an indication of the book's popularity and of the need it served. There followed a series of influential books in English, often specifically addressed to an audience of midwives: *Childbirth, or the happy deliverie of women* (1612), a translation of Ambroise Paré's pupil and son-in-law Jacques Guillimeau's French text of 1609, Jacob Rueff's *The Expert Midwife* (1637), a translation of the Latin text (1554)), Nicholas Culpeper's *Directory for Midwives*, 1651, and, for a different audience, William Harvey's *De generatione animalium,* (1651, Latin), translated into English in 1653. *The compleat midwife's practice enlarged*, was compiled by Nicholas Culpeper, an apothecary who practised in Spitalfields (Eccles 1982: 13), and supposedly recorded the experience of Dr Chamberlain, Sir Theodore Mayern (who supported Chamberlen's scheme to incorporate the London midwives) (Aveling 1977: 50), and Culpeper himself, as well as "others of foreign nations." The midwifery books of the period furnish illustrations both of births and also of the uterus, but because the illustrators did not have access to the science of anatomy (William Harvey was one of the first to have dissected a female body and to have seen the reproductive organs with his own eyes (Rich 1976: 144)), the representations correspond to received tradition rather than what could be observed. Even so, the valorization of vision that characterizes the Baconian program finds its way into the language of the male-authored midwifery books. Nicholas Culpeper, in *A Directory for Midwives*, says that men need not have the eyes of a lynx to see the injuries done to men and women by hiding the rules of medicine from them; on the contrary, anyone can see it, even though he be "as blind as a mole" (1651: 3). Culpeper also derides much of what appears in midwifery books (even though he repeats it), observing that Galen never saw a woman anatomized and yet "our Anatomists follow him as a little God-a-mighty and his *ipse dixit* serves the turn; and so the blind leading the blind" (1651: 3). He goes on to say that he himself watched a woman being cut open after she had died in childbed, and this becomes one of the sources of his authority.

Although the midwifery books are ostensibly designed to aid female midwives by providing information to which they might otherwise not have access, in fact the elaborate apologies in the prefaces to the books make it apparent that the motives of the translators are more complex. The translators' explanations attempt to diffuse possible criticisms of prurience or lascivious interest in the subject matter and content of the book that would become through the vehicle of translation available to a much wider audience for the first time. The anonymous translator of Jacques Guillimeau's *Child-birth, Or, The Happy Delivery of Women*, for instance, is careful to defend himself against possible charges both from the medical community and also from women in general:

> If therefore it bee thought prejudiciall either to the literary common wealth of *Physicke*, that I have exported and made common a commoditie, which the learned would have had private to themselves: or, if I have beene offensive to women, in prostituting and divulging that, which they would not have come to open light, and besides cannot be exprest in such modest termes, as are fit for the virginity of pen and paper, and the white sheetes of their child-bed.
>
> (Guillimeau 1635: np)

Using metaphors of commodification and trade, the translator excuses himself for having put into circulation for a general literate public the specialized knowledge previously limited to physicians. These translated midwifery tracts play a crucial mediating role between this educated medical community, who would have read classical medical authorities as well as contemporary treatises written in Latin, and the English midwife, who, if literate, would be unlikely to be able to read Latin, Greek, or the languages of the Continent. Her knowledge would have been primarily oral, passed among women skilled in midwifery, so that, although the apology is directed to physicians, the translation was at least as much an encroachment on the oral and practical knowledge that was the province of the midwife. The second part of the defense is directed at women in general, lest their modesty be offended by the "prostituting" of their secrets. The translation violates that secrecy, rendering it no longer virgin, as if the white sheets of child-bed and the blank page were being simultaneously subject to the outrage of having what is hidden made manifest and visible, publicized, published, put into circulation.

In the preface to Jacob Rueff's *The Expert Midwife*, the translator proleptically addresses his critics, preempting the charge that they might claim that "it is unfit that such matters as these should bee published in a vulgar tongue, for young heads to prie into" (Rueff 1637: Sig. A4). Despite the censure his translation might provoke, he deems it worthwhile nevertheless, considering the great danger to which childbirth exposes both mother and infant. Indeed, he casts himself in the role of saviour, since he understands that for the most part all women are unlearned "any further than to understand their owne native language" (Rueff 1637: Sig. A1). Midwives thus have no access to the very knowledge he considers most important: they cannot understand the business in which they are employed

> without the knowledge of many particulars concerning both the mother and the Infant, which they can never attaine unto, but either by the use of bookes penned by skilful Physitians & Chirurgians, or by conference with the learned and skilful (which can hardly, or not at all, in most places be had), or else by practicall & long experience, which though it bee the surest mistresse, yet it is the dearest and hath cost the lives of many, both in this kinde and in otherwise, before knowledge could be therby obtained.
>
> (Rueff 1637: Sig. A2).

Here we see a distinction that is to have increasing prominence in the midwifery books (and one that was invoked by Mrs Shaw and Mrs Whipp in their petition against Chamberlen) between practical experience – associated with lack of learning and the oral tradition of midwifery – and theoretical knowledge, connected with learning, classical medicine, and with the new science and the medicalization of midwifery. Whatever scruples the translator possesses about pandering to the lascivious curiosity of those who would pry into nature's secrets, specifically, of woman's hitherto hidden sexual nature, are laid to rest when he considers the "millions" who would "perish for want of helpe or knowledge" (Rueff 1637: Sig. A4).

Yet the translator's motives are not without self-interest; in projecting how many lives might be saved by the dissemination of medical knowledge that his text will make available, he suggests that "perhaps also a great deale more worke might be made for men-midwives, then yet is, although there bee too much already, and some perhaps for private profit have too farre already incroached upon woman's weaknesses and want of knowledge in these peculiar businesses" (Rueff 1637: Sig. A4v). Although he protests that his intentions are honest and, although he bequeaths his "labours" to "Grave, modest, and discreet women," it is difficult not to read his reference to men-midwives as an advertisement for a lucrative new area to be exploited. While we are assured that there is already more than enough work for men-midwives, nonetheless we are told that greater circulation of knowledge will ensure the survival of more children, which will in turn engender the work of delivering their offspring for male midwives. One need enquire no further about the motives of these men-midwives than to see that the translator recognizes that some have already exploited the profession "for private profit." The metaphor the translator employs to describe the midwife's practical experience (as opposed to the theoretical knowledge he makes available) inscribes a hierarchy: where learning culled from years of experience is described as a "mistress" whose service is capricious, arduous, and costly, theoretical knowledge, the emerging "master discourse," is efficient and beneficent, saving both time and lives. Where the "mistress" of practical experience evokes the tyrannical lady of amatory tradition, it also suggests the female teacher, thus registering a world of rudimentary feminine instruction that is about to be replaced with a system of written, masculine, and rationalized education.

While the implicit debate is between practical experience and theoretical knowledge, the authoritative figure most often cited by male midwives and physicians is Nature. William Harvey castigates those "giddy and officious midwives," who, fearful that they will seem unskilled or who are themselves impatient, cover their hands with oil and "distend[ ] the parts" (Harvey 1981: 404), seeking to accelerate what should be a natural process. Invoking Harvey as his model, Percivall Willughby in his *Observations in Midwifery*,[10] echoes this sentiment, advising midwives to "observe the wayes and proceedings of nature":

> The womb is a place locked up. Let midwives so deale with their travailing women, so will the birth be more easy, and the child not pulled to pieces, or destroyed, nor the woman torn, or ruinated by the midwife's struglings, or stretching of their bodies. In fiting time nature will open the womb.
>
> (1863: 276)

Nature is here imaged as the ultimate midwife, for it is she who will open the womb in due course. This depiction effects a shift of authority from the experience of actual midwives to a figure to which the physician now has a privileged access. The scientific and medical writings of the period tend to represent nature as a disorderly woman in need of control, a concealer of secrets, or a hoarder of riches (Merchant 1990: 169–70; Bordo 1987: 109); while Willughby's representation seems at first to be more beneficent, it casts the human midwives as inferior and ignorant of nature's secrets. By aligning himself with Nature, Willughby, professing to offer his own expertise to midwives, dislodges them from their position of authority, and seems to speak on behalf of nature.

The increasing medical control exerted over the female body in labor is paralleled by the appropriation of the midwives' voices in the obstetrical books of the early seventeenth century, which are spoken almost exclusively by men, who, however sympathetic to women and female midwives, nevertheless effect a kind of usurpation.[11] Yet the complaint voiced by Mrs Shaw and Mrs Whipp about Chamberlen's lack of practical experience, especially in ordinary births that do not require the intervention of instruments, is a powerful charge, for theoretical knowledge did not possess an automatic promise of success in the arena of childbirth. This problem is strikingly evident in Nicholas Culpeper's *Directory for Midwives*, where he admits to knowing nothing practical: "I have not medled with your Callings nor Manual Operations, lest I should discover my Ignorance like *Phormio* the Phylosopher, who having never seen Battel, undertook to read a Military Lecture before *Hannibal*" (Eccles 1982: 13). Nevertheless, he says that he has "conceived a few thoughts," which he hopes "to bring to perfect birth"; among them, he asserts that the ideal midwife should first know her ignorance, and then he argues that "God speaks not now by voice to men and women as formerly he did, but he speaks in, and by men" (Culpeper 1651: A2). One anonymous critique of Culpeper's text described it as "desperately deficient" and that kind of response may well have inspired *The Complete Midwife's Practice Enlarged* (Culpeper 1680). The title page of this revised work assures us that the "experience" of Sir Theodore Mayern, Dr Chamberlain, and Nicholas Culpeper are represented, along with that of "foreign nations." Judging from the frontispiece's portrait of Louise Bourgeois, and from the subtitle, which proclaims that the book contains instruction by the Queen of France's midwife to her daughter, Culpeper sought to capitalize not only on famous English practitioners, but specifically on the experience of a renowned female midwife. It is these "solid experiences" that authorize *The Complete Midwife's Practice*, and, although Culpeper acknowledges her presence, his own voice (and the "secrets kept close in the Breast of Mr Nicholas Culpeper") and hers often merge and become indistinguishable. As he tells his readers, the occasion of the book is to "make it a great exemplary... where Medicine married to the Midwife's industry, may teach every one the admirable effects of the Divinity of this art of Midwifery" (Culpeper 1680). It is a marriage that casts the midwife as a wife notable for her "industry," subsuming her under the rule of patriarchal medicine. As an intertexual union, the voices are linked, allowing Culpeper to bring his thoughts to their "perfect birth."

II

In his discussion of prophecy in *The Discoverie of Witchcraft* (1584), Reginald Scot (1964) offers an etymological interpretation of the Hebrew word "Ob," commonly translated as "Pytho," "Pythonicus spiritus," or, less properly, as "Magus" (120).[12] "Ob" literally means bottle, and it is associated with oracular utterance because "the *Pythonists* spake hollowe; as in the bottome of their bellies, whereby they are aptlie in Latin called *Ventriloqui*" (Scot 1964: 120). Ventriloquism, literally the act of appearing to speak from the abdomen or belly, is for Scot closely linked to prophecy, for in both cases the voice proceeds from a locus other than the organs of speech, since the ventriloquized voice originates in another place (the stomach) or being (a deity or evil spirit). We have already seen that woman's putatively unlimited capacity for speech associates her with the power of voice, and, in the case of prophecy, her ability to be a receptacle or mouthpiece for discourse other than her own is closely tied to cultural constructions of gender and, specifically, to female physiology. Voice or language appears to emerge from her body in a process analogous to birth; the woman is impregnated or filled with voice (as, in Christian tradition, Mary becomes the receptacle of the Word); she produces what issues from the belly. I now turn to a series of poems and texts that associate ventriloquism, poetic inspiration, and the origin of the voice with pregnancy and childbirth, for, as I will claim, the use of the metaphor derives both from an established tradition and also from the particular historical and cultural circumstances of the early modern period.

The *locus classicus* for this metaphor is Plato's *Theaetetus*, a dialogue whose very structure is informed by the trope of midwifery. As Socrates himself reminds Theaetetus, his mother, Phaenarete, was a midwife, and, by his own admission, he professes to practice the same art (Plato 1961: 853–4).[13] By claiming to follow in his mother's footsteps, he not only constructs a maternal origin for his skill, but encroaches on a traditionally female arena of knowledge and expertise. The difference is that his patients are men, not women, and where female midwives deal with the body, Socrates is concerned "with the soul that is in travail of birth" (Plato 1961: 855). In the transvestism of this transgression, the real art of midwifery is converted into a vehicle for a higher purpose; its function is not material (the birth of human bodies) but transcends that "lower" physical function in order to facilitate the delivery of true knowledge. The experience of conceptual birth is represented simultaneously as exactly the same as a woman's labor and also more intense in terms of the experience of pain. Those who seek Socrates's company, then, "have the same experience as a woman with child; they suffer the pains of labor, and by night and day, are full of distress far greater than a woman's" (Plato 1961: 855–6). The main instrument of his skill in assisting the birth of wisdom in others is the dialogic process, a process of questioning and insistent probing that often engenders the pains of labor, with surprising results.

> Those who frequent my company at first appear, some of them, quite unintelligent, but, as we go further with our discussions, all who are favored by heaven make progress at a rate that seems surprising to others as well as to themselves, although it is clear that they have never learned anything from me. The many admirable truths they bring to birth have been dis-

> covered by themselves from within. But the delivery is heaven's work and mine. The proof of this is that many who have not been conscious of my assistance... suffered miscarriage of their thoughts through falling into bad company, and they have lost children of whom I had delivered them by bringing them up badly, caring more for false phantoms than for true.
>
> (Plato 1961: 855)

It is Socrates's calling, one that humbly seeks to efface itself but that is a position of extraordinary potency, "to bring on these pangs or to allay them" (Plato 1961: 856). Like a midwife, Socrates assists at the births of others but claims that he himself is constrained from giving birth: "of myself I have no sort of wisdom, nor has any discovery ever been born to me as the child of my soul" (Plato 1961: 855). Yet, despite his disclaimers, he aligns his skill in midwifery with divine power, for, while he may create no direct offspring, he controls conceptual fertility or barrenness, the safe delivery of ideas, and the survival and health of intellectual progeny: in short, the life of the mind itself.

These descriptions of the fertile mind, the conception of thought, and the safe delivery of well-formed ideas continued to manifest themselves in sixteenth- and seventeenth-century uses of the trope to describe the birth of voice or poetry. Because speech, especially excessive and irrepressible speech, was associated with female physiology, it is not surprising that it should emanate from woman's body as the natural and inevitable culmination of her sexual nature, childbirth. Jacques Guillimeau, for example, in his 1635 tract on midwifery reiterates the current assumption that male and female children have a different relationship to speech even from their first entry into the world. The length of umbilical cord remaining attached to the child after the cord had been severed was thought to be closely related to the size of the sexual organs and the tongue, and it was therefore deemed necessary to cut a girl's umbilical cord much shorter than a boy's:

> Some do observe, that the Navell must be tyed longer, or shorter, according to the difference of the sexe, allowing more measure to the males: because this length doth make their tongue, and privie members the longer: whereby they may both speake the plainer, and be more serviceable to Ladies. And by tying it short, and almost close to the belly of females, their tongue is less free, and their naturall part more straite: and to

> speake the truth, the Gossips commonly say merily to the midwife; if it be a boy, *Make him good measure*; but if it be a wench, *Tye it short*.
>
> (Guillimeau 1635: 99)

In Joseph Swetnam's notorious misogynist tract, *The Arraignment of Lewd, Idle, Froward, and Unconstant Women*, he speaks of women's inability to contain a secret as analogous to the involuntary urge to give birth: "if thou unfoldest any of a secret unto a woman, the more thou chargest her to keep it close, the more she will seem, as it were, with child, till she have revealed it among her gossips" (Swetnam 1615: 73). What is contained and confined within the hiddenness of her body is made manifest in a process of externalization that is coterminous with her feminine nature, the ability to bring what is inside out and to make the unknown known. Although Swetnam's accusation is obviously a negative version of Socrates's dialogic birthing, both use the image of childbirth as a process that makes knowledge available, the mechanism that gives the secret or as yet unknown thought an audible being and a linguistic currency. As Patricia Parker has convincingly argued, the dilation or generation of the text is frequently represented by the pregnant female body, which both postpones and promises the appearance of "issue." The hermeneutical dilating of a text, the enlarging of its "matter" by interpretation, is also associated with *mater*, the maternal response to the biblical injunction to "increase and multiply" (Parker 1987: 15). Edmund Spenser furnishes a caricatured version of this conjunction, for instance, in the hideous birth scene of the monster Error, in which it vomits up both its offspring and a proliferation of textual matter.

The relationship between thought and the physiological process of birth, as evidenced in numerous tracts on midwifery, underlines this linkage: it is a commonplace of Renaissance medical treatises that the imagination exerts a powerful influence on the uterus, and it is partly for that reason that women are especially associated with creativity, even though they themselves cannot control the power that their physiology gives them. It was supposed that what a woman thought or was exposed to during her pregnancy had an effect upon the developing fetus, so that, for example, Nicholas Culpeper explains the birth of monsters as resulting either from the woman's having beheld such monsters while she was pregnant, or having seen pictures of them, or created them in her imagination. He recounts an anecdote of a woman in Pisa who was wont to kneel in front of a picture of John the Baptist, the prophet being dressed in animal skins, and she brought forth a child covered with hair like a camel (Culpeper 1651: 140). Robert Burton provides a similar catalogue of examples in *The Anatomy of Melancholy* that details the effects of a mother's moods and cravings on her unborn child, as well as her capacity to imprint what she sees upon the fetus, so that, for instance, if she sees a rabbit, her child will have a hare-lip (1977: 215). The belief in the power of an external image to shape or misshape the child was strong enough that when Elizabeth, wife of Henry VII, gave birth to prince Arthur in 1486, she delivered the child in a room hung with plain tapestries, for it was specified that tapestries with images were unsuitable for women in childbirth (Cunnington and Lucas 1972: 16–17).

Where women had no control over the imagination that could shape in strange or monstrous ways a developing human fetus, men could appropriate birth in a way that bypassed the wayward uterus completely. Like Athena emerging from Zeus's head, Sin is born from the left side of Satan's head in *Paradise Lost*, a cerebral and relatively painless procedure in comparison to the violence of Sin's delivery of Death, or her continual birthing of the monsters who thereafter inhabit and disrupt her womb. Her genitals are transformed into a hideous nether region that resounds with the cacophonic sound of the monsters who are "hourly conceiv'd" and "hourly born" (Milton 1957: II: 796–7), whereas the poetic progeny that are born from the male body are shaped into linguistic and vocal coherence. Sir Philip Sidney's opening sonnet in *Astrophil and Stella* details the poet's difficult search for expression of his innermost feelings. After seeking "fit words" and after a fruitless study of possible literary models, Astrophil almost despairs;

> Thus great with child to speake, and helplesse in my throwes,
> Biting my trewand pen, beating my selfe for spite,
> "Foole," said my Muse to me, "looke in thy heart and write."

Like a woman, Astrophil is powerless to control the physiological process that possesses him, for he is "helplesse" in his pains of labor, striving to externalize what he knows is within him. It is his muse, in the role of midwife, who delivers him from his "throwes" by reminding him that what he seeks to express is already inside of him. As Barbara Johnson notes, what emerges "by a sort of poetic Caesarian section... is the poem we have, in fact, already finished reading" (Johnson 1987: 196–7). The feminized poet in labor supercedes the maternal figure of instruction, "step-dame Studie," subverting the power the mother holds to introduce the child to language and the rudiments of education[14] and substituting the pregnant poet, whose labor results in the perfectly crafted sonnet. The opening of Sonnet 37 echoes this trope of birth in its cataloguing of pregnancy symptoms: "My mouth doth water, and my breast doth swell,/ My tongue doth itch, my thoughts in labour be." Here the conflation of speech imagery and labor is striking, for the tongue "itches" with an urgency like Swetnam's woman, who can no more contain her secret than she can a child ready to be born. "My breast doth swell" is a curiously hermaphroditic image, standing both for a male breast distended with emotion about to be translated into language and for the swollen breasts of the pregnant woman.[15] But if, in these two examples, writing is a giving of life to language, so then, in the logic of reversibility, does erasure take away that life; later in the sonnet sequence, Astrophil describes erasing his newly composed words as a kind of infanticide, where these "poore babes their death in birth do find" (50).

The possibility of infanticide also stands behind Milton's reference to textual production as childbirth in the *Areopagitica*, where censorship becomes abortion. Until book licensing was instituted,

> books were ever as freely admitted into the world as any other birth; the issue of the brain was no more stifled than the issue of the womb; no envious Juno sat cross-legged over the nativity of any man's intellectual offspring... But that a book, in worse condition than a peccant soul, should be to stand before a jury ere it be born to the world and undergo yet in darkness the judgment of Rhadamanth and his colleagues, ere it can pass the ferry backward into light, was never heard before.
>
> (1957: 725)

To send this freshly conceived text back again (should it fail to meet the judges' approval) before it has even been born seems to be a crime against nature (it is an affront both to the maternal function, registered in Juno's unnaturally restricting cross-legged position, and the innocent life of the child) and unjust in a religious and legal sense, because it forces a proleptic trial, one that precedes rather than follows a life. Yet if childbirth – and the tropological language that draws on it – is the mechanism that makes the hidden manifest, for Milton, conception and childbirth is imaged less as a dichotomy between inside and outside than as a threshold, a passage between life and death. To block this passage by refusing entrance into the world, either literally (where Juno, the deity presiding over childbirth, prevents the birth) or legally (by imposing a premature trial), consigns the unborn text (or child) to a kind of limbo, an infinitely suspended state that is neither unborn nor born, thus stifling creativity and the life of the mind. To image textual censorship as abortion is a curious linkage, which seems on the one hand rhetorically to heighten the sacrilege of book licensing by likening it to murder. On the other hand, the silencing of women in seventeenth-century culture, whether implicitly by ideological means or by direct injunction, was also a pervasive form of censorship. Figuring this suppression of female language as restricted birth underlines the association of voice or text with women and emphasizes the way in which both the procreative and linguistic function fall under the law of patriarchy.

Birth as a limen or threshold that permits passage between life and death is the animating idea in Milton's final sonnet, "Methought I saw my late espoused Saint." Much of the commentary that surrounds the sonnet has focused on the identity of the dead wife and has sought to explain the sonnet in terms of its biographical context; is Milton referring to his first wife, Mary Powell, who died three days after the birth of her fourth child, or does he allude to Katherine Woodcock, his second wife, who died almost three months after childbirth? If the sonnet refers to Mary Powell, then the poem seems invested with an intensity and tenderness of sentiment at odds with the settlement accorded to her children in Milton's nuncupative will (Huntley 1967: 468). Yet Katherine Woodcock did not, in fact, die in childbed, but of consumption (Parker 1945: 237), and after the period of purification alluded to in Leviticus. Rather than enter into the controversy about which wife the poem alludes to, I would argue that the very difficulty of assigning the poem to a particular wife is itself significant. Instead of a distinct identity that can be correlated with Milton's biography, we are given an indistinct representation of a beloved wife who dies in childbirth, an image rendered indeterminate not only because there are so few specific details, but also because the vision appears "veil'd" and therefore mediated by what the speaker's "fancied sight" constructs. Some critics have seized on this detail as a possible reference to Milton's blindness and therefore as a way of establishing the date for the sonnet, but "veil'd" also points to the conventional designation of a married woman as *nupta* (veiled), cognate with "nuptial" (from the Latin *nubo*, *nubere*, "to cover, to veil"). Marriage is thus associated with vision; to be married is to be veiled, because one is now another's, one man's property, and no longer accessible to the male gaze in general.[16] The proprietariness of Milton's description (the suspended "mine") and the suggestion that she is now free "from spot of child-bed taint" is what stabilizes her identity, for the "saint" of the sonnet is represented by means of her functions (wife and mother). Except for those general marks of recognition, she is described primarily in terms of similitude; she is likened to Alcestis, she reminds critics of Creusa, Beatrice, and Eurydice, and one argument identifying her as Katherine Woodcock locates a reference to the Virgin Mary (Milton 1957: 171, n.). Yet, in reading the sonnet, one is struck with the way these idealized allusions are manufactured at the expense of individual identity; the dead wife is replaced by a vision, a simulacrum, which is like visions of other literary or mythological figures, already types that stand for the qualities of excellence or purity that they possess. In other words, the logic of the sonnet is one of substitution, in which one figure is replaced by another, and the mechanism of this substitution is both metaphoric and also lies at the heart of cultural conceptions of pregnancy.

Patricia Parker, in a recent discussion of metaphor, has reminded us of the sense of transfer (as from place to place) and substitution implicit in the idea of metaphor (1987: 36–7). The sonnet is dense with allusions to figures of substitution and transfer: Alcestis, who gave her life so that her husband might live and who was brought back (transferred) from the dead by Herakles, Christ, who forfeited his life to ransom humanity, Orpheus and his attempt to reclaim Eurydice. These figures are gathered within the reference to the figure of the woman in childbirth, that body that has the power to give life, although sometimes (often, in the case of seventeenth-century childbirth, where puerperal fever contributed to the high mortality rate) at the expense of her own. Even Joseph Swetnam, in his *Arraignment* takes time from his diatribe against feminine evils to notice the extraordinary pain and risk associated with childbirth:

> Amongst all the creatures that God hath created, there is none more subject to misery than a woman, especially those that are fruitfull to beare children; for they... are continually overcome with paine, sorrow, & feare, as indeed the danger of child-bearing must needes be a great terrour to women.
>
> (1615: 57)

The power to bear life necessitates a ritual of purification. The danger that attended childbed suggests the sacrifice implicit in birth; in bringing forth new life, the mother may, like Alcestis, exchange her own for another. As Jonathan Goldberg has noted, "Euripedes' Admetus tells his father that Alcestis is truly his *mother*, for, by dying for him, she has given him life" (1986: 151). The allusions in the sonnet point not just to feminine figures who pass the untransgressable boundary between one life and the next (Creusa, Beatrice, Eurydice, Alcestis), then, but to the maternal figure who becomes herself a gateway or passage between life and death, allowing others to pass through her.[17]

This capacity is not limited to biological life, for she is also the source of poetic life, of the vision that allows sight beyond the veil, of the Orphic voice that can record this passage. Childbirth, as metaphor, is then transposed – as life was for Admetus and Alcestis – from wife to husband, so that, although she dies, the voice that is born survives her and becomes immortal, as the Orphic voice outlives the mutilation of his physical body. Just as the body of the mother becomes a medium or passage, so too does the body of Milton's sonnet become a conduit for other voices. As commentators have noticed, the first line of "Methought I saw my late espoused saint" echoes Ralegh's sonnet celebrating Spenser's *Faerie Queene* ("Me thought I saw the grave, where *Laura* lay") (Goldberg 1986: 147–9). The site of the vision in Ralegh's poem is Laura's tomb, but, in the course of the poem, the worship previously accorded to her is transposed to a usurping figure, the Faery Queene. The graces of Love and Virtue desert Laura to attend the queen, leaving Oblivion to guard the hearse; the soul of Petrarch weeps at the Faery Queen's approach and Homer's spirit trembles with grief at this theft. Milton thus echoes a sonnet whose subject is poetic rivalry and the displacement of a poet by his successors. Milton himself displaces Spenser, even as Spenser overshadowed Petrarch, and Petrarch's glory occluded Homer's. Milton makes the body of the dead wife both the medium of his vision and the basis of his intertexual allusion, for poets appear to succeed each other with the inevitability of generations. Where Ralegh's vision takes place in a burial chamber, Milton's is grounded in the body of a wife who dies in childbed, converting her capacity for giving birth into a capacity for poetic renewal, a transposition from female procreation to male creativity.

III

If the body of the woman who dies in childbed is the metaphorical source of the poetic voice for Milton, the speaker of Donne's "Elegy 19: To His Mistress Going to Bed" figures himself *as* a woman in the throes of childbirth at the opening of the poem. He then compares himself to a midwife in the closing lines, so that the elegy is framed by references to childbirth. That the poem is generated rhetorically by the metaphor of labor is registered in the tautological structure of the second line, "Until I labour, I in labour lie," where the chiasmic formulation replicates the sense of suspense characteristic of the poem's situation and of labor. The male speaker can be released only through a process that is not entirely within his control, for until he "labours" (archaic sense of pounding or beating) in the act of love, he lies in discomfort, as a woman does who seeks relief through giving birth. By usurping the role of midwife in the final section of the elegy ("Then since I may know,/ As liberally, as to a midwife, show/ Thyself"), the speaker also seeks the privileges of vision and knowledge that were in the Renaissance properly the province of the midwife. Men were explicitly excluded from this knowledge, as is made clear by the taboo against the man-midwife gazing upon the woman's body. This prohibition is evidenced by the translators' need to defend the publication of midwifery books, by anecdotes recounted by midwives that register women's shame and horror at having a man in the birth chamber, and also in the illustrations of birth scenes. There is one engraving published in an early eighteenth-century midwifery tract, for instance, in which the male midwife attending the birth is seated in front of a woman in labor. The lower half of her body is draped with a sheet, which is pinned around the man's neck, so that except for his head, he is enclosed within its draperies, effectively preventing him from looking directly at the laboring woman's genitalia.[18]

The speaker of Donne's poem desires to bring his mistress to the labor of love, to look upon the privacy of her body revealed to the gaze normally only in such circumstances as childbirth. This vision and the subsequent carnal "knowledge" he will have proleptically invokes the literal sense of generation: the act of love may beget a child and thus ultimately necessitate the attendance of a midwife. The woman is imaged as a "mystic book," a phrase that divides knowers into laypeople and initiates, and that may function as an oblique reference to the knowledge of the female body that was being circulated in obstetrical handbooks. Between the two allusions to childbirth that frame Elegy 19 lies the body of the poem itself which, like Sidney's sonnet No. 1, is analogically generated by these references to birth. The image of the elegy's central section alludes, of course, to a double colonization; on the one hand, to the lands England was exploring and claiming in the early seventeenth century ("O my America, my new found land"), and, on the other, to the body of the mistress the lover seeks to make his own ("My kingdom, safeliest when with one man manned,/ My mine of precious stones, my empery"). Medical colonization of the human body, like geographic exploration, "claims" the territories it discovers by naming them after the explorer. The human body is thus imprinted with the history of its own discovery, registered in the names given to particular organs or bodily processes (e.g. Fallopian tubes). The apostrophic "O" in "O my America" and the image of the mine (which also functions as a double possessive – "My mine") refer specifically to the female genitalia that the lover desires to conquer, a conjunction of colonization metaphors that points toward the historical transition from midwifery as a specifically female area of knowledge and specialization to its metamorphosis into a branch of distinctively male medicine.

Where Elegy 19 borrows the trope of childbirth to frame its voyeuristic exploration of the female body, the power of the imagination to shape an unborn child (a power that is often cited in midwifery books with respect to monstrous births) becomes the basis for Donne's elaborate conceit in "A Valediction: of Weeping." Here the lover's tears are impregnated with the image of the beloved:

> Let me pour forth
> My tears before thy face, whilst I stay here,
> For thy face coins them, and thy stamp they bear,
> And by this mintage they are something worth,
> For thus they be
> Pregnant of thee;
>
> (1–6)

What the speaker sees (the beloved) is imprinted upon the tears that issue from his body, as if he were a pregnant woman giving birth to a child that had been influenced by the vision of what she saw. The effect is strangely bisexual; because the speaker is self-conscious about the imminence of his departure ("whilst I stay here") and because he projects the dangers he may encounter in a hostile world, he figures himself as male. Yet his assumption of feminine physiology effects a crossing, a transvestism, in which his empathy for the pain of the addressed woman metaphorically places him in the position of a woman giving birth. He occupies the relatively passive role of supplying matter (tears), which is stamped with her image, while she appears to act upon him, generating replications of her own image. The simile for the lovers' parting is, in keeping with the conceit, parturition: "When a tear falls, that thou falls which it bore,/ So thou and I are nothing then, when on a divers shore" (8–9). Even as the speaker seems to give himself over to grief, vicariously placing himself in the position of the woman who is abandoned by her lover or by the child who leaves her body at birth, he distances himself from that position through the intellectual intricacy of the poem. In other words, the poem foregrounds its own metaphoricity, creating a linkage of sympathy and similitude between lover and beloved, but the nature of similitude also posits difference (two things are like one another because they are not the same as one another). Docherty has asserted that, whereas "[m]ale lovers look into the mirror of their lover's eye, or womb, and see a reflection of themselves (or of their sons as representations of themselves), thus supposedly guaranteeing a stable, transhistorical identity" (1986: 200), woman is the prior condition that guarantees both the product of poetry and the writer's masculinity. While Donne certainly repudiates the feminine in some of his poetry, and where some lines suggest the danger and shame of becoming a woman, as in Elegy 4, where the speaker says that "the greatest stain to man's estate/Falls on us, to be called effeminate" (61–2), he is elsewhere (as in "A Valediction: of Weeping") extraordinarily self-reflexive about his relation to gender, about his naming the feminine as his source, even about his willingness to occupy – however provisionally – the place to which he assigns women.

Readers of Donne's poetry have often remarked on the plenitude of images that represent the merging of lovers: the compass and the "gold to aery thinness beat" of "A Valediction: forbidding Mourning," the interinanimated souls of "The Ecstasy," or the phoenix in "The Canonization," but the psychic union of the lovers in "A Valediction: of Weeping" is represented in a conceit of pregnancy and birth. The poem seems to figure what Julia Kristeva – borrowing from Plato's *Timaeus* – has called the *chora*, the utopian space occupied by the mother and child before the child enters the Symbolic, language, or the Law of the Father.[19] The paradigmatic expression of the chora is pregnancy itself, where the child is still enclosed within the womb, and where the body of the mother and child are contiguous. This space, which Kristeva describes as an "'enceint' separating (the pregnant woman) from the world of everyone else" (1980: 240), is thus a kind of protective enclosure that encompasses both mother and child, even though it also always contains an inevitable separation or division between mother and child. Donne's poems are, of course, full of these choric spaces – the "little room" that is the womb in the Holy Sonnet "Annunciation," the "one little room, an every where" in "The Good Morrow" or the bedroom of "The Sun Rising" – images of a merging that would defy change and separation. The pregnant tears of "A Valediction: of Weeping" give way to (or birth to) the blank round globe of the second stanza, a world that is peopled solely by the lovers and affected only by their (Petrarchan) storms of emotion. Yet this world is also, as the New Critics so memorably demonstrated, the poem itself, a work born of and inspired by the grief the speaker expresses; like the tear impregnated with the beloved's image, so, too, is the poem a reflection (carried emblematically in the sorrow that issues from the poet) of the lovers, an enclosed space that preserves their union even as they face inevitable separation. Elaine Scarry has suggestively said that Donne repetitively materializes language and interiorizes it within the body, seeking, especially in the Valediction poems, to establish a way of representing the body during absence (Scarry 1988: 79–81). As Kristeva has reminded us in "Stabat Mater," the body of the Virgin Mary is only synecdochically available, accessible in the ear (which signifies listening and compassion), the breast (which stands for maternity and nourishment), and tears (the privileged sign of sorrow). Tears and milk are, she says, "metaphors of nonspeech, of a 'semiotics' that linguistic communication does not account for" (1987: 249). In a sense then, Donne's tears are a kind of doubling, expressing, on the one hand, the semiotics of sorrow, feminine (and maternal) silence, and the unrepresentability of grief, and, on the other, the carefully fashioned male appropriation of that semiotics of silence in the language of the poem.

If pregnancy and generation are tropes that (apotropaically) shield the lovers from change and separation, they also serve as a metaphor for the generation of the text. Donne is especially self-reflexive about the inspiration and conception of poetry in the verse letters, where his Muse is frequently invoked in terms of her sexual status – her barrenness, her fecundity, her chastity, her progeny.[20] In a letter to

Mr B.B., Donne urges his addressee to marry his Muse, and "multiply"; he, himself, is divorced from his Muse, "the cause being in me,/ That I can take no new in bigamy" (20–1), and therefore both his "will" and his "power" are crippled.

> Hence comes it, that these rhymes which never had
> Mother, want matter, and they only have
> A little form, the which their father gave;
> They are profane, imperfect, oh, too bad
> To be counted children of poetry
> Except confirmed and bishoped by thee.
>
> (23–8)

Reiterating the Aristotelian dichotomy that sees matter as feminine and form as masculine, the poet designates his poetic offspring as lacking content (matter) because they are without a feminine source (*mater*); although the paternal influence yields some form, they are sickly and imperfect. Renaissance physiology privileged the connection between women and the imagination because of the uterus, which was putatively susceptible to the influence of both the moon and the imagination. While this impressionability meant that pregnant women were vulnerable to the image-making capacity of the imagination, as we have seen, it also gendered the imagination as feminine, so that, although women themselves did not have access to or control over the power their physiology bestowed on them, they were nevertheless the locus of imaginative creativity. It was the uterus – which was sometimes characterized as having a life of its own – that produced the female qualities of insatiable sexual desire and garrulity, and it was woman's combination of moist and cold humours that disposed her to changeability, inventiveness, and to the special retentiveness of her memory (Maclean 1980: 41–2). This may help to explain Donne's obsession with female changeability, which he both fears and desires (as Docherty has argued (1986: 51–87)), his fascination with the sexual status of his Muse, and his interest in the pregnant female body. Perhaps no other of Donne's poems so explicitly express this ligature of speech, sexuality, and pregnancy than his two elegies written to commemorate the death of Elizabeth Drury.

The imbrication of poetic voice and the representation of the feminine in the *First* and *Second Anniversaries* of 1611 and 1612 is both rich and relatively unexplored.[21] As virtual set pieces articulating the sense of epistemological crisis of the early seventeenth century

("The new philosophy calls all in doubt"), the *Anniversaries* stand at the beginning of the English tradition of funeral elegy,[22] and their preoccupation with voice – with the distinctive voice of the elegiac poet, whose emerging reputation depends upon his skill in the art of lamentation, and with the now voiceless, deceased subject of elegy, whose continued life in the memories of the bereaved depends upon the surrogate voice of the poet – is complicated by gender. That is, where in an elegy like "Lycidas" the act of mourning Edward King's lost promise also celebrates Milton's emergent poetic ability,[23] Donne's elegiac voice is empowered by the ghostly muse of Elizabeth Drury in an act of appropriation that relies simultaneously (and paradoxically) on her virginity and her maternal qualities. The *Anniversaries* are full of metaphors of her sexuality and fecundity, but, because they are also preoccupied with bodies, disease, and explicit medical terminology, I claim that Donne's references to pregnancy and birth are contiguous with the discourses of theology and physiology, which themselves furnish a linkage between pregnancy and voice.

The *Anniversaries* have been the subject of critical controversy since they were published, primarily because of the perceived gap between the extravagant hyperbole of their expression and the relative insignificance of their occasion, the death of a young girl Donne probably never even met.[24] Ben Jonson summed up this outrage in his judgment that the *First Anniversarie* was "profane and full of Blasphemies," and he told Donne that "if it had been written of the Virgin Marie it had been something," to which Donne supposedly replied "that he described the Idea of a Woman, not as she was" (Jonson 1975: 462). Jonson's insight, if not his criticism, is apt, however, for the iconography of the Virgin suffuses both poems, in their linkage of maternity and virginity, in their explicit fascination with Mary, "the blessed mother-maid," and in their simultaneous obsession with physical procreation or conception and the desire to transcend it. (Although Jonson chastises Donne for his blasphemy, he was not above using the comparison himself on appropriate occasions; his 1630 "Epigram to the Queen, then Lying In," begins by citing the Angel Gabriel's address to Mary, "Hail Mary, full of grace," and argues that the words are as fittingly addressed by the poet to the "mother of our prince" (208).) The linkage between the Virgin Mary and Elizabeth Drury is, in fact, crucial to Donne's representation of the relationship between Elizabeth Drury and himself, which is figured in the emergence of the poetic voice from her simultaneously pure and maternal body. This focus provides a way of understanding how the poet constructs her as his own discursive origin, a source that he simultaneously acknowledges, appropriates, and also obliquely denigrates, an ambivalence toward female sexuality and power that is manifested throughout his poetry. Even in the *Anniversaries*, which celebrate the transcendent purity of Elizabeth Drury, there is a prevalent strain of misogyny, as in the conventional sentiment that the "first marriage was our funeral:/ One woman at one blow killed us all,/ And singly, one by one, they kill us all" (1: 105–7). Purified and exonerated from the charge levelled against ordinary women, Elizabeth Drury, like the Virgin, "could drive,/ The poisonous tincture, and the stain of Eve,/ Out of her thoughts, and deeds; and purify/ All, by a true religious alchemy" (I: 179–82). Donne's figuration of his relationship to the dead girl he celebrates, in fact, displays some of the symptoms of paranoia and empowerment described by Kristeva in "Stabat Mater," a text that is particularly pertinent to my discussion.

Kristeva's juxtaposition of the semiotic and cultural history of the Virgin and psychoanalytic theories of language and the maternal in "Stabat Mater" is enacted theoretically and visually. Like a ventriloquized text (and I will argue that the *Aniversaries* are ventriloquized in their appropriation and use of the feminine voice), "Stabat Mater" is double-voiced; the text is divided into two columns that are distinguished from one another by typeface and discursive style. While the right-hand column appears to be a historical, analytic account of the Virgin (one that draws on Marina Warner's *Alone of All Her Sex: The Myth and Cult of the Virgin Mary*), the left-hand column seems initially to be a rhapsodic, lyrical record of Kristeva's own experience of childbirth (Jacobus 1986: 167). The doubleness of the text replicates both the split between theoretical discourse and poetic expression, and also the split of the maternal body, which is divided within itself (even as it at once expresses and represents itself as text). This neat dichotomy is continually ruptured, however, by the intrusions of the analytic into the poetic column, and the irruption of the poetic in the theoretical text, as if the discourses were bounded by a permeable membrane that could not sustain their separateness. "Stabat Mater" thus figures itself as a kind of maternal body that encompasses the Freudian silence on maternity and the myth of the Virgin, both discourses that support from opposite perspectives the power of the imaginary, preverbal mother that provides a fantasy of plenitude designed "to compensate for the actual poverty of language and its inability to situate or articulate the (maternal) speaking subject" (Jacobus 1986: 169). While Kristeva's account moves toward the transhistorical (even as it refers to Warner's historical study), elements of her psychoanalytic analysis seem nevertheless to offer insight into Donne's specific historical circumstances.

If, as Kristeva asserts, a "mother is a continuous separation, a division of the very flesh" (1987: 254), evoking the separation from the mother in primary narcissism, or the division of language itself, her analysis of the myth of the Virgin must also confront the division of death. One of the most attractive aspects of the myth, according to her, is its homologization with the life of Christ; where Christ suffered, died, and was resurrected, Mary "experiences a fate more radiant than her son's: she undergoes no calvary, she has no tomb, she doesn't die and hence has no need to rise from the dead" (1987: 242). Where for the seventeenth century, the maternal, as epitomized by childbirth, stood for mortality and the inevitability of death, the Virgin fulfills the paranoid fantasy of being exempt from time or death because of the Assumption, which allows her to be translated directly to Heaven. On the one hand, physical birth signifies death for Donne; as he says in the *First Anniversarie* and in his Holy Sonnet "Annunciation," the womb is a prison of flesh, and the body is "a poor inn,/ A province packed up in two yards of skin" (175–6), threatened by sickness and its "true mother, age." On the other hand, death itself becomes a birth or liberation from the shackles of the flesh, and it is this translation, or elegiac conversion of death into life, that Donne seeks to effect. In this process, he not only links Elizabeth Drury to the Virgin, but he models himself on the mother-maid as well, borrowing her capacity to act as intermediary between the carnal and the spiritual, her consolatory qualities (and her capacity for sorrow), and her maternity that is not subject to death. Paranoia is a protective mechanism, whereby projection shields the subject by replacing what is threatening with a megalomaniacal fantasy of power (or by displacing a threat to an other not the subject). The relationship of men and women to the myth of the Virgin is complementary but not symmetrical; it subtended and supported the connection between the sexes by providing a means of satisfying feminine paranoia (through the fantasy of power) and male paranoia about women (by bifurcating femininity and maternity). Given its capacity to isolate maternity from female sexuality in general and to separate maternity from mortality, we can begin to see both how the myth of the Virgin satisfied certain cultural needs and also why the representation of Elizabeth Drury is imbricated with that of the Virgin.

The *Anniversaries* are, after all, elegies, and their subject is ostensibly death; more specifically, they are elegies written for the parents of a dead child. Elizabeth Drury functions as a kind of counter in the monetary sense, an object which can be endowed with value and exchanged. She is lost to her parents through death, but returned to life through the poetic resurrection Donne effects in the *Anniversaries*. The poetic rebirth that Donne engineers is designed in turn to secure him the patronage of the Drury family, so that the dead girl serves as a kind of intermediary. Kristeva argues that the body of the Virgin is synecdochized in the ear, which associates her with hearing and voice (1987: 248), signifying her capacity to intercede on behalf of petitioners. In this way, in her association with art and patronage (250), and with her maternal and liminal status, she becomes a go-between, an intermediary between mortal and immortal life ("this commerce 'twixt heaven and earth" (I: 399)), between poets and patrons. In the *Second Anniversarie*, Donne apostrophizes his soul, speaking of his "new ear" that will hear the angels' song when his soul sees the "blessed mother-maid" (II: 339). The exchange implied by the patronage system was, however, complicated by Donne's personal circumstances; he had captured the interest of the Sir Robert and Lady Drury with his shorter "Funerall Elegie," which contained the animating idea for the *Anniversaries*, and so, when Sir Robert asked Donne to accompany him on an extended journey to the continent, it was difficult for Donne to refuse, even though it meant a long separation from his wife and family (Bald 1970: 240–2, Bald 1986: 85–103). According to Walton's admittedly imprecise rendition, Ann Donne "was then with child and otherways under so dangerous a habit of body as to her health that she professed an unwillingness to allow him any absence from her, saying 'her divining soul boded her some ill in his absence,' and therefore desired him not to leave her." (Her premonitions were grounded in experience; she was pregnant twelve times in sixteen years of marriage, and she died in 1617, just five days after giving birth to a still-born child). Nevertheless, Donne made plans for his wife and children to stay with her younger sister on the Isle of Wight, and readied himself for departure. It was apparently during this interlude, when he was in London, waiting to leave that he composed *An Anatomy of the World*, and it was almost certainly in print when he and the Drurys at last journeyed to the continent in November, 1611 (Bald 1970: 244). He must have begun work on *Of the Progres of the Soule* soon after he arrived in Amiens, and it was published early in 1612. According to Walton's account, it was at this time that Donne's "ecstasy" occurred, the vision in which he saw his "dear wife pass twice by me through this room with her hair hanging about her shoulders and a dead child in her arms." As he learned twelve days later from the urgent messenger he dispatched, his wife had indeed been delivered of a still-born child "after a long and dangerous labor," on the same day and "about the very hour" that Donne saw the apparition. Although it is difficult to reconcile Walton's account with the chronology of Donne's letters,[25] it is clear that Donne left with the Drurys when his wife was both pregnant and also fearful about her health and that of the child she carried, and Donne's correspondence does suggest a preoccupation with her condition. Where Walton's recounting of the episode implies a sympathy so powerful that it was capable of generating visions, we can at least see a kind of parallel, in which Ann's pregnancy produced a still-birth child, whereas Donne's sympathy delivered two elegies laced with references to pregnancy and birth.[26]

The metaphoric framework of the *First Anniversarie* is given to us by its subtitle, "An Anatomy of the World." Although the anatomy was a fashionable kind of writing in the Renaissance that referred as much to a systematic analysis or satiric exposure as an actual dissection, Donne registers its literal sense both in his obsessive concentration on bodies and decay and also in his witty reminder near the end of the poem that the carcass he is anatomizing will putrefy and smell if he is not selective in his dissection.[27] The function of an anatomy is, of course, to make visible to the eye what could otherwise not be seen (as William Harvey puts it, to make available to light, ocular inspection, and reason the hidden secrets of nature (Harvey 1981: 8–9)). The body that he examines in the *First Anniversarie* is ostensibly that of the world, and, yet, there is a complex overlapping with the figure of Elizabeth Drury. Most obviously, according to the conceit of the poem, she is the balm or preservative of the earth; with her death, the world decays. The radical loss of coherence both in the physical and social worlds are attributed to her death, for she had the capacity to reunite the fragments by magnetic force, but with that power no longer accessible, the world has become increasingly chaotic and dispersed. Yet her physical body is conflated with the world's, and synecdochized, it continues to inform Donne's description of it, as in the lines "she whose rich eyes, and breast,/ Gilt the West Indies, and perfumed the East" (1: 229–30). As the animating spirit of the world, she is also matter or *mater*, the nourishing mother, and her departure from the world compromises its ability to produce life:

> The clouds conceive not rain, or do not pour
> In the due birth time, down the balmy shower.
> Th'air doth not motherly sit on the earth,
> To hatch her seasons, and give all things birth.
> Spring-times were common cradles, but are tombs;
> And false conceptions fill the general wombs.
> (1: 381–6)

No longer the nurturing life of the earth, she becomes instead the animating spirit of the anatomized world of the poem. In "A Funeral Elegy" the anatomized body is the poem itself, the "carcase verses" (14) that cannot contain her soul. Anatomy is, after all, a partitioning of the body, and the division of the poem into parts by means of the reiterated lament, "she, she is dead; she's dead," as well as the word-play on "part"/ "partake" (434), become ways of propagating or increasing the text, just as birth is a way of propagating the self. What is lost to the macrocosmic world, then, is displaced into the poem, where Donne draws on and shapes its generative properties.

The *Anniversaries* do not celebrate Elizabeth Drury's maternity, however, but her virginity, and, paradoxically, her ability to propagate texts is dependent upon that sexual purity. Like the Virgin, her fecundity is a-sexual. While the hymen is itself a figure of partition, and virginity is thus aligned with textual dilation or increase, it is also true that, for Donne, poetry is only produced by a chaste muse. His figuring the dead girl as his poetic source can thus only be accomplished by a kind of transsexual exchange, in which the spirit of Elizabeth Drury impregnates Donne's muse:

> Immortal Maid, who though thou would'st refuse
> The name of mother, be unto my Muse
> A father, since her chaste ambition is,
> Yearly to bring forth such a child as this.
> These hymns may work on future wits, and so
> May great grandchildren of thy praises grow.
> (2: 33–8)

Elizabeth Drury becomes the male, inseminating principle, which by analogy makes Donne's muse the bearer of these annually produced progeny. The anniversary poems that he promises are likened to life returning after the deluge, a Lethe flood that has caused the world to forget the name of its departed soul; Donne dedicates his life to remedying that amnesia, but his motives are not unselfish. As he tells us, "my life shall be,/ To be hereafter praised, for praising thee." As at least one critic has pointed out, the poem is obsessed with nomination, with naming Elizabeth Drury (Docherty 1986: 228); yet despite the repetitions of "she" and the lavish periphrastic descriptions, she is never named directly. The question of whose fame or name verse enrolls is not a simple one for the *Anniversaries*, or, for that matter, for elegy in general. Where funeral elegy conventionally laments a dead person, the name that is commemorated is as often that of the mourner or elegist rather than the mourned. Grief never subordinates Donne's fierce sense of ego or his awareness of the patronage system. Claiming that she died too young to speak (at age 14), while yet *infans* (without speech), Donne seems to assume a kind of prophetic stance, allowing her to speak through him. Far from becoming a transparent medium, however, Donne functions as the privileged translator, relaying a voice that only he can hear and only he can interpret:

> Nor could incomprehensibleness deter
> Me, from thus trying to imprison her.
> Which when I saw what a strict grave could do,
> I saw not why verse might not do so too.
> Verse hath a middle nature: heaven keeps souls,
> The grave keeps bodies, verse the fame enrols.
> (1: 469–74)

Like a patron herself, albeit a ghostly one, Elizabeth Drury becomes a kind of muse, who, like the mother of the muses, Mnemosyne, presides over a commemoration, a recreation through the action of memory. If the governing metaphor of the *First Anniversarie* is the anatomy of the body, the progress is the organizing principle of the *Second Anniversarie*, where the speaker follows Elizabeth Drury in her progress to heaven, to becoming at the end of the poem "the trumpet, at whose voice the people came" (2: 528), the embodiment of voice. She is the proclamation, (the speaking before – *proclamare*), the text, and he is the mouthpiece, the voice who articulates her muteness. In an apostrophe to his soul, the speaker berates his soul for its ignorance, for knowing neither how it will die or how it was "begot" (2: 256). The puzzle in the catalogue of ignorance that follows is the relationship between inside and outside; how the stone enters "the bladder's cave" without breaking the skin, how the blood flows from one ventricle to the other, and how putrid matter gathers in the lungs (2: 270–80). The paradigm for the link between inside and outside is the body–soul relationship, which is the conundrum not only of life and death, but also of subjectivity. The speaker places himself in a privileged position with respect to these questions, for, like the anatomist, he has a specialized access; not through the "lattices of eyes" or the "labyrinths of ears" (2: 296–7) does he know, but directly, as is possible only in heaven. Elizabeth Drury is the embodiment of knowledge, she "who all libraries had thoroughly read" (2: 303), and who is imaged as "written rolls/ Where eyes might read upon the outward skin,/ As strong records for God, as minds within" (504–5). And it is this figure of knowledge, whose inside, or invisibility, can be read by eyes, that the speaker claims to translate.

That Donne never knew the person he was elegizing and that his depiction of her remains so idealized as to lack any human specificity at all enhances his ability to usurp her speechlessness, her absence, and to colonize her dead spirit, as it were. He apostrophizes her, employing the trope that is the figure of voice and that animates the dead or inanimate (Culler 1985: 40):

> blessed maid,
> Of whom is meant whatever hath been said,
> Or shall be spoken well by any tongue,
> Whose name refines coarse lines, and makes prose song,
> Accept this tribute, and his first year's rent,
> Who till his dark short taper's end be spent,
> As oft as thy feast sees this widowed earth,
> Will yearly celebrate thy second birth,
> That is, thy death.
>
> (1: 443–51)

The lines invert the conventional definition of life and death, producing a familiar religious paradox where death engenders the new life of the soul. This paradox also illuminates the operations of patronage; it is Elizabeth Drury's death, after all, that occasions the poems, which in turn secure him the potentially regenerating favor of the Drurys. Yet Donne's use of the inversion provides a new context: "Our body's as the womb,/ And as a midwife death directs it home"

(1: 453–4). What is specific to woman (the womb) is generalized to all humanity; anyone who has a body also has a womb, from which Death, as the midwife, delivers new life. In the same way, Donne, as poetic midwife, delivers life from death, serving as what he calls that "middle nature," which makes manifest what has been hidden from other human eyes, the interpreter figure between life and death. All bodies become wombs, and the midwife, Death, oversees a process of spiritual birth, in which the poet is complicit. Like Kristeva's Virgin Mary, whose power depends on her overcoming her own death and on the separation of the maternal function from ordinary female sexuality, the poet is linked to a maternity that has no repercussions of mortality, no contamination of the feminine. He, too, becomes a midwife, an intermediary, and liminal figure, who stands poised between this world and the next, impregnated with the ghostly voice of Elizabeth Drury.

4

VENTRILOQUIZING SAPPHO, OR THE LESBIAN MUSE

I'll tell thee now (dear love) what thou shalt do
To anger destiny, as she doth us,
How I shall stay, though she esloign me thus,
And how posterity shall know it too;
How thine may out-endure
Sibyl's glory, and obscure
Her who from Pindar could allure,
And her, through whose help Lucan is not lame,
And her, whose book (they say) Homer did find, and name.

John Donne (1971)[1]

When in John Donne's "Valediction: of the Book," the male speaker urges his mistress to compose the "annals" of their love, he also implicitly interrogates both the status and viability of female authorship. He advises his beloved to chronicle their passion so that she might achieve fame as an author and "out-endure Sybil's glory," casting into obscurity even those women he cites as paradigmatic examples of feminine literary preeminence: "Her who from Pindar could allure,/ And her, through whose help Lucan is not lame,/ And her, whose book (they say) Homer did find and name" (7–9). Although the speaker ostensibly praises these three women, suggesting that their talents either surpassed or helped to shape the poetic genius of Pindar, Lucan, and Homer, his rhetoric ironically deflates the encomium. He describes the women periphrastically but declines to name them, substituting instead the names of the men whose reputations have supplanted theirs. This elision of the proper name within the poem mimetically reproduces the historical effacement of the women's identities, underlining and reenacting the mechanism through which their accomplishments were originally eclipsed. The speaker initially seems to be asserting that Homer plagiarized his poems, but the qualification "they say" introduces an element of indeterminacy, and the acts of "finding" and "naming" blur the distinctions of poetic property and effectively neutralize the implicit censure of Homer's alleged appropriation. The speaker's complicity in the erasure of the women's identities is furthered by his treatment of his mistress, for he suggests that she could overshadow only female authors whose literary reputations have already been forgotten and buried: the Theban poet, Corinna, who putatively beat Pindar in a literary competition, Lucan's wife, Polla Argentaria, who was supposed to have helped him complete (and versify) the *Pharsalia*, and, perhaps most egregious of all, Phantasia, the woman who was reputed to have composed both the *Iliad* and the *Odyssey* and from whom Homer allegedly plagiarized them (Gardner 1965: 192–3). That the poem is framed by a series of imperatives to write underscores the irony that informs the situation; what the speaker exhorts of his mistress he has already accomplished. His instructions function, then, as a proleptic completion of the act he invites his addressee to undertake. His persistent emphasis on the permanence of the book that will record their love ("as long lived as the elements") is also ironically undercut both by his references to actual threats (the Vandals and Goths, as well as the elements themselves) and by the material instability of Donne's poem itself, with its multiple variants and textual inconsistencies. While he seems to promise his mistress a status that would rescue her from the oblivion to which Corinna, Polla Argentaria, and Phantasia have been relegated, the act of offering firmly resituates her on the margins of discourse, where she is confined as the nameless, faceless handmaiden to poetic accomplishment.

Donne alludes to these connections between the politics of gender and the poetics of plagiarism in "A Valediction: of the Book," but he makes them his central subject in the poem enunciated in the Sapphic voice, "Sappho to Philaenis."[2] This neglected text has disturbed and offended critics and editors, and until very recently[3] they have by turns ignored it, questioned its authenticity, and censured its subject matter. Herbert Grierson, for example, the first editor to identify its genre as a heroical epistle, called it "passionate and eloquent in its own not altogether admirable way" (1912: 2, 91), while Helen Gardner consigned it to the *Dubia*, for she judged it "too uncharacteristic of Donne in theme, treatment, and style to be accepted as unquestionably his," and furthermore, she found it difficult to imagine him "wishing to assume the love-sickness of Lesbian Sappho" (1965: xlvi). As the language of these judgments makes clear, its exclusion from the canon of Donne's poetry appears to have been based more on moral objections than textual evidence, since its presence in numerous manuscripts that purport to be collections of his poetry and in the first edition of Donne's poems (1633) would seem to support its authenticity (Gardner 1965: xlv – xlvi). If we are to take the manuscript evidence seriously and consider "Sappho to Philaenis" as Donne's, how can we account for its different style and for the uncharacteristic submersion of his own distinctive poetic "voice" and unabashedly "masculine expression"[4] in the accents of a Greek lesbian woman poet? Given the male poet's clear recognition of the female author's ultimate invisibility in "A Valediction: Of the Book," why should Donne choose to speak in the feminine voice, thus risking both the neglect accorded to women writers in general and the censorship associated with Sappho in particular?[5]

I will suggest some answers to these questions by analysing both Donne's poem and the various subtexts with which it is filiated. Because all of the texts I treat are marked by their emphasis on feminine speaking and their ambiguous or unknown authorship, I also focus on the intertextual problem of transvestite ventriloquism; in this case, the male author's appropriation of the feminine voice. I argue that the issue of ventriloquistic speech informs all of these texts and is not incidental to the debates about their attribution, since the questions of literary voice and authorial property are closely related to gender, to the historical possibility of women's speech and writing. This problem is complicated and intensified by the texts' linkage to Sappho on the one hand and to their history of suppression and faulty transmission on the other, for the representation of lesbianism in Western literature is also a history of censorship. Indeed, James Holstun has recently alluded to the absence of references to lesbianism not only in literary sources but also in legal records and philosophical tracts as a phenomenon of "voicelessness" (1987: 836),[6] an epithet that precisely describes the strategies of silencing I will be investigating.

Donne's poem is a verse letter, written, the title tells us, by Sappho to another woman, Philaenis. The letter describes the erotic union of the women, and the ideal world created by their love explicitly excludes men (and by extension the male author). Further, the poem's form and the Sapphic voice turn out not to be Donne's invention at all, but are instead borrowed from Ovid's fifteenth epistle in the *Heroides*. Like Donne's poem, the attribution of Ovid's Sapphic letter was uncertain until quite recently; the question of authorship was complicated because the epistle became separated from the rest of the *Heroides* and was not rediscovered until the fifteenth century.[7] But the difficulties in assigning an author to the voice that speaks do not stop here; the Ovidian epistle, it could be argued, is about the very questions that have surrounded the poem's transmission and attribution throughout its history. The issues of poetic property and authorial signature are inscribed within the text, in the citations from the historical Sappho's poetry that are woven into Ovid's letter, in its purported status as autobiography, and in its thematizing of voice. Thus, although my argument is structured like a traditional source study in its investigation of Donne's primary subtexts, Ovid's *Heroides 15* and Lucian's *Amores*, it is fundamentally intertextual in Barbara Johnson's sense of that distinction: source studies, she asserts, tend to speak "in terms of a transfer of property ('borrowing')," while intertextuality tends to speak "in terms of misreading or infiltration, that is, of violations of property" (1985: 264). In these texts, the issue of literary property is further complicated both by the ventriloquistic cross-dressing of the speakers and by the representation of intertextual violation as erotic.

I

It is a commonplace of Donne criticism that his mastery of the persona is a result of scrutinizing Ovid's complex manipulation of narrative voices.[8] I want to examine this assertion with specific reference to Donne's "Sappho to Philaenis" and to its Ovidian subtext,[9] for both poems are, in a sense, about their own borrowed voices and the problematized status of poetic property. Sappho's epistle to Phaon is situated at the end of the single *Heroides*, Ovid's collection of verse complaints supposedly written by mythological heroines to the lovers who have abandoned them. It differs from the preceding fourteen, however, for whereas Ovid insinuates in the other epistles that he has liberated the heroines from the tyrannical bonds of the narratives that had confined and defined them (as Dido's letter differentiates itself from the Virgilian account in the *Aeneid* on which it depends), ostensibly allowing them to assume control over their own representations through their manipulation of language, Sappho's case is unique. She alone among these famous women is a poet in her own right, one so pre-eminent that Plato called her the tenth Muse, Longinus praised her for the sublimity of her style, Horace admired her poetry, and Catullus translated her (Jacobson 1974: 281–2; Stigers 1977: 83–102). Only in Sappho's letter does Ovid make use of the speaker's own writings, because only here do the roles of fictional and actual author coalesce. Ovid knew Sappho's poetry and his epistle is full of its echoes, but whereas "echo" suggests a disembodied voice capable only of repetition, Ovid's radical reinscription of Sappho bears the marks of sexual mastery and theft. His ventriloquistic appropriation of her voice subordinates Sapphic meter to the demands of his own elegiac lines, and the portrait that he presents provided an indelible legacy that displaced the authority of her own words, blurring the boundaries between "authentic" and constructed discourse.

Ovid's epistle played a central role in perpetuating an image of Sappho that was probably originally fashioned by the middle and new comedy (Jacobson 1974: 281). The candor and passion of her poetry became an object of ridicule for these playwrights, who made her into a caricature of love-longing and sowed the seeds for the reputation of immorality and licentiousness that was still attached to her name in the Renaissance.[10] It is in these parodic portraits that Sappho is first connected with Phaon, the ferryman upon whom Venus bestowed preternatural beauty; made desperate by her unrequited desire for him, Sappho reportedly threw herself off the Leucadian cliff. The story was retold by poets of the new comedy, but Ovid's version of Sappho's story is the one that has survived, bequeathing a detailed account that carries the weight of authenticity through its pseudo-autobiographical narratorial voice. Ovid's Sappho conforms to the Heroidean paradigm of the abandoned woman, and she displays an intense, indeed humiliating, erotic yearning, given the context of Phaon's disdain. The dynamic of power within the poem relies on a sexual subjugation that entails poetic submission, and we must read Ovid's concern with the question of poetic ownership, then, as relating partly to the potency of the reputation he seeks to subordinate to his own in his desire to establish himself as a love poet. His use of the feminine voice allowed him to challenge the epic and patriarchal ethos of Augustan Rome (just as eroticism undermines the stability of epic in the *Metamorphoses*),[11] but the constructed voice in *Heroides 15* must assert itself against the real Sappho's poetic voice, which continually threatens to usurp Ovid's mastery.

Sappho's initial response to Phaon's abandonment of her is a frozen grief that admits no expression, neither tears nor words. ("[L]acrimae deerant oculis et verba palato,/ adstrictum gelido frigore pectus erat" (111–12) (My eyes had no tears, my tongue no words, a clear chill gripped my heart.))[12] Even though Sappho does speak and eloquently describe her own suffering, it is not in her habitual discourse that she does so. Her voice, as she continually reminds us, is silenced:

> Nunc vellem facunda forem! dolor artibus obstat,
> ingeniumque meis substitit omne malis.
> non mihi respondent veteres in carmina vires;
> plectra dolore tacent, muta dolore lyra est.
>
> (195–8)
>
> (I wish I were eloquent now! Sorrow checks my art
> and all my genius is halted by my grief.
> My old power for poetry will not come at my call;
> my plectrum is sorrowing and silent, sorrow has hushed my lyre.)

Even while she laments the diminishment of verbal power that psychic pain has imposed upon her, she recalls the poetic skill that she once possessed, expressing the pride that she takes in her lyric gift in fiercely competitive terms: not even Alcaeus, her contemporary and countryman, garnered greater praise. Although nature has denied her physical beauty, making her short ("brevis") and dark-complexioned ("non candida"), her corporeal deficiencies were nevertheless compensated for by her poetic ability. Her poetry had the capacity to mold and shape perceptions, so that, while she lacked conventional beauty, she appeared alluring to Phaon when she sang to him. Indeed, she speaks of her poetry as an aphrodisiac; she remembers singing her lyrics to Phaon, and, while she sang, he stole kisses. Sappho tells us that she excelled at this amorous play:

> tunc te plus solito lascivia nostra iuvabat,
> crebraque mobilitas aptaque verba ioco,
> et quod, ubi amborum fuerat confusa voluptas,
> plurimus in lasso corpore languor erat.
>
> (47–50)
>
> (Then, more than ever, my wanton play delighted you,
> my constant motion, my observances of delight,
> and, with the body's exhaustion, that languor beyond languor
> in us both, after that final, fine confusion of our desire.)

Her regard for her own erotic skill is matched by her awareness of the lyric power that was hers, for her descriptions of passion incited and fed the desire of her listeners, allowing her to transform herself and her audience, literally to enchant them.

Ovid, however, divests Sappho of this potent metamorphic gift and borrows it for himself, making her subject to the power that was once hers. His poem transforms the direction of Sappho's affections, leading her to disdain not only the formerly enticing Lesbian girls for the unattainable Phaon but also to chastise her previous lesbian affections in favor of a heterosexual attachment. That Ovid converts the object of Sappho's passion from the girls she addresses in her own songs (Anactorie, Cydro, Atthis) to a man who scorns her suggests a subjugation that is at once sexual (made all the more demeaning, given her praise of her sexual abilities) and poetic. Sappho's songs are silenced within the poem's fiction by Phaon and literally by Ovid; in this way Ovid aligns himself with Phaon, since Sappho must yield to his poetic authority in the same way that she succumbed to Phaon's erotic mastery. Ovid thus provides a narrative logic for Sappho's switch from song to elegy, for, though she herself claims to be better suited to the lyric mode, her sorrow makes her prefer elegy ("elegiae flebile carmen" (7) (elegy is the music for pain)). Ovid superinscribes a new metrical style over her silence, which, while uncharacteristic of the historical Sappho, is nevertheless appropriate to the occasion he has fashioned for her speaking.

Fittingly, then, the epistle opens with a reference to poetic signatures: Sappho's first words are a question to her lover as to whether her style is instantly recognizable. The query, posed as it is by Ovid speaking through Sappho, has a pungent irony since Sappho's fame as a lyric poet depended at least in part on the verse form that carries her name, the Sapphic stanza. Ovid's witty remark calls attention to his suppression of Sapphic meter in favor of his own elegiac couplets, to the translation from Greek to Latin, and to the transformation of gender from female to male poet. In the process, it points to the question that subtends the poem: who is speaking and to whom does the speaking belong? Clearly, the poet is neither Sappho, despite the echoes of her verse and despite the speaker's identification of herself as Sappho; nor is it Ovid, despite the poem's conforming to the demands of his newly invented genre of the mythological complaint and to the elegiac meter that characterizes the other letters in the collection. In a sense, Sapphic and Ovidian signatures are superimposed on one another in a palimpsestic transparency, and the usurpation that has made Ovid's ventriloquized speech possible is thus thematized in the text.

The textual violation that has occurred, the splicing together of the Greek lyric fragments in this new context, is figured, appropriately, in a buried allusion to the Philomela myth, for in both cases sexual seduction or rape becomes a prelude to the theft or literal extirpation of the tongue, a kind of linguistic rape.[13] Indeed, Sappho claims that in this landscape of abandonment no birds warble their sweet complaints: "sola virum non ulta pie maestissima mater/ concinit Ismarium Daulias ales Ityn./ ales Ityn, Sappho desertos cantat amores – /hactenus; ut media cetera nocte silent." (153–6) (Only the nightingale, only Philomel, whose terrible grief took vengeance/ most terrible against her husband, laments for Itys her son./ The nightingale sings of Itys, her abandoned love is Sappho's song:/ Only that; all else is as silent as the dead of night.) Ovid's lines actually refer to Procne (the most mournful mother), and Verducci's mistranslation thus transposes the "terrible grief" and the subsequent revenge to Philomela. Verducci's rendering confuses the family lineage by making Itys Philomela's son, yet her translation does nevertheless make visible (and audible) what Ovid's lines elide, namely, the rape and mutilation (of Philomela) that provoked Procne's horrific vengeance. In a sense, Ovid's focus on Procne reenacts the silencing of Philomela; the tongueless sister stands as a mute but powerful presence in the poem, in the same way that Sappho herself appears as a silenced voice within the epistle.

Ovid has in one sense perpetrated a corresponding theft of Sappho's tongue; her letter is as much a lament for her extinguished voice as it is a complaint about Phaon's abandonment. Yet, even while the Ovidian allusion carries the traces of silencing, it also focuses insistently on Procne's mourning of Itys, a grief suffused with the memory of maternal savagery. Procne's murder of her child becomes an act of vengeance that links the organ of speech (the tongue) with the organ of eating; the revenge for Philomela's rape and muting was, of course, to kill the son, who resembled his father, and to have the father unknowingly consume the child. This act of cannibalization, the father's literal ingestion of the child's body, offers a trope for intertextuality. While the Daulian bird laments the death of Itys, the dismembered body that Sappho now mourns is the corpus of her poems that has been cut and scattered, only to be remembered in a different, Ovidian shape. The reference to Itys alludes not only to the myth of Procne and Philomela, then, but perhaps even more powerfully, to Sappho's use of the myth in her own poetry ("oh, Irana/ why... me?/ daughter of Pandion/ swallow?" (Sappho 1966: 83)); Ovid thus invokes a myth of silencing and cannibalization at the very moment that he reenacts it by echoing or incorporating her verse.[14] The violence that lies at the heart of these intertextual maneuvers is thus recorded in a self-reflexive gesture, as if Ovid recognized his own complicity in the suppression of the Sapphic voice. The doubleness of his elegy acknowledges his own competitive, masterful silencing, even as it registers Sappho's lament and the mournful voices of the other muted or transformed women in the poem.

Ovid speaks from "the place of the silenced woman" through the figure of woman (Johnson 1985: 280), but the voice remains hermaphroditic, denying the possibility of "authentic" female speech through its distorted, travestied expression of feminine desire. Having subordinated Sappho's voice to his own and used her to demonstrate his poetic mastery, Ovid has no further use for the querulous caricature of longing that he has created. The genre of the erotic complaint, a form initially defined but ultimately undone by its repetitive, formulaic character, eventually offers itself to precisely this kind of parody. With a form unable to sustain the escalating intensity it generates except by inscribing the very caricature it invites, Ovid must have realized the limits of the genre he claimed to have created, and whatever risks he incurred are shifted on to the ventriloquized feminine voice, particularly Sappho's, whose own poetic gifts are held up to comic scrutiny. Ovid has his Sappho vow to dedicate her lyre to Apollo before she jumps off the Leucadian rock, a fittingly hyperbolic symbol both of his own departure from the genre of erotic complaint and of his neutralization of the threat that Sappho's reputation represents. Sappho leaves behind the epitaph she wrote for posterity, in which she bequeaths her lyre to Apollo. As Paul de Man has argued, prosopopeia is the dominant figure of epitaphic discourse, for it creates the fiction of "the voice-from-beyond the grave," conferring a mask or face (*prosopon poien*) that makes one's name "as intelligible and memorable as a face" (1979: 926–7). Here, however, the Sapphic voice that speaks registers only its resolution not to speak, so that the trope of prosopopeia (which is also the figure of voice), offers an empty mask, a name without a referent. The inscription carries the authoritative weight of Sappho's final words, a memorial that engraves a place and an instrument for a later poet to inhabit and use, petrifying her relinquishment of her own poetic gift in perpetuity.

II

Although John Donne can no more speak for – or in the place of – Sappho than Ovid can, since both poets' ability to represent her voice depends upon her silence, Donne appears to challenge the erotic subjugation perpetrated by Ovid, acting out his rivalry with his predecessor in the art of love poetry upon the body (or in the voice) of Sappho. Donne's subversion of Ovidian authority begins with the filiation of his poem with Ovid's through their genre, but this similitude serves merely to accentuate the difference within. "Sappho to Philaenis" masquerades as a recuperation of the original Sappho, since, inverting Ovid's distortion of her sexual preference, it represents her as lesbian. Donne's Sapphic epistle is, then, addressed to Philaenis, an obscure Greek writer from the island of Leucas, and, although it reproduces the situation of the Ovidian letter through its apostrophe to an absent lover, the beloved is now a woman. Apart from the tenuous geographical link between Sappho and Philaenis (Leucas), there appears to be little historical or poetic reason for this choice of companion, since neither Sappho nor Ovid mention Philaenis, and antiquity furnishes us with only a few references to her lost writings.

Who is Philaenis and why should Donne pair her with Sappho? Since only one critic who has discussed this poem has attempted to identify her, I want first to suggest a source for her and, then, to offer an explanation for the appropriateness of that context.[15] Most of what little we do know about Philaenis can be gleaned from two epigrams in the *Greek Anthology*, where she figures, significantly, at the center of a debate on disputed authorship. The first (345), ascribed to Aeschrion, is articulated in her voice; it situates her tomb on a headland, overlooking the sea, and, from beyond the grave, she addresses passing sailors, exhorting them not to insult or mock her. She swears that she was neither lascivious nor a "public woman," and she attributes the writings (the subject matter of which she professes not to know) associated with her name to Polycrates, an Athenian possessed of an evil tongue. The second epigram (450), composed by Dioscorides, is also enunciated by Philaenis and again protests against the slander that attached itself to her name. She denies that she authored an obscene treatise that was "offensive to ladies," and, after swearing to her chaste and modest nature, pronounces a hypothetical malediction on the writer who may have composed the work to shame her and ruin her reputation. Apparently, the work with which her name is connected is a kind of erotic guidebook that furnished its readers with explicit information about diverse sexual practices and positions. It is not clear, however, that Philaenis ever had a historical existence; the name may have stood simply for the prototypical harlot, and it may have been affixed to the pornographic work as a pseudonym (Vessey 1976: 79–81). Nevertheless, the similarities between this "constructed" Philaenis and Sappho are instructive: both women wrote erotic works, both women were therefore presumed to be immoral and licentious, and, in both cases, their alleged sexual notoriety made the identity of the author and the attribution of the work questionable. (In Sappho's case, it was posited that there were actually two women of this name from Lesbos, one a courtesan and one a poet, a dualism whose sustained life has haunted criticism of Sappho's poetry.)[16]

Although Philaenis is vehement in her denial of sexual misconduct, her references to heterosexual relationships only has led at least one critic to suppose that her silence elides a greater sin: that she was a lover of women. This supposition is supported by a depiction of her supplied in the pseudo-Lucianic dialogue, the *Amores* or *Affairs of the Heart*.[17] A debate on the virtue of heterosexual love for men as opposed to pederasty, the dialogue has at its center a brief digression on lesbianism in which Charicles defends the right of women to love each other:

> if males find intercourse with males acceptable, henceforth let women too love each other. Come now, epoch of the future, legislator of strange pleasures, devise fresh paths for male lusts, but bestow the same privilege on women, and let them have intercourse with each other just as men do. Let them strap to themselves cunningly contrived instruments of lechery, those mysterious monstrosities devoid of seed, and let woman lie with woman as does a man. Let wanton Lesbianism – that word seldom heard, which I feel ashamed even to utter – freely parade itself, and let our women's chambers emulate Philaenis, disgracing themselves with Sapphic amours.
>
> (Lucian 1979: VIII 195)

The passage is important most obviously because it provides a linkage between Sappho and Philaenis within an explicitly lesbian context, one which may have furnished Donne directly or indirectly with the subject and treatment of his poem. Even more interesting, however, are the implications of this defense, in which women appear to achieve sexual autonomy through their employment of the dildo as a pseudo-phallus and are not only thus freed from their dependence upon the capriciousness of male desire but are compensated for their anatomical lack and apparently also accorded some of the symbolic power associated with the phallus. (This representation also encodes the common supposition that heterosexual intercourse is the only form of pleasure, and that lesbian love is thus an inferior copy of the original (Butler 1991; Faderman 1981: 31–7).) Charicles subverts his magnanimous gesture, however, through the strong moral censure that modifies his description, infiltrated as it is with terms of outrage ("monstrosities," "wanton," "ashamed," "disgracing"). His suggestion of sexual independence for women turns out to be doubly ironic, first, in his "conferring" independence on women and, second, by making that autonomy a ludicrous example of the social depravity male homosexuality might foster were it to replace conjugal love as the dominant mode of sexual relations.

Charicles is nevertheless praised by his audience for his impassioned rhetoric in defense of women, and the terms of their approbation are significant: Callicratidas claims that, if the political and legal spheres were open to women, they would have elected Charicles as their champion for his rhetorical zeal. Not even those women considered outstanding for wisdom and verbal power, not even "Sappho, the honey-sweet pride of Lesbos" herself (Lucian 1979: VIII 197), could have pleaded their case with such vehemence. Indeed, Callicratidas argues that Charicles's passion gives him the right – even the duty – to speak on behalf of women, for, after all, he can do it more forcefully than they can themselves. Clearly, there is an analogy between women who become men by means of a mechanical device that duplicates the phallus and men who speak on behalf of women (or in ventriloquized feminine voices, which is the logical extension of this surrogacy). In each case, the difference between sexes is collapsed into a reconstruction of self as other, and, while it looks as if both men and women might gain independence through this process, it short-circuits the possibility of genuine difference. That women's sexual independence as it is constructed by these male speakers depends on their mimicry of the male anatomy points to the dangers of having men speak on behalf of or in the place of women; if women are excluded from legal and civic contexts and by extension exiled from the text, who is to ensure that their representatives can or will genuinely argue for their interests? What is at issue is not only whether it is possible to speak on behalf of or in the place of another, for advocacy is clearly a cornerstone of many political and legal systems, but the ethical implications of assuming this power.

Donne's "Sappho to Philaenis" seems to depict an idyllic version of lesbian love in which the women do not attempt simply to replicate heterosexual relations and take on male characteristics, as they do in the pseudo-Lucianic dialogue, but rather evolve a specifically feminine mode of erotic union within a utopian world that excludes men and which seeks to invent a language that will reflect its new ideology. As an address to the absent beloved, Philaenis, the poem employs apostrophe, what Jonathan Culler has called the figure of voicing (1985: 40). Apostrophe conventionally signals spontaneously adopted passion, the "turning away" from description or narration to direct address, and it is thus an appropriate figure in a reconstruction of the Sapphic voice. More importantly, apostrophe confers animicity or presence upon an inanimate object or absent addressee, transforming, in effect, object into subject; it functions, then, as a dialogue between subject and the implied new subject that is constructed by the apostrophe. The vocative of apostrophe enables the speaker to fashion a relationship with an object that in turn helps to constitute the identity of the speaker as poet, for the figure of voice dramatizes both its own speaking and its power to invest the inanimate or absent with life and presence (Culler 1981: 138–42). Yet this vitalizing force is ultimately illusory, since as Culler argues, "this figure which seems to establish relations between the self and the other can in fact be read as an act of radical interiorization and solipsism" (1981: 146).

"Sappho to Philaenis" follows a similar trajectory, moving from its opening, which reproduces the Ovidian complaint in its mourning for Philaenis's absence, to Sappho's conversion of that absence into presence, with the celebration of poetic language that this reanimation entails, and finally to a dramatization of the radical solipsism and narcissism of this recovery, in which the other turns out to be the self. What is enacted within the poem (between Sappho and Philaenis) points to an analogous relationship between author and speaker, where what appears to be Donne's generous bestowing of language and independence on Sappho, in direct contrast to Ovid's violations of her, turns out to be an act of colonization,[18] an act that is perhaps most clearly visible in the metaphor central to Elegy 19, where the mistress's body and the New World become versions of each other

("O my America, my new found land"). As this apostrophic formulation suggests, both mistress and land are mastered by man's exploration and possession of them. The "O" of apostrophe points not just to "undifferentiated voicing," nor to its emptying of "semantic reference" (Culler 1981: 142–3), then, but also to the cipher of the uncolonized land and to woman's "centric part." In a similar way in "Sappho to Philaenis," the otherness of a classical text (Ovid's) and the otherness of woman (Sappho) are domesticated and reshaped into an image of the self, a process that is mediated both by ventriloquism and by voyeurism.

"Sappho to Philaenis" opens with a lament not only for the beloved's absence, but also for the dwindling potency of poetic language in general. Like the Ovidian Sappho, this Sapphic voice wonders whether that "enchanting force" is "decayed," since, although verse can with Orphic power move or "draw" "Nature's work" against the laws of nature, it nevertheless cannot restore Philaenis. But an alternate reading of these lines suggests in addition the reciprocal attraction between an original in nature and its representation or copy "drawn" in verse, an interpretation that is supported by Sappho's later satisfaction with the poetic image of Philaenis that she fashions. She initially worries that the wax image of Philaenis that she carries in her heart will be destroyed in this crucible of desire, but it is instead radically reconfigured. The recreation of the absent beloved takes place as Sappho gazes in a mirror. Caressing her own body, she remarks on the similarity between herself and Philaenis, who are as alike, in fact, as the two halves of a single body:

> My two lips, eyes, thighs, differ from thy two,
> But so, as thine from one another do;
> And, oh, no more, the likeness being such,
> Why should they not alike in all parts touch?
> Hand to strange hand, lip to lip none denies;
> Why should they breast to breast, or thighs to thighs?
> Likeness begets such strange self-flattery,
> That touching myself, all seems done to thee.
> Myself I embrace, and mine own hands I kiss,
> And amorously thank myself for this.
> Me, in my glass, I call thee; but alas,
> When I would kiss, tears dim mine eyes, and glass.
>
> (45–56)

The identification between a body and its reflection or between an image and a copy marks in this passage a dissolution of boundaries, a blurring of difference, in which Sappho comes to master both Philaenis and herself through the objectifying, controlling power of the gaze. Although the passage is full of tactile imagery, in furnishing a comic rewriting of Ovid's description of Narcissus in the *Metamorphoses* and thus making the mirror central to Sappho's fantasy, the poem invokes the power of vision to construct the other. That is, Sappho's entrance into the scopic economy simultaneously displaces male desire, since she now assumes the normally male position of looker (with its ability to shape what it sees – "to make blind men see,/ What things gods are, I say they are like to thee" (17–18)), and makes her subject to it, for she is now also the recipient of that gaze (as the reflection of Philaenis).

This doubleness, which is made possible by the physical correspondence between self and other, leads Sappho to discover the body's bilateral symmetry, the perfect equivalence between its right and left halves. Symmetry gives rise to a new language that Sappho coins to describe Philaenis, for, as she implicitly argues, the most available idiom, Petrarchism, is no longer a sufficient or even accurate mode of praise. The Petrarchan blazon that itemizes the mistress's body parts through a catalogue of extravagant comparison cannot function without borrowing its terms from the external world; the blush of the mistress's cheek must be described with reference to the canonical roses and lilies. Rather than being "soft," "clear," "straight," or "fair" as "stars, cedars, and lilies are," then, Sappho claims that Philaenis is already perfect, sufficient unto herself. The language that Sappho employs is thus correspondingly symmetrical, a tautological idiom whose referent has already been named: Philaenis is beautiful not because she possesses the attributes of stars and flowers but because she is perfectly balanced, one half mimicking the other: "thy right hand, and cheek, and eye, only,/ Are like thy other hand, and cheek, and eye" (23–4).

The specular symmetry of this lesbian world stands in sharp contradistinction to that of the Ovidian epistle in which the boundaries between self and other were more clearly delineated, boundaries continually transgressed by acts of penetration, in which Ovid stole from Sappho's poetry, in which women are violated and savagely silenced. Ovidian eroticism carries with it a poetics based on an analogous ideology of violence and possession, and it is precisely against this ideology that Donne's poem seems to protest. Sappho's revision of the rhetoric of Petrarchan praise implicitly suggests a remedy to these intertexual rivalries through its fashioning of a world dominated by an unfamiliar erotic ethos. She praises love between women as a utopian union in which it is possible to love without possessing and to take pleasure without violating. The intrusion of men into this world is figured in terms of agriculture and theft, appropriations designed for self-gain. Lesbian love, on the other hand, is commendable precisely because it leaves no traces and entails no ownership: "of our dalliance no more signs there are,/ Than fishes leave in streams, or birds in air" (41–2).[19] Sappho proclaims Philaenis's body to be a natural paradise that already contains perfection, an image of the Golden Age in which the earth produced abundant food without cultivation and people lived in harmony without the need for laws to protects their rights and property. Why, then, should she admit the "tillage" of a "harsh rough man," an intrusion that signals simultaneously the agricultural appropriation of the earth and also points towards the sexual "tilling" of the female body that subtends the patriarchal order. The sense of property implicit in this heterosexual union is imaged as an indelible sign: for "men leave behind them that which their sin shows,/ And are as thieves traced that rob when it snows" (39–40). The metaphor is so suggestive of literary borrowing that Dryden used it to describe Ben Jonson's pillaging of his classical sources, asserting that Jonson's thefts could be tracked in the snows of the ancients.[20] Donne's ventriloquistic borrowing of Sappho's voice allows him to create an intertextuality that appears to be different from the Ovidian rivalry, in which poets steal from one another's work and where such plagiarism can be traced.

Yet the collapse of other into self, registered in Sappho's narcissistic absorption of Philaenis, also describes Donne's relationship to Ovid and Sappho, for they are both ultimately assimilated into a poem of his making. We might read the lines "Likeness begets such strange self flattery,/ That touching myself, all seems done to thee" (51–2), then, as a slippage between ventriloquized and authorial voices, in which Donne's characteristic pun on his name functions as a signature, transforming the "thee" to Donne. (It then becomes tempting – if sexually complicated – to read "restore/ Me to me; thee, my half, my all, my more" – as referring to Ann More.) This dislocation of voice reveals both the ventriloquist and the voyeur, the first producing speech that appears to emanate from a source other than the real speaker, and the other deriving pleasure from a looking that requires no participation (as Donne watches Sappho watching – and touching – herself). Both scopophilia and the borrowing of voices are mediated activities that necessitate no direct involvement; just as voyeurism is the wish to see without being seen, a mastery and form of possession of the object through the gaze, so is ventriloquistic appropriation of the feminine voice a mastery of the other, a censorship of its difference. Donne borrows the feminine voice as a way of acting out his rivalry with Ovid, but he controls its dangerous plenitude by domesticating its alterity and ultimately turning it into a version of himself.

That all of these texts are in various ways censored points to a crucial aspect of the feminine voice in general and of Sappho's reputation in particular: the suppression of actual feminine speaking enables and authorizes the fictional reconstruction of the (other) feminine voice, and ventriloquism thus functions as a poetic enactment of the mechanism of censorship at work within the broader cultural context. It is not in spite of the destruction of Sappho's verse, then, but partly because of it that she was so frequently acclaimed and imitated by subsequent poets (male and female), for it is upon her absence and silence (broken only by the surviving fragments of poems) that subsequent accounts of her could be and were inscribed.

Feminine speech and its literary representation in western culture have historically depended on a long and potent tradition, reflected, on the one hand, by the invectives against woman's irrepressible garrulity and, on the other, by the Pauline injunctions for feminine silence. Because woman's voice metonymically figures both her essential nature and her sexuality in this tradition, silence comes to stand for sexual continence, the closing of the double "mouths" of the feminine body.[21] That the connection between silence and chastity was an active nexus in the English Renaissance is evidenced not only by the wealth of pamphlet material on the subject but also by the copious references to and moral pronouncements on woman's speaking in literary contexts.[22] We might compare the description of Cordelia's voice in *King Lear* ("Her voice was ever soft,/ Gentle and low, an excellent thing in a woman" (5.3.271–2)), for instance, with that of Milton's Dalila in *Samson Agonistes*, who is likened to a hyena, the putatively bisexual beast whose ability to mimic the human voice lured men to their destruction (748).[23] Cordelia's linguistic restraint, registered not only in her decorous and pleasing voice when she does speak but also by her unwillingness to "heave [her] heart into [her] mouth" (1.1.90) in the first place, stands for a constellation of particularly feminine virtues: filial loyalty, modesty, chastity, the capacity to endure suffering, humility, and patience.[24] Dalila, conversely, is notoriously unfaithful, and her political treachery is intimately allied to her (presumably limitless) sexual promiscuity. Yet her seductively dangerous ability to counterfeit voices (registered in her parodically distorted reproductions of Samson's arguments) aligns her voice with Milton's own, for the feminine voice represents the rhetorical plenitude and versatility coveted by the poet. For a male author to assume the feminine voice is thus necessarily to confront in complex ways the "issue" of female sexuality, since the source of feminine verbal facility was thought to be coextensive with her erotic nature.

The imbrication of woman's putatively insatiable sexual desire and her uncontrollable urge to speak renders the appropriation of her voice a dangerous business for the male author, for it threatens to relegate him to the position of voyeur, unable either to satisfy her limitless desire or to control the voice he has borrowed. This threat is especially evident in male borrowings of the Sapphic voice, because the poet must face not only the otherness of her gender and sexual preference but also the legendary power of her reputation. His capacity to insert himself into her discursive space is dependent on the strategies he develops to mute or refashion her original voice, an intertextual rivalry which although similar to the competition between male poets and their precursors, both in its homage to her power and its complicity in her silencing, manifests itself as well in intersexual politics. Lesbianism complicates transvestite ventriloquism, since its presence in western culture has, of course, been heavily censored. Ovid makes Sappho heterosexual so that she will be vulnerable to his erotic and poetic mastery, whereas Donne marginalizes her within a utopian world that – despite its allusion to the fertility of the Golden Age – is narcissistically sterile. Although love between women leaves no "signs," Sappho's poetry is also without signature and without poetic "offspring." Indeed, male borrowings of the feminine voice seem to provide an intensified version of intertextuality, for, where a system of diachronic textual echoes and citations continually subverts the ontological security of a text, its discrete historical boundaries, and its status as self-contained property, the phenomenon of transvestite ventriloquism provides in addition a powerful critique of phonocentrism.[25] That is, while all textual "voices" are constructions, tenuously connected with their referents and ambiguously tethered to the authorial presence that supposedly stands behind them, critical discourse has traditionally relied on the implicit presence of a stable author who manipulates these personae or voices. Ventriloquistic cross-dressing, particularly when the borrowed voice belongs to an actual poet, transgresses the laws of gender, propriety, and property by undermining in a fundamental way the conventional relationships between author and voice, making visible in the process the radical contingency of poetic and authorial identity.

Why use the feminine voice for this interchange between male poets? Luce Irigaray, in her feminist rewriting of Lévi-Strauss, has argued that western patriarchal culture is organized and subtended by the exchange of women, who function as commodities to be passed between men. Within the social context, women have value only as they facilitate relations among men; the sociocultural endogamy "excludes the participation of that other, so foreign to the social order: woman.... Men make commerce *of* them, but they do not enter into any exchanges *with* them" (Irigaray 1985b: 172). Thus, although the poet purports to defer to the feminine voices that speak his texts (including the most potent of all, the voice of the muse), she is mastered within the economy of representation, and embodying the potential for signification as she does, she becomes the perfect medium of exchange. This is perhaps nowhere as clearly apparent as in Donne's verse letters, where the muse forms the basis of poetic transaction between the author and his (male) correspondents. In a letter to Roland Woodward, for instance, communication is effected through the voice of the muse:

> Zealously my Muse doth salute all thee,
> Enquiring of that mistique trinitee
> Wherof thou'and all to whom the heavens do infuse
> Like fyer, are made; thy body, mind, and Muse.
> Does thou recover sicknes, or prevent?
> Or is thy Mind travail'd with discontent?
> Or art thou parted from the world and mee
> In a good skorn of the worlds vanitee?
> Or is thy devout Muse retyr'd to sing
> Upon her tender Elegiaque string?
> Our Minds part not, joyne then thy Muse with myne,
> For myne is barren thus devorc'd from thyne.
> (Milgate 1967: 62)

Natural reproduction is here appropriated to the symbolic order, where the relations between the muses reenacts the heterosexual economy of which it is a reflection, providing poetic offspring through their disembodied commerce. Just as woman's reproductive value is subsumed under the monopolization of the proper name in order to insure the property and stability of the patriarchal order, so, too, are the transactions within the poetic order bounded and informed by an attention to property and ownership. Chastity is the keystone of Renaissance patriarchal culture, since sexual propriety alone determines the identity of the child as property of the father (Jonson's praise of Lady Sidney's chastity in "To Penshurst" provides a reminder of this fundamental organizing principle: "Thy lady's noble, fruitful, chaste withal./ His children thy great lord may call his own:/ A fortune in this age, but rarely known" (90–2)). Commerce between the muses is also governed by laws of sexual propriety, which provides a context within which we might begin to understand the strange conceit used in a letter to Donne, written by "T.W.," presumably, Thomas Woodward:

> Have mercy on me & my sinfull Muse
> Wc rub'd & tickled wth thyne could not chuse
> But spend some of her pithe & yeild to bee
> One in yt chaste & mistique tribadree.
> Bassaes adultery no fruit did leaue,
> Nor theirs wc their swolne thighs did nimbly weaue,
> And wt new armes & mouthes embrace & kis
> Though they had issue was not like to this.
> Thy Muse, Oh strange & holy Lecheree
> Beeing a Mayd still, gott this Song on mee.
>
> (Milgate 1967: 212)[26]

Woodward compliments not only the powers of inspiration Donne's muse possesses, but her chastity as well. Disdaining the base fruit that adultery (trangressive heterosexual congress) yields, the muses engage instead in tribadism, a lesbian exchange that merely simulates hetero-sexual intercourse; as a parodic version of the virgin birth, Donne's muse begets the verse poem on Woodward without ever impeaching her own virtue or threatening to trangress the boundaries of property/ propriety. In a heterosexual economy, sexual exchange that does not involve the phallus does not "count," is excluded from the circuit, and so cannot threaten the integrity of feminine virtue.[27] What is appropriated is the figure of the muse, whose reputation for chastity and fertility the (male) poets guard, since her capacity inspires the poet with words, with voice. Just as the muse provides inspiration in a figure distanced from the poet and over whom he purports to exert only partial control, so too is the feminine voice a distanced figure, an image of surrogacy, whose viability depends finally upon the silence of actual women.

III

I have argued that Donne's "Sappho to Philaenis" seems to present an idyllic world of lesbian congress, but that this utopian vision is a male construction of lesbianism. Not only does the poem encode a portrait of Sappho as slightly ridiculous in her lonely passion and finally enclosed within a symmetrical, almost tautological sterility, but it also uses a lesbian erotic ethics as an implicit strategy for overcoming a male poetic rival. Nevertheless, there are elements within the poem that strikingly anticipate recent feminist theory; my interpretation of Donne's poem as a voyeuristic illusion depends upon my supposition of a Renaissance context and a male author. Yet the epistle's fascination with the relationship between eroticism and language, its desire to abolish an exchange system that relies on women, even as it renders them invisible, and its emphasis on touching as a source both of erotic pleasure and epistemological understanding, links it to a feminist text to which it bears an uncanny resemblance, Luce Irigaray's "When Our Lips Speak Together." Just as Donne's Sappho laments the bankruptcy of language, its lack of resources for expressing an erotic passion that differs from or surpasses the heterosexual, so does Irigaray begin her lyrical apostrophe by condemning the poverty of language. Yet where Donne's Sappho envisions a paradise of homology and symmetry that is based on a celebration of the sameness of the female bodies, Irigaray makes sameness the principle of patriarchal domination, what Jane Gallop calls the "unicity of phallomorphic logic" (Gallop 1988: 94): "all round us, men and women sound just the same. The same discussions, the same arguments, the same scenes. The same attractions and separations. The same difficulties, the same impossibility of making connections. The same ... Same ... Always the same" (Irigaray 1985b: 205).

To continue to speak in that sameness would be to fail, for words would pass above "our bodies," and they would remain enveloped "in proper skins, but not our own" (Irigaray 1985b: 205). "When Our Lips Speak Together" alternates between the intimacy of direct address ("Don't you think so? Listen." "How can I touch you if you're not here?") and the encompassing plural that collapses boundaries between women ("If we keep on speaking sameness, if we speak to each other as men have been doing for centuries, as we have been taught to speak, we'll miss each other" (1985b: 205)). Irigaray's new feminine speaking relies, of course, on the relationship between the lips that speak and the lips of the female genitals (*labia minora* and *labia majora*), for this conjunction ensures that woman's voice will no longer be similar to and indistinguishable from man's voice, but that it will be rechannelled through the female body, a specifically sexualized female body.[28] As Irigaray continually reminds us, such a speaking is always a reversal ("So let's try to take back some part of our mouth to speak with" (1985b: 208)), a strategy of mimicry, that playful assumption of the role assigned to women by patriarchy. In this case, the double mouths of the feminine body, the site in the Renaissance of the control both of female sexuality and also of female speaking, are occupied subversively by Irigaray. They become the basis not only of a new sexuality, one that bypasses the Freudian binarism of clitoris and vagina and the unicity of the penis, but also of a new linguistic and significatory economy.

This economy is, according to Irigaray, based on principles of contiguity and association rather than on the notions of sacrifice and substitution that figure so prominently for Lacan (Whitford 1991: 180). Thus, rather than having the son–father relationship that organizes the Oedipal complex, which is based on renunciation and metaphoric substitution, the mother–daughter bond would be founded on metonymic identification, what is contiguous, associative, or combinatory (Whitford 1991: 180). Irigaray's juxtaposition of white and red blood crystallizes this distinction: white blood (*sang blanc*), which is a pun on *semblant* (the "other of the same"), stands for paternal genealogy, whereas red blood (*sang rouge*) figures the link between mother and daughter (Whitford 1991: 118–19). In this maternal order, there would be no need for the daughter to repudiate her mother (as lacking the phallus); it would now be possible for the mother and daughter to co-exist, just as it would now be feasible for women to relate without the rivalry necessitated by patriarchy. The notion of contiguity and metonymy are crucial, because they allow for multiplicity rather than a system of (metaphoric) replacement and substitution. This means not that women are fused with one another in a relationship that obliterates the individual subject, but that subject-to-subject relations among women could now exist. The difference made possible by this realm of multiplicity, which is signalled by the two lips, provides the basis "*both* for sexual difference (and thus of the sexual relation) *and* of a female homosexual economy" (Whitford 1991: 182). Diana Fuss glosses Irigaray's emphasis on multiplicity in Irigaray's own words: "Both at once." A woman is both singular and double, or, as Irigaray puts it, "*She is neither one nor two*" (Irigaray 1985b: 26; Fuss 1989: 58).

The problem of enumeration is precisely Irigaray's point, for the impossibility of fixing woman to a specific number that is mutually exclusive is what also prevents setting up a hierarchy of original and copy. Whereas my interpretation of the mirror scene in Donne's "Sappho to Philaenis" stressed Sappho's desire for a fusion that is continually undercut by the poem's rhetoric ("Likeness" begets "*self* flattery," "touching myself, all *seems* done to thee," "Me, in my glass, I *call* thee" (emphasis mine)), a rhetoric that emphasizes the impossibility of the endeavor, Irigaray subverts the logic of this relation:

> The fact that you live lets me know I am alive, so long as you are neither my counterpart nor my copy. How can I say it differently? We exist only as two? We live by twos beyond all mirages, images, and mirrors. Between us, one is not the "real" and the other her imitation; one is not the original and the other her copy. Although we can dissimulate perfectly within their economy, we relate to one another without simulacrum. Our resemblance does without semblances; for in our bodies, we are already the same. Touch yourself, touch me, you'll "see."
>
> (1985b: 216)

Where the mirror becomes the vehicle for union in Donne's epistle, a necessary supplement to the proclaimed doubleness and self-sufficiency of the female body, for Irigaray, the mirror is a sign of patriarchal mimesis. According to her, there is no need for an external representation of doubleness because the two lips already disturb and displace the economy of similitude. The specular image is thus a sign of a deathly sameness: "the strange way they divide up their couples, with the other as the image of the one. Only an image. So any move toward the other means turning back to the attraction of one's own mirage. A (scarcely) living mirror, she/it is frozen, mute" (1985b: 207). Although Donne's poem incorporates the tactile,[29] Sappho's summoning of the absent Philaenis still depends upon vision, and it is the tears which dim her eyes that eventually destroy the illusion of her lover's presence. Irigaray, by contrast, condemns this "age-old oculocentrism" (1985a: 48) that is the basis of Freudian distinctions of sexual difference, and she substitutes touch instead as the sense that will reshape perception in general. Again, the two lips provide the paradigm, since theirs is a perfectly mutual touching in which there is no distinguishable subject and object, no division into what is touched and what is touching. As she says in a phrase that registers a grammatical multiplicity of senses, "You will always have the touching beauty of a first time, if you aren't congealed in reproductions" (1985b: 214).

Irigaray's most radical reshaping of the Order of the Same in "When Our Lips Speak Together" is directed to language itself. She reflexively returns to the question of how to reclaim the phrase "I love you," how to put it differently. Ultimately, it entails inventing a language, finding a language of the body, a language accompanied by enough gesture and movement to resist the immobilizations of patriarchal definition, of petrification as statues (1985b: 214). Diana Fuss has suggested that her use of "statue" in this context refers to Irigaray's critique of Lacan's Seminar XX on women, most notably his infamous remark on St Theresa's *jouissance*: "you only have to go and look at Bernini's statue in Rome to understand immediately that she's coming, there's no doubt about it" (Mitchell and Rose 1982: 147). That Lacan should presume to understand women's pleasure from art and from an art created by a male artist ("In Rome? So far away? To look? At a statue? Of a saint? Sculpted by a man? What pleasure are we talking about? Whose pleasure?" (1985b: 91)) graphically displays the dangers of ventriloquism. By contrast to Lacan's interpretation of Bernini's statue, Irigaray offers the fluency of female language, a flux and current of words that continually resist solidification. Rather than defining what this language would sound like, she argues that the female voice is defined precisely by this fluidity, this lack of fixed boundaries, this definition that always resists definition.[30]

CODA

I have referred recurrently in this book to a genre that I have not named explicitly: the complaint. It could be argued that the complaint, particularly the complaint voiced by the seduced and abandoned woman, which descends ultimately from Ovid's *Heroides* and which flourished so pervasively in Renaissance (especially Tudor) England, is *the* paradigmatic ventriloquized text.[1] If one considers the feminine complaints, which range from Churchyard's "The Tragedy of Shore's Wife," Daniel's "The Complaint of Rosamond," some of the letters in Drayton's *England's Heroicall Epistles* and his "Matilda" to Shakespeare's *The Rape of Lucrece*, *A Lover's Complaint*, Donne's "Sappho to Philaenis," and Marvell's "The Nymph Complaining on the Death of her Fawn," it becomes clear that there is a profound affinity between the representation of the abandoned woman and male constructions of the feminine voice. In his study of the abandoned woman as a figure in poetry, Lawrence Lipking has suggested that abandonment is a feminine condition ("When a man is abandoned, in fact, he feels like a woman"), and while both male and female authors have contributed to the tradition, "almost every great male poet has written at least one poem in the voice of an abandoned woman" (Lipking 1988: xix–xxi). While Lipking does not emphasize the ventriloquized nature of the complaint (indeed, his study sometimes replicates the historical appropriations of the feminine voice that he analyses, especially in his final chapter, "Aristotle's Sister"), it is precisely its cross-dressed and fabricated nature that makes its depiction so revealing of gender construction. In the Renaissance complaint, in its Ovidian model, and in many subsequent variations on the genre, the complaint is deeply implicated in female sexuality and its consequences.

Feminine abandonment and the complaint that gives it articulation are rooted in an erotics that registers the discrepant power relations between the sexes. Because chastity is powerfully correlated with silence in the early modern period, the complaint inscribes a particular orientation towards sexuality, couched as it is so often is in a feminine voice that warns of the consequences of seduction or rape, that implicitly or explicitly counsels chastity, or that forecasts the bitter aftermath of erotic pleasure. Its ventriloquized status gives it a special force, since it seems to be spoken by its victim, but is almost always in the Renaissance the vehicle of a patriarchal didacticism, a way of controlling female desire and promulgating a particular version of female sexuality, one that relies on or responds to a forceful, sometimes violent male sexuality. Its passionately static nature, and its repetitive, often formulaic rhetoric depict a kind of cultural imprisonment of feminine erotic experience, and the very excesses of its expression seem confounded by the narrowness of experiential possibility.[2]

The complaint furnishes such a pervasive representation of the feminine voice that its querulous tone and exiled condition has come to define a version of woman. In fact, the complaint provides a poetic articulation of the metaphysical condition that Luce Irigaray has termed *déréliction*, a state of abandonment, like that of Ariadne on Naxos, "left without hope, without help, without refuge" (Whitford 1991: 78). As Margaret Whitford explains, where "the fundamental ontological category for men is *habiter* (dwelling)," whether in "grottoes, huts, women, towns, language, concepts, theories," women's ontological status is dereliction, abandonment, a state that prevents their emergence as subjects (Whitford 1989: 112). Irigaray argues that language is one of the fundamental dwelling places in culture, a "house of language which for men even constitutes a substitute for his home in a body," but because "woman is used to construct it," "it is not available to her" (Whitford 1989: 112). While Irigaray is describing a metaphysical plight, whose remedy is really the creation of a female symbolic. I want to apply her term here in a much more limited sense.

Throughout this book I have juxtaposed early modern ventriloquizations of the feminine voice and twentieth-century feminist theorizations of voice. What I have sought to show is the continuity between historical appropriations and representations of feminine speaking and the characteristics recent feminists have attributed to woman's voice. Far from describing the unchanging, essential qualities of women's speech, however, I have argued that our interpretations of a female or feminine voice need to take into account the gender of who is speaking. Ventriloquism, as it is employed by writers of the early modern period, is a powerful strategy of silencing, of speaking on behalf of another, of disrupting the boundaries of a propertied utterance. Just as it has been used in patriarchal culture to mute or shape feminine speaking, feminists, particularly French feminists, are reappropriating ventriloquism to infiltrate, interrogate, and dismantle a language and a cultural lexicon that have confined women to a marginal and metaphoric status. In a sense, Irigaray's diagnosis of women's dereliction is a way of occupying the state of abandonment accorded to women by philosophical, mythological, and poetic discourses, an occupation that may well be a mimetic reversal of that condition of exile.

NOTES

INTRODUCTION: THE VOICE OF GENDER

1 One exception is Gail Reitenbach's (1990) "'Maydes are simple, some men say': Thomas Campion's Female Persona Poems," which analyses Campion's ventriloquized poems both with respect to their status as song and in relation to critical discussion of the dramatic monologue.

2 For an extensive discussion of the relationship between literary imitation and the imagery of rebirth, see Greene (1982).

3 Richard Lanham sees the Renaissance obsession with Ovid as a function of its valorization of the rhetorical mode – as opposed to the "serious" mode. The rhetorical mode privileges language, contingency, and the social, and both its educational system, which is based on imitation, and its practice of composition produce texts that seem to dramatize or at least thematize their relationship to earlier texts. See Lanham on the rhetorical mode (1976: 1–35) and on Ovid's relation to Virgil (1976: 48–64). Jacobson (1974), Verducci (1985), and Brownlee (1990) discuss the intertextual nature of the *Heroides*.

4 I am grateful to Victor Chan for bibliographic guidance and for his insights into this image.

1 TRAVESTIES OF VOICE: CROSS-DRESSING THE TONGUE

1 Elaine V. Beilin's (1987) *Redeeming Eve: Women Writers of the English Renaissance*, *Her Own Life: Autobiographical Writings by Seventeenth-Century Englishwomen* (1989), Katharina M. Wilson's (1987) collection, *Women Writers of the Renaissance and Reformation*, Ann Rosalind Jones's influential essays on the female Renaissance lyric, such as "Surprising Fame: Renaissance Gender Ideologies and Women's Lyric" (in *The Poetics of Gender*), the recent collection of essays from *English Literary Renaissance*, *Women in the Renaissance*, and (although covering a slightly later period) Elaine Hobby's *Virtue of Necessity: English Women's Writing 1649–88*, are examples of this important kind of gynocritical study. The influential volume *Rewriting the Renaissance:*

The Discourses of Sexual Difference in Early Modern Europe devotes its third section to "The Works of Women: Some Exceptions to the Rule of Patriarchy," and *The Renaissance Englishwoman in Print: Counterbalancing the Canon* features a number of essays on female Renaissance authors, as well as a bibliography of women writers from 1500–1640. Ann Rosalind Jones's recent study, *The Currency of Eros* (1990), provides both a critique of the gynocritical paradigm as advanced by Showalter and a theoretically powerful rationale for studying female writers. Jones invokes a model of cultural negotiation that is based on a Gramscian definition of hegemony, which sets up a dialogue or series of negotiations between dominant groups or institutions and less powerful groups (Jones 1990: 2–3). Where Showalter's gynocritical paradigm reinscribes a stable, individual subject, Jones's analyses are richly historicized and contextualized within class, institutional, and discursive frameworks.

2 As Tania Modleski has argued in "Feminism and the Power of Interpretation: Some Critical Readings," feminism and pluralism would seem to be antithetical, since pluralism emphasizes the "sovereignty of the individual subject and his right and ability to choose among any number of viable alternatives" (1986: 122), and feminism emphasizes the constraints on interpretation. Showalter seems to criticize the freedom of choice implicit in pluralism at the same time that she retains the stability of the female subject for her gynocritical project.

3 For an insightful treatment of postfeminism in theory and film, see Modleski's *Feminism Without Women: Culture and Criticism in a "Postfeminist" Age*. Modleski also discusses Showalter's introduction to *Speaking of Gender*, giving it a darker reading than I do, for she claims that Showalter marginalizes feminism, making it into a conduit to gender studies (1991: 5). Her focus on Showalter's text as a symptom of a larger postfeminist trend allows her to foreground what is certainly a disturbing feature, a sense that feminism has now become a stage, and that gender studies may be the new promised land. Nevertheless, there is nothing inherent in gender studies, or in Showalter's description of it, that is incompatible with feminism or a focus on women; I am not advocating gender studies as a replacement for feminism, but rather as a way of enlarging a gynocritical theory that relies on humanist theories of the stable subject.

4 When Showalter first introduces him, she identifies him as a member of a husband and wife team, who are engaged in the joint project of trying "to outline a model of women's culture" (1981: 261). Thereafter, she refers only to two essays written by Edwin Ardener.

5 Although I am interested in structures of doubleness, I am not advocating a system of binarities. Rather, ventriloquistic speaking has closer affinities with Marjorie Garber's designation of transvestism as the "third," "a mode of articulation, a way of describing a space of possibility. Three puts in question the idea of one; of identity, self-sufficiency, self-knowledge" (Garber 1992: 11). Ventriloquism may also be loosely related to Emile Benveniste's description of the "middle voice." Whereas grammatical voice customarily defines "diathesis," the

position or arrangement of the subject in the verb, and whereas verbs are usually distinguished by active or passive voice (who speaks and who is spoken), in the historical Indo-European, there was a third designation, the middle voice (Benveniste 1971: 145). Benveniste argues that, in the active voice, the subject performs an action in which s/he is not located, while, in the middle voice, the process centers on the subject, "the subject being inside the process" (Benveniste 1971: 148) (e.g. speaking, being born). One crucial distinction, then, is agency, since agency is curiously suspended in the middle voice, the subject being neither the instigator of the action nor the recipient of it. I would claim that ventriloquism occupies a similarly suspended state with respect to agency. See also Goldberg's discussion of the middle voice (Goldberg 1986: 8–9).

6 See especially Phillip Stubbes's *Anatomie of Abuses* for examples of this rhetoric. For two recent treatments of transvestism, see Stephen Greenblatt's "Fiction and Friction" and Marjorie Garber's *Vested Interests: Cross-Dressing & Cultural Anxiety*.

7 Louis Montrose notes that Belphoebe is compared both to Diana and also to Penthesilea, but the Amazonian allusion is invoked only to be mastered ("that famous Queene/ Of *Amazons*, whom *Pyrrhus* did destroy" (21.3.31)) (1983: 77), whereas Radigund flourishes unchecked by men.

8 For an account of the history of this error, and for an analysis of Spenser's and Sidney's treatments of it, see Victor Skretkowicz, "Hercules in Sidney and Spenser" (1980).

9 The thematizing of speech is apparent in the narrative of Hercules's birth, where a jealous Juno keeps her legs crossed and her fingers interlocked so that Alcmena cannot be delivered of her child. Galanthis, a servant, realizes what is happening and tricks Juno into loosening her hands and legs, thus allowing Hercules to be born. As a revenge on Galanthis for her part, Juno transforms her into a weasel, and in return for using her deceitful voice to aid her mistress, Galanthis is condemned to give birth through her mouth (Ovid 1977a: 25). While it is Hercules who is associated with eloquence in the Renaissance, it is worth noticing both how his nativity is associated with speech, and how a woman is punished with a birth process analogous to speech.

10 For the debate on whether women were suited to rule, see Benson (1985), Jordan (1987), Phillips (1941), and Roberts (1990).

11 Josephine A. Roberts (1990) provides an analysis of Radigund in relation to the debates about women's ability to rule and the dangers of gynocracy. She argues that the figure of Radigund needs to be read in context, and that the critical tendency to see in Radigund Spenser's disparagement of female rule must be qualified by his more positive portrayal of Britomart's inherent (but never actualized) ability to govern (1990: 192). While I agree with Roberts in general about Spenser's representation of women and political power, I claim that the Radigund episode nevertheless appears to carry both a burden of personal bitterness and an admonition, a chastising of the transgression of private affection into political action.

12 For a fuller discussion of the significance of weapons, see Sandra Clark

(1985: 170–1) and Linda Woodbridge's analysis of the pacifism of the Jacobean court (1984: 144, 168).

13 For an excellent transposition of Althusser's definition of ideology to gender, see de Lauretis (1987: 6–11).

14 The relationship between the author's sex and the pamphlets from the debate on women (especially Swetnam's and his respondents') has been addressed by Henderson and McManus. While their attention is focused primarily on female pseudonyms and their use, rather than anonymous pamphlets, their arguments still have relevance here. Arguing that men use female pen names when there is some benefit to be derived (such as their incursion into a generic territory dominated by women – like the Gothic romance), they assert that in the Renaissance, "a female name on a defense treatise was an anomaly which would enhance neither the prestige nor the sales of the work" (1985: 21). Henderson and McManus go on to notice that there is ample precedent for men to write defenses of women under their own names or anonymously, and that the "consistency of tone, the attitude toward men, and the passionate conviction" of the pamphlets they examine (which have female signatures affixed to them) "support their authors' claims to be women" (1985: 21). Although I sympathize with this position, the sincerity and passion of the speaker hardly seems like a standard by which to judge the gender of the author, and, furthermore, this formula doesn't explain the complicated question of authorship in *Haec-Vir*.

15 Given the similarities between their strategies (although not their interpretations), Kofman's attack on Irigaray throughout *The Enigma of Woman* provides a disturbing subtext. Even though Kofman is astute about recording Freud's own revisions of his writings – which themselves argue for the provisionality of textual truth – and even though she enters Freud's voice with impunity when she ventriloquizes him, she nevertheless berates Irigaray for using the French rather than the German text of "Femininity." She argues that "going back to the German text is not a matter of trying to 'save' Freud at all costs... but only of manifesting the minimal intellectual honesty that consists in criticizing an author in terms of what he has said rather than what someone has managed to have him say" (Kofman 1985: 14).

2 FOLLY AND HYSTERIA: DUPLICITIES OF SPEECH

1 See *A short, yet, sound commentarie; written on that woorthie worke called; The Prouerbs of Salomon* (Anon 1589: Sig. C3) and John Marbeck, *A Booke of Notes and Commonplaces* (1581: 503). Terence Cave's analysis of Erasmus's *Lingua* and his reading of Folly's voice brilliantly reveal the duplicity at work in Renaissance ideas of the tongue. Cave also emphasizes Erasmus's recognition of the alimentary and sexual functions of the tongue, a depiction that aligns Folly herself with the synecdoche of the tongue, and as I go on to argue, female speech with the body (Cave 1979: 164–7).

2 For a concise formulation of this position, see Derrida's (1973) essay "The Voice That Keeps Silence" in *Speech and Phenomena and Other Essays on Husserl's Theory of Signs* and Christopher Norris's (1982) explication of phonocentrism in *Deconstruction: Theory and Practice*.

3 The style of this utterance is what Clarence Miller has called "casual-sophistical" (1988: 280). Claiming that there are three styles which correspond roughly to the tripartite structure of *Folly*, Miller observes that the casual-sophistical style predominates in the first section, and its stylistic features are rhetorical questions, parentheses, and afterthoughts – all characteristics that would enhance the supposedly extemporaneous nature of Folly's speech.

4 Sister Geraldine Thompson notes this slippage, for instance (1973: 66), as does Miller (Erasmus 1979: xii).

5 For a theoretical analysis of the linkage between laughter, the mother, and the infant, see Kristeva's "Place Names" (1980: 280–6) and her comments on laughter as a rupture in the symbolic in *Revolution in Poetic Language* (1984: 222–5). In both cases, laughter is linked to the drives, to the "riant, porous boundary" (1980: 284) between child and mother, and hence to the chora. Laughter stands for Kristeva as, among other things, a vocalization that precedes and then co-exists with language, a semiotic disposition that begins as "riant spaciousness" (1980: 283). Laughter is thus associated with the imaginary or the semiotic, the maternal body, and the drives, and it reemerges in the symbolic as an irruption that carries traces of this semiotic disruption, of a non-linguistic but expressive vocalization. The affinities between Kristeva's description of the semiotic (and laughter), the maternal, and the artistic and Erasmus's characterization of those touched by madness or ecstasy are striking.

6 It is also true that, against this double-voiced discourse of disguise, Erasmus sets up a nostalgic, utopian vision of unitariness. He images a golden age when there was no need for multiple languages or grammar or rhetoric, a time before the madness that motivates scientific or geographical exploration was born. It is in this context that he speaks of a Nature that loathes disguise and hates artifice (Erasmus 1979: 51–2). While this portrait of Nature seems antithetical to Erasmus's insistence on illusion, it is akin to Folly's depiction of herself as always recognizable and unchanging. As desirable as this correspondence between appearance and being is, Erasmus implicitly argues that it is not attainable through nostalgic return, but, paradoxically, only through the doublenesses of human folly, language, and history.

7 Robert Burton offers a similar account in *The Anatomy of Melancholy*, which he names the melancholy of Maids, Nuns, and Widows (Burton 1977, 1: 414). In his *Disputations Touching the Generation of Animals*, William Harvey sees the uterus as an organ of desire, which, if not satisfied by marriage, will produce hysterical passions that may become so intense that the woman will seem to be moonstruck or possessed by an evil demon (Harvey 1981: 44). He notes that, in some cases of hysteria, the afflicted women suffered prolapses of the uterus, and that this had a positive effect, since the uterus could be chilled by the external air, and

the womb would then return to its proper place (1981: 413).

8 "Le rire de la méduse" appeared in *L'arc* in 1975, the same year that *La jeune née* was published, so the overlap between the two texts is perhaps not surprising. What interests me is the fluidity of Cixous's treatment of her other texts at certain points in *La jeune née* and her foregrounding of the authorial relation at others. Her citation of her *Portrait du Soleil* in the "Exchange," for instance, juxtaposes her interpretation and ventriloquization of Dora with Freud's, a strategy that "silently" questions what it means to have a feminist appropriate the hysteric's voice after Freud has "colonized" that discourse for the purposes of (male) psychoanalytic theory.

9 My interpretation of what Cixous is doing through her identificatory strategies differs markedly from Toril Moi's reading. Moi says that this "constant return to biblical and mythological imagery signals her investment in the world of myth: a world that, like the distant country of fairy tales is perceived as pervasively meaningful, as closure and unity. The mythical or religious discourse presents a universe where all difference, struggle and discord can in the end be satisfactorily resolved" (1985: 116). In fact, a large part of the so-called mythological section that Moi refers to is Cixous's feminist re-working of the *Oresteia*, in which she interrogates the cultural myth of the family (paternal, filial, and maternal roles). Her reading explicitly challenges Engels's and Freud's ideas about the origin of the family, particularly its transition from matriarchy to patriarchy, and, in doing so, Cixous reveals how western cultural myths about familial structure, justice, and the law come to acquire the status of mythic truth. Her return to classical texts, then, is not a search for the comforts of closure and unity, but a radical (in the etymological sense of the word) gesture of destabilization.

10 That Moi uses a Derridean theoretical paradigm is evident from her choice of words: "Woman, in other words, is wholly and physically present in her voice – and writing is no more than the extension of this self-identical prolongation of the speech act" (1985: 114). The notion of self-identity is an aspect of phonocentrism but not of *écriture feminine* as propounded by Cixous. As Moi goes on to say in the next sentence, a woman's voice is not her own, but is an echo of another voice (1985: 114), and the origin of *this* voice is unrecoverable (Clément/Cixous 1986: 93).

11 Domna Stanton has perceptively analysed Cixous's references to the mother as a metaphor. Stanton's difficulty with Cixous's program lies not in its purported biological essentialism, but in the nature of metaphor itself, which, as a trope of similitude, seems to reaffirm both an ontology and a philosophy of sameness (Stanton 1986: 161).

12 My understanding of Cixous's project has been greatly enhanced by Margaret Whitford's interpretation of Irigaray's writing (1989). Whitford's analysis answers the charges of essentialism that have been levelled against Irigaray (and, by extension, Cixous) by reorienting understanding; she argues that Irigaray seeks to bring about a change in the symbolic, and that what she has been accused of advocating in fact constitutes her diagnosis of what is wrong (1989: 106).

3 MATRIX AS METAPHOR: MIDWIFERY AND THE CONCEPTION OF VOICE

1 Elaine Showalter's (1979, 1981) distinction between "feminist critique" and "gynocritics," operates, as I have claimed in Chapter 1, on an implicit definition of voice and authorship as stable categories. Where Anglo-American critiques of French feminist writing have accused theorists like Hélène Cixous and Luce Irigaray of essentialism, of describing an *écriture feminine* that emerges from a biologically female body, in fact, as Alice Jardine (1985) has argued, French feminism has tended to be preoccupied with subjectivity and enunciation in ways that should modify this charge. In "The Laugh of the Medusa," Cixous speaks of writing in "white ink," a phrase that has been interpreted as mother's milk because Cixous appears to gloss it that way herself. While it certainly operates as a metaphor of the female body, it is also an intertextual echo of Jacques Derrida's "White Mythology." For Derrida, white mythology is a metaphysics or "white ink" "which reassembles and reflects the culture of the West," an invisible inscription that asserts itself even as it erases itself (1982: 213). Although I cannot examine all the implications here, it seems clear that Cixous's formulation must be read as a more complicated and multivalent utterance than it might at first appear. See Jones (1985) and Whitford (1989) for two different treatments of the problem of essentialism.

2 Jonathan Goldberg's important study, *Voice Terminal Echo*, for example, never explicitly addresses the question of gender, even though his frequent allusions to Ovidian myth refer to women (Echo, Philomela, and Medusa). Notable exceptions are Elaine Showalter's *Speaking of Gender* and Nancy K. Miller's treatment of authorship in *Subject to Change*.

3 See especially Derrida's "White Mythology" and Paul de Man's *Allegories of Reading*. Hayden White has memorably argued, for instance, that narratives of history are fundamentally tropological, and he employs the four "master" tropes to distinguish among modes of nineteenth-century historical consciousness.

4 The books and essays include Rich, Kristeva, Blumenfeld-Kosinski, Friedman, Suleiman, Treichler, Smith. One obvious reason for this focus is the influx of women into the academic profession, which is, of course, both the result of and a contributing element in the development of the feminist movement. This demographic change has prompted a consideration of women and the role of gender in disciplines that have traditionally excluded women's experience. For a discussion of late twentieth-century issues associated with childbirth, see Treichler (1990). Katharine Eisaman Maus's essay "A Womb of His Own: Male Renaissance Poets in the Female Body" (1991), which I read after I had written this chapter, examines the trope of male birth in some of the same ways that I do. Where her focus is spatial – the interior of the female body as a place of refuge – my emphasis is on the usurpation of what issues from that body (child/voice).

5 See Marcus's discussion of Mary Tudor's pregnancies.

6 In her autobiography Alice Thorton describes the nine children she bore, providing a graphic account of the pain and danger childbirth engendered for both mother and child in the seventeenth century (Graham 1989: 147–64). See also Dorothy McLaren's (1986) discussion of fertility and lactation from 1570–1720 for an analysis of class, infant mortality, fertility, and wet-nursing.

7 For a discussion of contraception, abortion, and infanticide, see McLaren.

8 Chamberlen's aspirations for gain in midwifery were frustrated, but he continued to evolve schemes for gain, which included the design and regulation of baths and bath stoves, a proposal for the propelling of carriages by wind, and a grant for the invention and perfection of phonetic writing (Aveling 1977: 59–105).

9 For a history of the representation of caesarean birth in the period, see Blumenfeld-Kosinski (1990). Her study provides an instructive case-study of surgical intervention in child-birth, and there are certainly many points of intersection between that history and the medicalization of midwifery, not only through the inclusion of men and surgeons at childbirth, but also through the addition of technology. While neither technology nor men necessarily implied the colonization of childbirth, it was nevertheless true that the caesarean offered a metaphoric fantasy (grounded, of course, in the actual surgical procedure) of a birth that bypassed nature and the female body ("not of woman born"). Eve's birth from Adam's side in *Paradise Lost* (VIII: 465 ff) contains echoes of a caesarean (woman born from a male body though an incision in his side), and there are complex associations with the caesarean in Marvell's "An Horatian Ode." Cromwell is linked to Caesar in the poem (101), and his star "like the three-forked lightening, first/ Breaking the clouds where it was nursed,/Did thorough his own side/ His fiery way divide" (13–16), as if, in a violent natural image, he were giving birth to himself.

10 Written around 1672, *Observations on Midwifery* probably circulated in manuscript, but was not actually published until the nineteenth century.

11 The intersection between transvestism and gynecological knowledge is staged in a revealing anecdote recounted by Jacques Guillimeau in *Childbirth, or, the Happy Delivery of Women*. He cites examples of prominent midwives in biblical or classical literature, and among them is Agnodicea, an Athenian woman, who, despite a law that forbade women access to the study of medicine, wished to become a physician. She cut off her hair, disguised herself as a man, and apprenticed herself to a male physician. Once she had learned "physicke," she offered to assist a woman who was troubled in her "naturall parts," but the afflicted woman refused out of modesty because she assumed that the physician was a man. Agnodicea then revealed herself to be a woman and cured her patient; indeed, she thereafter became so successful in curing Athenian women of their gynecological ailments, that her male colleagues were no longer called to assist women. They retaliated, accusing her of seducing her female patients. When she put aside her garments, showing herself to be a woman, they accused her of an even greater transgression: studying medicine, which was, of course, forbidden by law. The Athenian women heard of Agnodicea's plight, and they came in a body to the Areopagites,

pleaded on her behalf, and were ultimately successful in having the law prohibiting women from practising "physicke" revoked (Guillimeau 1635: 80–1). Despite the happy ending, the story reveals both how difficult it was for a woman to study medicine (she must cross-dress to do so), and how bitterly contested and competitive the practice was. That Agnodicea should be charged with sexual misconduct suggests that the medical and sexual treatments of the female body are not as distinct as medical discourse claims; medicine can be used to regulate female sexual behavior, just as sexuality can exert a disciplinary function within medical circles.

12 I am indebted to Thomas M. Lennon for calling this reference to my attention.

13 That Socrates's mother was a midwife was known in the Renaissance; Jacques Guillemeau cites this fact in his tract on midwifery, *Childbirth, or, the Happy Delivery of Women*.

14 I realize that this formulation seems to argue against the psychoanalytic paradigm in which the mother is associated with an Imaginary, prelinguistic world against which the child must eventually turn in order to enter the Symbolic order. The psychoanalytic paradigm seems counter to the crucial role the mother plays in language acquisition (registered in the phrase "mother tongue") and early education, both in early modern England, and in twentieth-century North American culture. For a theoretical treatment of this question, see Silverman, especially her discussion of Kristeva's "Place Names" (Silverman 1988: 72–140).

15 Although I would not want to generalize from a few examples, it seems likely that a female poet's use of the pregnancy/birth trope would be freighted with different connotations. When Sidney's niece, Lady Mary Wroth, employs the metaphor – as she does in sonnet 35 of *Pamphilia to Amphilanthus* – it expresses the anxiety associated with false hope: "Faulce hope which feeds butt to destroy, and spill/ What itt first breeds; unaturall to the birth/ Of thine owne wombe; conceaving butt to kill,/And plenty gives to make the greater dearth." The metaphor captures both the uncertainty of what resides in the womb ("unaturall") and the possibility of its loss, both sentiments that must have occurred frequently to women in the period. Edward, Lord Herbert of Cherbury, sent Lady Mary a poem congratulating her on the birth her child by the Earl of Pembroke that draws on both the literal and metaphoric senses of childbirth; where he adds poetic "feet" to prose, she has the ability "as everybody knows," to "Add to those feet fine dainty toes" (Wroth 1983: 26).

16 The veiled woman also points, of course, to the enticing figure who attracts partly because of her unknowability. See Derrida, *Spurs* (1979: 49 ff), on the image of truth as a veiled woman in Nietzsche's writings.

17 Julia Kristeva calls pregnancy "the threshold of culture and nature" and refers to the transitional function of the maternal as a "middle" or "interval," a border or crossroads (1987: 259, 254).

18 This engraving is reproduced in Donnison (1988: 101), and in Ehrenreich and English (1973: 20).

19 Kristeva offers a number of different definitions of the chora; in addition

to the one I am working with here that figures the oneness of mother and child and refers to a moment in the subject's psychic development, she offers a second explanation, one that posits the internalization of the mother, so that the chora becomes a "mobile receptacle," organizing and regulating the subject's drives (see 1984: 25–30). In "Place Names," Kristeva appears to offer a third interpretation of the chora, in which it becomes the site to which the subject relegates the mother; in this definition, the chora is associated most clearly with the semiotic, the repressed in language that resurfaces in poetic or psychotic language. For a fuller discussion, see Silverman (1988: 102–9).

20 Marvell's epigrammatic poem, "Upon a Eunuch: A Poet," enunciates the generative substitution that produces poetry:

> Don't believe yourself sterile, although, an exile from women,
> You cannot thrust a sickle at the virgin harvest,
> And sin in our fashion. Fame will be continually pregnant by you,
> And you will snatch the nine sisters from the mountain;
> Echo too, often struck, will bring forth musical offspring.

While the poet does not give birth to his poems, his ability to write seems to be based on his status as a eunuch, a condition that renders his sexuality indeterminate (he is neither man nor woman). Yet, even though the poet is castrated, he impregnates Fame and causes Echo to produce offspring, a kind of perversion (or transcendence) of nature reminiscent of "The Mower Against Gardens," where the eunuch figures and where the cherry procreates without a sex.

21 Thomas Docherty's analysis is an exception. His interpretation is similar to mine in the sense that he, too, concentrates on the confusion or overlapping of Donne's name or voice and that of Elizabeth Drury. However, where I focus on maternity, pregnancy, and virginity, he discusses the relationship in terms of a marriage, the intersection between the notions of the medium, the hymen, and the angel (1986: 227–31).

22 There has, of course, been a great deal of debate about the genre of the *Anniversaries*. Frank Manley discusses this problem in *John Donne: The Anniversaries*.

23 See Stanley Fish's analysis of voice in *Lycidas* (Fish 1981), which examines the disruptions in the coherence of the first-person voice as a tension between personality and anonymity.

24 Much subsequent criticism has focused on identifying the idea represented by the woman, whether as historical figure (Queen Elizabeth), as archetype or symbol (Astraea, the Virgin, Christ, the indwelling logos), as allegory (Lady Wisdom, Lady Virtue, Lady Justice), as saint (Lucy, pattern of Christian regeneration and illumination), or in terms of traditions like Neoplatonism and Petrarchism (Lewalski 1973: 108).

25 See Bald (1970: 249–52). The child was buried on 24 January, but Donne was still ignorant of what had happened in April. Nevertheless, Donne's letters do indicate his profound concern for the health of his wife and child.

26 Bald cites a letter from Lady Burghley, Sir Robert's sister, which speaks of Lady Drury's "great belly" (Bald 1986: 103). The pregnancy was

apparently a rumor, but it appears that at least others – if not the Drurys – were preoccupied with the possibility that she would have another child.

27 His step-father was, after all, John Syminges, who had been President of the Royal College of Physicians several times (Bald 1970: 37), the house he moved to when he was eleven adjoined St Bartholomew's Hospital (Carey 1981: 136), and he may well have had the chance to observe dissection first hand. His witnessing of executions seems to be registered in the viscerality of his simile of the beheaded man that opens the *Second Anniversarie*. For an account of the cultural history of anatomies and "spectacular" nature of the anatomy theatre and its audience, see Sawday (1990). See also Don Cameron Allen's essay on Donne's knowledge of Renaissance medicine (Allen 1975).

4 VENTRILOQUIZING SAPPHO, OR THE LESBIAN MUSE

1 All quotations from Donne's poetry, unless otherwise noted, are from this edition.

2 "Sappho to Philaenis" is not the only instance of his assumption of the feminine voice, of course; such poems as "Woman's Constancy" and "Confined Love" see the question of fidelity from a feminine perspective, and in "Break of Day" it is a woman who speaks the *aubade*, translating the sun's voyeuristic gaze into words (for "light hath no tongue"), just as Donne in turn gives voice to the woman. In Holy Sonnet No. 14, the speaker occupies the position of the Petrarchan lady who is besieged by the lover. Although the lover is in this case God, the ultimate union is imaged in paradoxically erotic terms; unless "enthral[ed]," the speaker never will be free nor ever chaste unless "ravish[ed]" by God. The erotic conquering that the speaker so ardently desires entails an entering, possessing, and radical refashioning that has in western culture tended to be the prerogative of the male. In both of these poems, Donne is writing within well-established conventions, and the employment of the feminine perspective as central inverts and remakes tradition, establishing Donne as master rather than slave of inherited forms. The male poet's use of the feminine voice in these cases would thus seem to afford a means of countering a received poetic tradition whose authority always threatens to overwhelm the poet's singular identity.

3 John Carey, who calls it "the first female homosexual love poem in English," discusses the poem as it thematically replicates Donne's obsession with union and merging (1981: 270–1). G.R. Wilson has included it in his discussion of mirror imagery in Donne's poetry (1969: 107–21), and Florence Verducci refers to it in her analysis of Ovid's Sapphic epistle (*Ovid's Toyshop of the Heart*: Epistulae Heroidum). The most sustained and important essay on "Sappho to Philaenis" is James Holstun's article "'Will You Rent Our Ancient Love Asunder?': Lesbian Elegy in Donne, Marvell, and Milton."

4 The phrase is, of course, from Thomas Carew's *Elegie*, which has

generated a tradition of Donne as a typically "masculine" poet, one whose style is marked by force (even violence, according to Samuel Johnson's famous definition of metaphysical wit) and an apparent disregard for the sweetness and regularity of conventional verse. Ben Jonson provides a characteristic example of this categorization of style according to gender in *Timber* (1975: 395–6).

5 Much recent feminist work on Sappho has focused on her power as a female precursor for women figures, as the originary figure in a matrilineal poetic genealogy. See Susan Gubar's "Sapphistries" (1984), and Joan DeJean, "Sappho's Leap: Domesticating the Woman Writer" (1985), and "Fictions of Sappho" (1987).

6 Holstun (1987: 836). He cites Judith Brown's study, *Immodest Acts: The Life of a Lesbian Nun in Renaissance Italy*, which has noted the paucity of references in legal, literary, and philosophical records to lesbianism (a nineteenth-century term) (1987: 835–6). Even assuming that one could overcome the "conceptual distortions" incumbent on a reconstruction of lesbianism in the early modern period, Holstun argues, unless the mechanism of its "voicelessness" is revealed and unless "we take care not to perpetuate the exclusion of lesbianism" by taking the isolated cases as "ignorable oddities" (1987: 836), we risk complicity in the larger structure of censorship. My own argument about Ovid and Donne sees the treatment of Sappho by subsequent poets (and some critics) as a heightened version of a general suppression of the female voice, a project of cultural silencing which would, of course, be especially threatened by the preeminence of Sappho's reputation and by the erotic self-sufficiency of lesbian love. See also Lillian Faderman's (1981) *Surpassing the Love of Men*, which, in writing a history of lesbian love, seeks both to break the silence surrounding lesbianism and to analyse its changing representations.

7 The manuscript history of the Sapphic epistle was separate from that of the *Heroides*; besides excerpts from it in the twelfth-century *Florilegium Gallicum*, the letter appears in only one medieval source in conjunction with the other fourteen Ovidian epistles, and the evidence suggests that it was copied from a different source. From 1420 onwards, it is to be found in some 200 manuscripts, all derived from a common source. Daniel Heinsius established its order in the *Heroides* by placing it in the fifteenth position in his edition of 1629. See Reynolds's *Texts and Transmissions: A Survey of the Latin Classics* (1983: 268–72) for a detailed history, Albert R. Baca, "Ovid's Epistle from Sappho to Phaon (*Heroides 15*)," (1971: 29–38), and Howard Jacobson, *Ovid's* Heroides (1974) for the arguments about its transmission.

8 For more extensive treatments of Donne's Ovidianism, see Leishman (1959), Gill (1972), and Armstrong (1977).

9 Howard Jacobson has focused on the poetic relationship between Ovid and Sappho, and his discussion of the Sapphic echoes in Ovid's letter is invaluable (1974: 277–99). Linda S. Kauffman in *Discourses of Desire: Gender, Genre, and Epistolary Fiction* explores the poem as a travestied expression of female desire (1986: 50–61), and Florence Verducci's *Ovid's Toyshop of the Heart* provides a detailed analysis of the epistle in relation to the other Heroidean letters.

10 With the exception of a few metrical experiments (Ben Jonson's line from *The Sad Shepherd*, "But best the dear good angel of the spring,/ The nightingale" and Sidney's translation of Sappho's ode into anacreontics in the Second Eclogues of the *Arcadia*), it appears that most Renaissance poets knew Sappho only as she was mediated by the portrait of her in Ovid's epistle. Lyly's *Sapho and Phao*, for instance, depends heavily on the biographical details that Ovid supplies.

11 This is an argument familiar from Lanham, which recognized Ovid's challenge to the legitimating stability of Virgil's *Aeneid* (1976: 48–64), a subversion that is apparent in Ovid's intercalation of erotic incidents in his retelling of Aeneas's adventures in the *Metamorphoses.*

12 All citations from *Heroides 15* are from Verducci's text and translation.

13 Patricia Klindienst Joplin's (1984) analysis of the Philomela myth reveals the crucial role that gender and power play in the story, elements that she claims were elided in Geoffrey Hartman's reading (1970), which tends to mystify rather than expose the violence that subtends the myth. She argues persuasively that the Philomela story is about the exchange of woman, an issue that makes it particularly pertinent to the issue of literary property I am discussing.

14 Joan DeJean cites an ancient commentator on Lucian who compares Sappho to a nightingale: "As far as Sappho's body went, she was exceedingly disgusting to behold, being short and of dark complexion – resembling a nightingale whose tiny form was enshrouded in shapeless wings" (1989: viii).

15 Don Cameron Allen's learned note on Philaenis (1964: 188–91) offers three plausible sources, one of which is the *Greek Anthology*. He suggests that Donne may also have found her in Martial's epigram (VII, 66), which describes her as "play[ing] handball and lift[ing] weights in the dusty palaestra and whose supra-masculine drinking and eating were exceeded by her perverted lust for young girls of whom she devoured eleven at a sitting" (1964: 190). Calderinus's commentary on Martial (which Donne almost certainly knew) connects Sappho and this athletic Philaenis and refers indirectly to a second Philaenis, the author of erotic poetry. Cameron argues that these two figures, as well as the chaste and defamed Philaenis of the *Greek Anthology*, combined in Donne's mind to form his Philaenis. Although Cameron does not mention it, there is a second reference to Philaenis in Martial's epigrams (VII, 70), where she appears as a *tribade*; in the epigram just preceding (VII, 69), which praises the taste and learning of Theophila as transcending that of her sex, there is a reference to Sappho. Sappho herself would have praised Theophila's verses, we are told, but Theophila was more chaste than Sappho. The proximity of Sappho and Philaenis in these two epigrams, together with the idea of praising (or loving) another woman poet, provides another conjunction that may have influenced Donne's choice of Philaenis.

16 Aelian provides one of the earliest references to the "double" Sappho in his *Varia Historia*. In the words of Abraham Fleming's English translation of 1576, "*Plato* the sonne of *Aristo*, numbreth *Sapho* the Versifyer, and the daughter of *Scamandronymous* amonge such as were wise, lerned

and skilful. I heare also, that there was another *Sapho* in *Lesbus*: which was a stronge whore, and an arrant strumpet" (quoted in *Works of John Lyly*, 1967, 2: 365). Twentieth-century critics, such as Robinson (1924) have expressed their disbelief that anyone as licentious as Sappho was reputed to have been could have written such exquisite poetry.

17 Michel Foucault (1986) examines this dialogue in some detail. He does not comment on the discussion of lesbianism, however, but focuses instead on the opposition between heterosexual love and male homosexuality.

18 Thomas Docherty has a perceptive discussion of women in Donne's poetry in terms of the metaphor of colonization (1986: 51–87), an idea that has been compellingly articulated by Hélène Cixous in "The Laugh of the Medusa," where she suggests that woman has been constructed as the "dark continent" (1981: 47).

19 Thomas Docherty refers to a passage in *Measure for Measure*, where fish become a metaphor for female genitals (1986: 236), and this sense may underwrite the erotic fantasy of "The Bait," where the fish amorously swim to the woman, happier to catch her than she it. Donne uses a similar image in a verse epistle to Sir Henry Wotton, where he recommends that Wotton behave "as/ Fishes glide, leaving no print where they pass,/ Nor making sound" (Milgate 1967: 56–7).

20 Dryden 1964: 333. Grierson notes that "Sappho to Philaenis" is very probably the source of Dryden's metaphor (1912: 2: 91).

21 Lee Patterson has explored this linkage in relation to Chaucer's Wife of Bath, a discussion to which my own formulation is indebted (1983: 656–95). For a more extended treatment, see Patricia Parker's (1987) analysis of the anatomical and rhetorical aspects of dilation.

22 See especially Joseph Swetnam's comments on speech and sexuality (1615), Linda Woodbridge's analysis of the pamphlet literature (1984), Henderson and McManus's treatment of the gender controversy (1985), and Lisa Jardine's examination of the specific ligature of eroticism and female speech in her chapter on the figure of the shrew (1983).

23 Gloss of the Geneva Bible to Ecclesiastes xiii, 18. Quoted in Milton 1957: 569. J.J.M. Tobin refers to the hyena's traditional attributes of bisexuality, capacity for mimicry, and uncleanness, as well as its association with Circean enchantment (1977: 89–90).

24 Ian Maclean provides a detailed summary of the tradition that associates women with these qualities (1980). He locates one origin for the tradition in Aristotle's *Nichomachean Ethics*, where these particular virtues appear to be regarded as involuntary and hence "imperfect," effectively "exclud[ing] [women] from Aristotle's moral universe" (1980: 51).

25 See Goldberg (1986) for a theoretical meditation on the problematic of voice in Renaissance texts.

26 I am indebted to Gordon Braden for calling my attention to this verse letter.

27 In "Fiction and Friction" Stephen Greenblatt analyses two instances of transvestism and supposed lesbianism in France. In the first instance, an incident reported by Montaigne, a woman dresses as a man, marries a woman, but is then discovered to be a transvestite. Condemned for using

"'illicit devices to supply her defect in sex'" (Greenblatt 1988: 66), she is convicted and executed. In the second case, a servant dressed as a woman claims to be a man, but the sex of the man is disputed. The couple is accused of sodomy, and the "man" is charged with being a "tribade," who has "abused" his female lover with his unnaturally enlarged clitoris (Greenblatt 1988: 73–4). In both cases, the supposed lesbianism seems to have been condemned because prosthetic devices were employed. In T.W.'s letter, however, the lesbian union seems to be chaste precisely because its eroticism involves "tickling" and "rubbing" (the etymology of tribade is, of course, from the Gk. *tribas*, "rubbing"), rather than penetration.

28 Jane Gallop argues that in French, *lèvres* always refers (also) to the mouth, and that the application of *lèvres* to the vulva (*les lèvres de la vulve*) is necessarily figurative (Gallop 1988: 98).

29 Elaine Scarry has drawn attention to Donne's extraordinary emphasis on touch, which she argues is his model for the senses (Scarry 1988: 88). While this is true, his sense of touch is often mediated or supplemented by vision.

30 Irigaray's idea of female language has been condemned by feminists like Toril Moi (1985) because it was seen to be essentialist (since it emanated from a supposedly essential female body). Both Diana Fuss (1989) and Margaret Whitford (1991) have challenged this reading in ways that have far-reaching implications for future Anglo-American readings of French feminists texts. My own reading emphasizes the dimension of mimicry at work in Irigaray's texts; by providing a historical context for her metaphor (the two lips, the double mouths), I argue that she is subversively employing a traditionally patriarchal definition of women.

CODA

1 For an analysis of Tudor complaints as a genre, see Dubrow (1986).

2 For an account of a female poet using the model of Ovid's *Heroides* subversively, that is, occupying the same position to which Ovid's ventriloquism has assigned her, see Ann Rosalind Jones's discussion of Isabella Whitney (Jones 1990: 43–57).

REFERENCES

Allen, Don Cameron (1964) "Donne's Sappho to Philaenis," *English Language Notes*, 1: 188–91.
—— (1975) "John Donne's Knowledge of Renaissance Medicine," in *Essential Articles for the Study of John Donne's Poetry*, ed. John R. Roberts, Hamden, CT: Archon Books.
Anon (1589) " *Short, yet, sound commentarie; written on that woorthie worke called; The Prouerbs of Salomon*, London.
Arms, Suzanne (1975) *Immaculate Deception*, Boston: Houghton Mifflin.
Armstrong, Alan (1977) "The Apprenticeship of John Donne: Ovid and the *Elegies*," *ELH*, 44: 419–42.
Althusser, Louis (1971) *Lenin and Philosophy*, trans. Ben Brewster, New York: Monthly Review Press.
Aveling, J.H. (1977) *The Chamberlens and the Midwifery Forceps*, London: J. and A. Churchill (1882 rpt), New York: AMS Press.
Baca, Albert R. (1971) "Ovid's Epistle from Sappho to Phaon (*Heroides 15*)," *Transactions and Proceedings of the American Philological Society*, 102: 29–38.
Bacon, Francis (1960) *The New Organon and Related Writings*, ed. Fulton H. Anderson, Indianapolis: Bobbs-Merrill.
Bakhtin, Mikhail (1981) *The Dialogic Imagination*, trans. Caryl Emerson and Michael Holquist, Austin: University of Texas Press.
Bald, R.C. (1970) *John Donne: A Life*, Oxford: Oxford University Press.
—— (1986) *Donne and the Drurys* (1959, rpt), Westport, CT: Greenwood Press.
Barthes, Roland (1978) *A Lover's Discourse: Fragments*, trans. Richard Howard, New York: Hill & Wang.
Beilin, Elaine V. (1987) *Redeeming Eve: Women Writers of the English Renaissance*, Princeton: Princeton University Press.
Belenky, Mary Field, Clinchy, Bythe McVicker, Goldberger, Nancy Rule, and Tarule, Jill Mattuck (1986) *Women's Ways of Knowing: The Development of Self, Voice, and Mind*, New York: Basic Books.
Belsey, Catherine (1985) *The Subject of Tragedy, Identity and Difference in Renaissance Drama*, London: Methuen.
Benson, Pamela Joseph (1985) "Rule Virginia: Protestant Theories of

Female Regiment in *The Faerie Queene*," *English Literary Renaissance*, 15: 277–92.

Benveniste, Emile (1971) *Problems in General Linguistics*, trans. Mary Elizabeth Meek, Coral Gables, FL: University of Miami Press.

Blumenfeld-Kosinski, Renate (1990) *Not of Woman Born: Representations of Caesarean Birth in Medieval and Renaissance Culture*, Ithaca: Cornell University Press.

Bordo, Susan (1987) *The Flight to Objectivity: Essays on Cartesianism & Culture*, Albany: State University of New York Press.

Brown, Judith (1986) *Immodest Acts: The Life of a Lesbian Nun in Renaissance Italy*, New York: Oxford University Press.

Brownlee, Marina Scordilis (1990) *The Severed Word: Ovid's* Heroides *and the* Novela Sentimental, Princeton: Princeton University Press.

Burton, Robert (1977) *Anatomy of Melancholy*, New York: Vintage Books.

Butler, Judith (1991) "Imitation and Gender Insubordination," in *Inside/Out: Lesbian Theories, Gay Theories*, New York: Routledge: 13–31.

Byatt, A.S. (1990) *Possession*, London: Vintage.

Carew, Thomas (1989) *The Poems of Thomas Carew*, ed. Arthur Vincent, New York: Charles Scribner's Sons.

Carey, John (1981) *John Donne: Life, Mind and Art*, London: Faber & Faber.

Castle, Terry J. (1979) "Lab'ring Bards: Birth *Topoi* and English Poetics 1660–1820," *Journal of English and Germanic Philology* 78: 193–208.

Cave, Terence (1979) *The Cornucopian Text: Problems of Writing in the French Renaissance*, Oxford: Clarendon Press.

Chamberlen, Peter (1647) *A Voice in Rhama, Or, The Crie of Women and Children*, London.

Child, Francis James (ed.) (1965) *The English and Scottish Popular Ballads*, New York: Dover.

Cixous, Hélène (1981) "The Laugh of the Medusa," in *New French Feminisms*, ed. Elaine Marks and Isabelle de Courtivron (1980, rpt), New York: Schocken Books: 245–64.

Cixous, Hélène and Clément, Catherine (1986) *The Newly Born Woman*, trans. Betsy Wing, Minneapolis: University of Minnesota Press.

Clark, Alice (1968) *Working Life of Women in the Seventeenth Century* (1919, rpt.) London: Frank Cass & Co. Ltd.

Clark, Sandra (1985) "*Hic Mulier, Haec-Vir*, and the Controversy over Masculine Women," *Studies in Philology*, 82 (2): 157–83.

Culler, Jonathan (1981) *The Pursuit of Signs: Semiotic, Literature, Deconstruction*, Ithaca: Cornell University Press.

—— (1985) "Changes in the Study of the Lyric," in *Lyric Poetry: Beyond New Criticism*, ed. Chaviva Hosek and Patricia Parker, Ithaca: Cornell University Press: 38–54.

Culpeper, Nicholas (1651) *A Directory for Midwives*, London.

—— (1680) *The Compleat Midwife's Practice Enlarged*, London.

Cunnington, Phillis and Lucas, Catherine (1972) *Costume for Births, Marriages, and Deaths*, New York: Barnes and Noble.

DeJean, Joan (1985) "Sappho's Leap: Domesticating the Woman Writer," *L'Esprit Créateur*, 15: 14–21.

—— (1987) "Fictions of Sappho," *Critical Inquiry*, 13: 787–805.
—— (1989) *Fictions of Sappho 1546–1937*, Chicago: University of Chicago Press.
De Lauretis, Teresa (1987) *Technologies of Gender: Essays on Theory, Film, and Fiction*, Bloomington: Indiana University Press.
De Man, Paul (1979) *Allegories of Reading: Figural Language in Rousseau, Nietzsche, Rilke, and Proust*, New Haven: Yale University Press.
—— (1979a) "Autobiography as De-facement," *MLN*, 94, 5: 919–30.
Derrida, Jacques (1973) *Speech and Phenomena and Other Essays on Husserl's Theory of Signs*, trans. David B. Allison, Evanston: Northwestern University Press.
—— (1979) *Spurs: Nietzsche's Styles*, trans. Barbara Harlow, Chicago: University of Chicago Press.
—— (1982) "White Mythology: Metaphor in the Text of Philosophy," in *Margins of Philosophy*, trans. Alan Bass, Chicago: University of Chicago Press.
Docherty, Thomas (1986) *John Donne, Undone*, London: Methuen.
Dollimore, Jonathan (1991) *Sexual Dissidence: Augustine to Wilde, Freud to Foucault*, Oxford: Clarendon Press.
Donne, John (1971) *The Complete English Poems*, ed. A.J. Smith, Harmondsworth: Penguin.
Donnison, Jean (1988), *Midwives and Medical Men: A History of the Struggle for the Control of Childbirth*, London: Historical Publications Ltd (2nd edn).
Dryden, John (1964) *An Essay on Dramatic Poesy*, *Selected Works of John Dryden*, ed. William Frost (1953, rpt), New York: Holt, Reinhart & Winston.
Dubrow, Heather (1986) "A Mirror for Complaints: Shakespeare's *Lucrece* and Generic Tradition," in *Renaissance Genres: Essays on Theory, History, and Interpretation*, ed. Barbara Kiefer Lewalski, Cambridge, MA: Harvard University Press: 399–417.
Eagleton, Terry (1987) "Response," in *Men In Feminism*, ed. Alice Jardine and Paul Smith, New York: Methuen: 133–5.
Eccles, Audrey (1982) *Obstetrics and Gynaecology in Tudor and Stuart England*, London: Croom Helm.
Ehrenreich, Barbara and English, Deirdre (1973) *Witches, Midwives, and Nurses: A History of Women Healers*, New York: Feminist Press.
Eliot, T.S. (1957) "The Three Voices of Poetry," in *On Poetry and Poets*, London: Faber & Faber.
—— (1975) "The Metaphysical Poets," *Selected Prose of T.S. Eliot*, ed. Frank Kermode, London: Faber & Faber: 59–67.
Erasmus, Desiderius (1979) *The Praise of Folly*, trans. Clarence H. Miller, New Haven: Yale University Press.
Faderman, Lillian (1981) *Surpassing the Love of Men: Romantic Friendship and Love Between Women from the Renaissance to the Present*, New York: William Morrow.
Farrell, Kirby, Hageman, Elizabeth H., and Kinney, Arthur F. (eds) (1988) *Women in the Renaissance: Selections from the English Literary Renaissance*, Amherst: University of Massachusetts Press.

Ferguson, Margaret W., Quilligan, Maureen and Vickers, Nancy J. (eds) (1986) *Rewriting the Renaissance: The Discourses of Sexual Difference in Early Modern Europe*, Chicago: Chicago.

Fish, Stanley (1981) "*Lycidas*: A Poem Finally Anonymous," in *Glyph 8*, Baltimore: Johns Hopkins University Press: 1–18.

Foucault, Michel (1984) "What Is An Author?" in *Foucault Reader*, ed. Paul Rabinow, New York: Pantheon Books: 101–20.

—— (1986) *The Care of the Self*, trans. Robert Hurley, New York: Random House.

Freud, Sigmund (1957) "Mythological Parallel to a Visual Obsession," in *Complete Psychological Works of Sigmund Freud*, trans. J. Strachey, London: Hogarth Press, Vol. 14: 337–8.

Freud, Sigmund and Breuer, Josef (1974) *Studies on Hysteria*, trans. James and Alix Strachey, Harmondsworth: Penguin.

Friedman, Susan Stanford (1989) "Creativity and the Childbirth Metaphor: Gender Difference in Literary Discourse," in *Speaking of Gender*, ed. Elaine Showalter, New York: Routledge: 73–100.

Fuss, Diana (1989) *Essentially Speaking: Feminism, Nature and Difference*, London: Routledge.

Gallop, Jane (1988) *Thinking Through the Body*, New York: Columbia University Press.

Garber, Marjorie (1992) *Vested Interests: Cross-Dressing and Cultural Anxiety*, New York: Routledge.

Gardner, Helen (ed.) (1965) *John Donne: The Elegies and The Songs and Sonnets*, Oxford: Clarendon Press.

Gilbert, Sandra M. and Gubar, Susan (1979) *The Madwoman in the Attic: The Woman Writer and the Nineteenth-Century Literary Imagination*, New Haven: Yale University Press.

Gilbert, Sandra M. and Gubar, Susan (eds) (1979) *Shakespeare's Sisters: Feminist Essays on Women Poets*, Bloomington: Indiana University Press.

—— (1985) *The Norton Anthology of Literature by Women*, New York: W.W. Norton.

Gill, Roma (1972) "*Musa Iocosa Mea*: Thoughts on the *Elegies*," in *John Donne: Essays in Celebration*, ed. A.J. Smith, London: Methuen.

Gilligan, Carol (1982) *In a Different Voice*, Cambridge, MA: Harvard University Press.

Goldberg, Jonathan (1981) *Endlesse Worke: Spenser and the Structures of Discourse*, Baltimore: Johns Hopkins University Press.

—— (1986) *Voice Terminal Echo*: *Postmodernism and English Renaissance Texts*, New York: Methuen.

Goreau, Angeline (1984) *The Whole Duty of a Woman: Female Writers in Seventeenth-Century England*, Garden City: Dial Press.

Graham, Elspeth, Hinds, Hilary, Hobby, Elaine, and Wilcox, Helen (1989) *Her Own Life: Autobiographical Writings by Seventeenth-Century Englishwomen*, London: Routledge.

Greek Anthology, The (1953) trans. W.R. Paton (1917, rpt.), Cambridge, MA: Harvard University Press.

Greenblatt, Stephen (1988) "Fiction and Friction," in *Shakespearean Negotiations: The Circulation of Social Energy in Renaissance England*,

Berkeley: University of California Press.
Greene, Thomas M. (1982) *The Light In Troy: Imitation and Discovery in Renaissance Poetry*, New Haven: Yale University Press.
Grierson, Herbert (ed.) (1912) *The Poems of John Donne*, Oxford: Oxford University Press.
Gubar, Susan (1984) "*Sapphistries*," *Signs*, 10: 43–62.
Guillimeau, Jacques (1635) *Childbirth, Or, the Happy Delivery of Women*, London.
Guillory, John (1990) "From the Superfluous to the Supernumerary: Reading Gender into *Paradise Lost*," in *Soliciting Interpretation: Literary Theory and Seventeenth-Century English Poetry*, ed. Elizabeth D. Harvey and Katharine Eisaman Maus, Chicago: University of Chicago Press: 68–88.
Harris, Barbara J. (1990) "Property, Power, and Personal Relations: Elite Mothers and Sons in Yorkist and Early Tudor England," *Signs*, 15: 606–32.
Hartman, Geoffrey (1970) *Beyond Formalism: Literary Essays 1958-1970*, New Haven: Yale University Press.
Harvey, William (1981) *Disputations Concerning the Generation of Animals*, trans. Gweneth Whitteridge, Oxford: Blackwell Scientific Publications.
Haselkorn Anne M., and Travitsky, Betty S. (eds) (1990) *The Renaissance Englishwomen in Print: Counterbalancing the Canon*, Amherst: University of Massachusetts Press.
Helgerson, Richard (1978) "The New Poet Presents Himself: Spenser and the Idea of a Literary Career," *PMLA*, 93: 893–911.
Henderson, Katherine Usher and McManus, Barbara F. (eds) (1985) *Half Humankind: Contexts and Texts of the Controversy about Women in England, 1540–1640*, Urbana: University of Illinois Press.
Hic Mulier, Haec-Vir (1620) *Three Pamphlets on the Jacobean Antifeminist Controversy*, intro. Barbara J. Baines, Delmar, NY: Scolars' Facsimiles & Reprints, 1978.
Hobby, Elaine (1988) *Virtue of Necessity: English Women's Writing 1649–88*, London: Virago Press.
Holstun, James (1987) "'Will You Rent Our Ancient Love Asunder?': Lesbian Elegy in Donne, Marvell, and Milton," *ELH*, 54: 835–67.
Homer (1975) *The Iliad*, trans. Robert Fitzgerald, New York: Anchor Books.
Huntley, John (1967) "Milton's 23rd Sonnet," *ELH*, 34: 368–81.
Hutcheon, Linda (1991) *Splitting Images: Contemporary Canadian Ironies*, Toronto: Oxford.
Irigaray, Luce (1985a) *Speculum of the Other Woman*, trans. Gillian G. Gill, Ithaca: Cornell University Press.
—— (1985b) *This Sex Which Is Not One*, trans. Catherine Porter, Ithaca: Cornell University Press.
Jacobson, Howard (1974) *Ovid's Heriodes*, Princeton: Princeton University Press.
Jacobus, Mary (1986) *Reading Woman*: *Essays in Feminist Criticism*, New York: Columbia University Press.
Jardine, Alice (1985) *Gynesis: Configurations of Woman and Modernity*, Ithaca: Cornell University Press.

Jardine, Lisa (1983) *Still Harping on Daughters: Women and Drama in the Age of Shakespeare*, Brighton: Harvester Press.
Johnson, Barbara (1985) "Les fleurs du mal armé: Some Reflections on Intertextuality," in *Lyric Poetry: Beyond New Criticism*, ed. Chaviva Hosek and Patricia Parker, Ithaca: Cornell University Press: 264–80.
—— (1987) *A World of Difference*, Baltimore: Johns Hopkins University Press.
Johnson, Samuel (1967) *The Lives of the Poets*, ed. George Birkbeck Hill, Clarendon (1905, rpt), New York: Octagon Books.
Jones, Ann Rosalind (1985) "Writing the Body: Toward an Understanding of *l'Ecriture feminine*," in *The New Feminist Criticism*, ed. Elaine Showalter, New York: Pantheon Books: 361–77.
——. (1986) "Surprising Fame: Renaissance Gender Ideologies and Women's Lyric," in *The Poetics of Gender*, ed. Nancy K. Miller, New York: Columbia University Press.
—— (1990) *The Currency of Eros: Women's Love Lyric in Europe, 1540–1620*, Bloomington and Indianapolis: Indiana University Press.
Jonson, Ben (1975) *Complete Poems*, ed. George Parfitt, New Haven: Yale University Press.
—— (1975) "Conversations with William Drummond of Hawthornden," *Ben Jonson: Complete Poems*, ed. George Parfitt, New Haven: Yale University Press: 459–480.
—— (1975) *Timber: or Discoveries, Ben Jonson: Complete Poems*, ed. George Parfitt, New Haven: Yale University Press: 373–458.
Joplin, Patricia Klindienst (1984) "The Voice of the Shuttle is Ours," *Stanford Literature Review*, 1 (1): 25–53.
Jordan, Constance (1987) "Woman's Rule in Sixteenth-Century British Political Thought," *Renaissance Quarterly*, 40: 421–51.
Jorden, Edward (1603) *A Briefe Discourse of a Disease Called the Suffocation of the Mother*, London.
Kahn, Victoria (1985) *Rhetoric, Prudence, and Skepticism in the Renaissance*, Ithaca: Cornell University Press.
Kauffman, Linda S. (1986) *Discourses of Desire: Gender, Genre, and Epistolary Fictions*, Ithaca: Cornell University Press.
Kegl, Rosemary (1990) "'Joyning my Labour to my Pain': The Politics of Labor in Marvell's Mower Poems," in *Soliciting Interpretation: Literary Theory and Seventeenth-Century English Poetry*, ed. Elizabeth D. Harvey and Katharine Eisaman Maus, Chicago: University of Chicago Press: 89–118.
Kofman, Sarah (1985) *The Enigma of Woman: Woman in Freud's Writings*, trans. Catherine Porter, Ithaca: Cornell University Press.
Kramer, Heinrich and Sprenger, James (1971) *Malleus Maleficarum*, trans. Montague Summers (1928, rpt) New York: Dover.
Kristeva, Julia (1980) "Motherhood According to Giovanni Bellini" and "Place Names," in *Desire in Language*, ed. Leon S. Roudiez, trans. Thomas Gora, Alice Jardine and Leon S. Roudiez, New York: Columbia University Press.
—— (1984) *Revolution in Poetic Language*, trans. Margaret Waller, New York: Columbia University Press.

—— (1987) "Stabat Mater," *Tales of Love*, trans. Leon S. Roudiez, New York: Columbia University Press.

—— (1989) *Black Sun: Depression and Melancholia*, trans. Leon S. Roudiez, New York: Columbia University Press.

Lanham, Richard (1976) *The Motives of Eloquence: Literary Rhetoric in the Renaissance*, New Haven: Yale University Press.

Laqueur, Thomas (1986) "Orgasm, Generation, and the Politics of Reproductive Biology," *Representations*, 14: 1–41.

—— (1990) *Making Sex: Body and Gender From the Greeks to Freud*, Cambridge, MA: Harvard University Press.

Leishman, J.B. (1959) *The Monarch of Wit* (1951, rpt), London: Hutchinson.

Lewalski, Barbara K. (1973) *Donne's "Anniversaries" and the Poetry of Praise*, Princeton: Princeton University Press.

Lewis, C.S. (1966) "Donne and Love Poetry in the Seventeenth Century," in *John Donne's Poetry*, ed. A.L. Clements, New York: Norton.

Lipking, Lawrence (1988) *Abandoned Women and Poetic Tradition*, Chicago: University of Chicago Press.

Lucian (1979) *Affairs of the Heart*, trans. M.D. MacLeod (1967, rpt), Cambridge, MA: Harvard University Press.

Lyly, John (1967) *The Complete Works of John Lyly*, ed. R. Warwick Bond, Oxford: Clarendon Press.

Maclean, Ian (1980) *The Renaissance Notion of Woman: A Study in the Fortunes of Scholasticism and Medical Science in European Intellectual Life*, Cambridge, MA: Cambridge University Press.

Marbeck, John (1581) *A Book of Notes and Commonplaces*, London.

Marcus, Leah S. (1989) "Erasing the Stigma of Daughterhood: Mary I, Elizabeth I, and Henry VIII," in *Daughters and Fathers*, ed. Lynda E. Boose and Betty S. Flowers, Baltimore: Johns Hopkins University Press: 400–17.

Martial (1919) *Epigrams*, trans. Walter C.A. Ker, London: William Heinemann.

Marvell, Andrew (1976) *The Complete Poems*, ed. Elizabeth Story Donno (1972, rpt), Harmondsworth: Penguin.

Maus, Katharine Eisaman (1991) "A Womb of His Own: Male Renaissance Poets in the Female Body," in *Sexuality and Gender in Early Modern Europe: Institutions, texts, images*, ed. James Grantham Turner, Cambridge, MA: Harvard University Press.

Merchant, Carolyn (1990) *The Death of Nature: Women, Ecology, and the Scientific Revolution*, (1980, rpt), San Francisco: Harper & Row.

McLaren, Angus (1984) *Reproductive Rituals: The Perception of Fertility in England from the Sixteenth Century to the Nineteenth Century*, London: Methuen.

McLaren, Dorothy (1986) "Marital Fertility and Lactation 1570–1720," in *Women in English Society 1500–1800*, ed. Mary Prior (1985, rpt), London: Methuen: 22–53.

Milgate, W. (1967) *John Donne: The Satires, Epigrams, and Verse Letters*, London: Oxford University Press.

Miller, Clarence (1988) "Styles and Mixed Genres in Erasmus' *Praise of Folly*," in *Acta Conventus Neo-Latini Guelpherbytani*, eds Stella P.

Revard, Fidel Rädle, and Mario A. Di Cesare, Binghamton: Medieval and Renaissance Texts and Studies: 277–87.

Miller, Nancy K. (1988) *Subject to Change*, New York: Columbia University Press.

Milton, John (1957) *Complete Poems and Major Prose*, ed. Merritt Y. Hughes, Indianapolis: Odyssey Press.

Mitchell, Juliet and Rose, Jacqueline (1982) *Feminine Sexuality: Jacques Lacan and the école freudienne*, New York: W.W. Norton.

Modleski, Tania (1986) "Feminism and the Power of Interpretation," in *Feminist Studies/Critical Studies*, Bloomington: Indiana University Press: 121–38.

—— (1991) *Feminism Without Women: Culture and Criticism in a "Post-feminist" Age*, London: Routledge.

Moi, Toril (1985) *Sexual/Textual Politics: Feminist Literary Theory*, London: Methuen.

Montrose, Louis Adrian (1983) "'Shaping Fantasies': Figurations of Gender and Power in Elizabethan Culture," *Representations*, 1 (2): 61–94.

Norris, Christopher (1982) *Deconstruction: Theory and Practice*, London: Methuen.

Olsen, Tillie (1965) *Silences*, New York: Dell.

Ong, Walter J.S.J. (1977) "Transformations of the Word and Alienation," in *Interfaces of the Word: Studies in the Evolution of Consciousness and Culture*, Ithaca: Cornell University Press: 17–49.

Orgel, Stephen (1989) "Nobody's Perfect: Or Why Did the English Stage Take Boys for Women?" *The South Atlantic Quarterly*, 88, (1) 7–29.

Ovid (1975) *Tristia. Ex Ponto*, trans. Arthur Leslie Wheeler, Cambridge, MA: Harvard University Press.

—— (1976) *Fasti*, trans. Sir James George Frazer, Cambridge, MA: Harvard University Press.

—— (1977a) *Metamorphoses*, trans. Frank Justus Miller, Cambridge, MA: Harvard University Press.

—— (1977b) *Heroides and Amores*, trans. Grant Showerman, Cambridge, MA: Harvard UP.

Parker, Patricia (1987) *Literary Fat Ladies: Rhetoric, Gender, Property*, London: Methuen.

Parker, William Riley (1945) "Milton's Last Sonnet," Review of English Studies, 21: 235–28.

Patterson, Lee (1983) "'For the Wyves love of Bathe': Feminine Rhetoric and Poetic Resolution in the *Roman de la Rose* and the *Canterbury Tales*," *Speculum*, 58 (3): 656–95.

Phillips, James E., Jr (1941) "The Background of Spenser's Attitude Toward Women Rulers," *Huntington Library Quarterly*, 5: 5–32.

Plato (1961) *Theaetetus*, *The Collected Dialogues of Plato*, ed. Edith Hamilton and Huntington Cairns, Princeton: Princeton University Press.

Reff, Theodore (1967) "Redon's *Le Silence*: An Iconographic Interpretation," *Gazette des Beaux Arts*, 6: 359–68.

Reitenbach, Gail "'Maydes are simple, some men say': Thomas Campion's Female Persona Poems," in *The Renaissance Englishwoman in Print: Counterbalancing the Canon*, ed. Anne M. Haselkorn and Betty S.

Travitsky, Amhest: University of Massachusetts Press: 80–95.
Reynolds, L.D. *et al.* (eds) (1983) *Texts and Transmissions: A Survey of the Latin Classics*, Oxford: Clarendon Press.
Rich, Adrienne (1976) *Of Woman Born: Motherhood as Experience and Institution*, New York: W.W. Norton.
Richardson, Samuel (1980) *Pamela*, ed. Peter Sabor, Harmondsworth: Penguin.
Roberts, Josephine A. (1990) "Radigund Revisited: Perspectives on Women Rulers in Lady Mary Wroth's *Urania*," in *The Renaissance Englishwoman in Print: Counterbalancing the Canon*, ed. Anne M. Haselkorn and Betty S. Travitsky, Amherst: University of Massachusetts Press (1990): 187–207.
Robinson, David M. (1924) *Sappho and Her Influence*, Boston: Marshall Jones Company.
Rueff, Jacob (1637) *The Expert Midwife*, London.
Sacks, Elizabeth (1980) *Shakespeare's Images of Pregnancy*, London: Macmillan.
Said, Edward (1986) "Intellectuals in the Post-Colonial World," *Salmagundi*, 70–1 (Spring–Summer): 41–81.
Sappho (1966) *The Poems of Sappho*, trans. Susy Q. Groden, Indianapolis: Bobbs-Merrill Educational Publishing.
Sawday, Jonathan (1990) "The Fate of Masya: Dissecting the Renaissance Body," in *Renaissance* Bodies: The Human Figure in English Culture c. 1540–1660, eds Lucy Gent and Nigel Llewellyn, London: Reaktion Books: 111–35.
Scarry, Elaine (1988) "Donne: 'But yet the Body is his booke,'" in *Literature and the Body: Essays on Populations and Persons*, ed. Elaine Scarry, Baltimore: Johns Hopkins University Press.
Scot, Reginald (1964) *The Discoverie of Witchcraft*, Fontwell, Arundel: Centaur Press.
Shakespeare, William (1974) *The Riverside Shakespeare*, ed. G. Blakemore Evans, Boston: Houghton Mifflin.
Showalter, Elaine (1977) *A Literature of Their Own: British Women Novelists From Bronte to Lessing*, Princeton: Princeton University Press.
—— (1979) "Toward A Feminist Poetics," in *The New Feminist Criticism*, ed. Showalter, New York: Pantheon Books: 125–43.
—— (1981) "Feminist Criticism in the Wilderness," in *The New Feminist Criticism*, ed. Showalter, New York: Pantheon Books: 243–70.
—— (1983) "Critical Cross-Dressing; Male Feminists and the Woman of the Year," in *Men in Feminism*, eds Alice Jardine and Paul Smith, New York: Methuen, 1987: 116–32. Originally published in *Raritan* (Fall 1983).
Showalter, Elaine, (ed.) (1986) *The New Feminist Criticism*, New York: Pantheon Books.
—— (1989) *Speaking of Gender*, New York: Routledge.
Silverman, Kaja (1988) *The Acoustic Mirror: The Female Voice in Psychoanalysis and Cinema*, Bloomington: Indiana University Press.
Skretkowicz, Victor (1980) "Hercules in Sidney and Spenser," *Notes and Queries*, 225: 306–10.
Smith, Hilda (1976) "Gynecology and Ideology in Seventeenth-Century

England," in *Liberating Women's History*, ed. Berenice A. Carroll, Urbana: University of Illinois Press: 97–114.

Spencer, H.R. (1927) *The History of British Midwifery*, London: Bale Sons & Danielsson.

Spenser, Edmund (1978) *The Faerie Queene*, ed. Thomas P. Roche, Jr, New Haven: Yale University Press.

Stanton, Domna C. (1986) "Difference On Trial: A Critique of the Maternal Metaphor in Cixous, Irigaray, and Kristeva," in *The Poetics of Gender*, ed. Nancy K. Miller, New York: Columbia University Press.

Stigers, Eva Stehle (1977) "Retreat From the Male: Catullus 62 and Sappho's Erotic Flowers," *Ramus*, 6: 83–102.

Stone, Lawrence (1977) *The Family, Sex and Marriage in England 1500–1800*, Harmondsworth: Penguin.

Stubbes, Phillip (1583) *Anatomie of Abuses*, London.

Suleiman, Susan Rubin (1985) "Writing and Motherhood," in *The (M)other Tongue: Essays in Feminist Psychoanalytic Interpretation*, ed. Shirley Nelson Garner, Claire Kahane, and Madelon Sprengnether, Ithaca: Cornell University Press.

Swetnam, Joseph (1615) *The Arraignment of Lewd, Idle, Froward, and Unconstant Women*, London.

Thompson, Sister Geraldine (1973) *Under Pretext of Praise: Satiric Mode in Erasmus' Fiction*, Toronto: University of Toronto Press.

Tobin, J.J.M. (1977) "A Note on Dalila as 'Hyaena'," *Milton Quarterly*, 11: 89–90.

Treichler, Paula A. (1990) "Feminism, Medicine, and the Meaning of Childbirth," in *Body/Politics: Women and the Discourses of Science*, ed. Mary Jacobus, Evelyn Fox Keller, and Sally Shuttleworth, New York: Routledge.

Updike, John (1989) *S.*, Harmondsworth: Penguin.

Veith, Ilza (1965) *Hysteria: The History of a Disease*, Chicago: University of Chicago Press.

Verducci, Florence (1985) *Ovid's Toyshop of the Heart: Epistulae Heroidum*, Princeton: Princeton University Press.

Vessey, Thomson D.W. (1976) "Philaenis," *Revue Belge de Philologie et d'Histoire*, 54: 78–83.

Vickers, Nancy (1985) "'The blazon of sweet beauty's best': Shakespeare's *Lucrece*," in *Shakespeare and the Question of Theory*, ed. Patricia Parker and Geoffrey Hartman, New York: Methuen: 95–115.

Virgil (1978) *Aeneid*, trans. H. Rushton Fairclough, Cambridge, MA: Harvard University Press.

Waller, Marguerite (1987) "Academic Tootsie: The Denial of Difference and the Difference It Makes," *Diacritics*, 17 (1): 2–20.

Whitford, Margaret (1989) "Rereading Irigaray," *Between Feminism and Psychoanalysis*, ed. Teresa Brennan, London: Routledge: 106–26.

—— (1991) *Luce Irigaray: Philosophy in the Feminine*, London: Routledge.

Willughby, Percival (1863) *Observations in Midwifery*, ed. Henry Blenkinsop, London: H.T. Cooke & Son.

Wilson, G.R. (1969) "The Interplay of Perception and Reflection: Mirror Imagery in Donne's Poetry," *Studies in English Literature*, 9: 107–21.

Wilson, Katharina M., ed. (1987) *Women Writers of the Renaissance and Reformation*, Athens, GA: University of Georgia Press.
Woodbridge, Linda (1984) *Women and the English Renaissance: Literature and the Nature of Womankind, 1540–1620*, Urbana: University of Illinois Press.
Woolf, Virginia (1929) *A Room of One's Own*, New York: Harcourt, Brace and World, Inc.
Wroth, Lady Mary (1983) *The Poems of Lady Mary Wroth*, ed. Josephine A. Roberts, Baton Rouge: Louisiana State University Press.

INDEX